Praise for *Going the Distance*

"Deeply analytical, brilliant in its exposition, Kevin Kennedy and Mary Moore's study of the dynamics underlying the growth—and failure—of long-lived dominant companies systematically traces the predictable challenges of governance and action that face all large businesses as they grow. Then with dead-on accuracy, they convincingly pinpoint the key strategies and leadership qualities that enable great companies to leverage those challenges into competitive advantage. More than a post-mortem on the high-technology economy, *Going the Distance* brings fresh, useful insight to the entire topic of successful leadership in the complex organizations that exist throughout our society. The need to foster throughout the organization what this study calls leadership DNA is certainly pressing in a fast-moving, competitive business environment. But the lack of well-coordinated cooperative reflection and action for the good of the whole can be equally damaging in a university, a city, or any large, complex entity. This is a rare book on management that offers lessons applicable to leadership excellence in a broad range of organizations."

—**Francis L. Lawrence,** President Emeritus,
Rutgers, The State University of New Jersey

"Growing a company is a complex business. This wonderful book can act as a guide, showing how to manage that complexity, and transform it from a problem into a strategic advantage. For those of us who've learned some of these lessons the hard way, Moore and Kennedy's book provides an invaluable framework and fills in the gaps. Anybody who wants to build a world-class business should have a close look at this book."

—**Jerry Fiddler,** Founder and Chairman,
Wind River

"So much to learn.... Every chapter gives insight that inspires and makes one look into his own mirror.... No CEO should be without it."

—**Jozef Strauss,** Chief Executive Officer,
JDS Uniphase Corporation

"*Going the Distance* provides real insight into what makes some companies prosper from startup to industry leader, while others fall off the track before they get there. If you want to avoid the pitfalls and take your company the distance without the suffering the inevitable trials that growth and complexity bring, this is required reading. I wish I had the benefit of this book as a new CEO."

—**Michael Brown,** Chairman,
Quantum Corporation

"Kennedy and Moore have created a pragmatic view of how companies grow, succeed, and fail. They provide a refreshing focus on how culture is truly essential to building sustainable leadership and attracting top talent. Interesting, provocative, and real."

—**Jeffrey E. Christian**, Chairman and Chief Executive Officer, Christian and Timbers

"This book offers unique perspective and insight into the challenges many a company will face during its life cycle. These real lessons can serve as a model of understanding for translating these challenges into marketplace opportunities for growth and sustainability."

—**Rod Adkins**, General Manager, Pervasive Computing Division, IBM Software Group

"*Going the Distance* provides a detailed structural analysis of complexity of business systems. Kevin and Mary provide a rare insight into building a deliberate practice linking strategy to execution."

—**Don Listwin**, Chief Executive Officer, Openwave Systems Inc.

"Entrepreneurs and CEOs will find this to be a practical guide, full of examples, of about what can go right and what can go wrong in building a company from startup to greatness."

—**Bill Elmore**, General Partner, Foundation Capital

"The authors put forward a compelling case for the variables that plant the seeds of decay for any enterprise. More importantly, the book provides a very pragmatic approach to building a dashboard with early warning indicators that could prevent these seeds from germinating."

—**Masood Jabbar**, Executive Advisor to the Chief Executive Officer, Sun Microsystems

"Moore and Kennedy capture exactly what is unique about Cisco System's success as a growth model. Unlike many leaders who either froze in place or thrashed back and forth as complexity rose with growth, the authors show us how Cisco turned what could have become a perfect storm into competitive advantage. *Going the Distance* offers managers a concise framework to identify and gain advantage from these same challenges in their own companies."

—**Christopher Meyer, Ph.D.**, author of *Fast Cycle Time* and *Relentless Growth*

"A highly original thesis around the life cycle of a corporation, with deeply analytical insights on what is very hard to grasp: the developing threads that prefigure future success or failure. The authors have struck a great balance between experience and corporate practice, on the one hand, analytical reasoning and seeking causes, on the other. Thoroughly enjoyable reading for anyone who, like the authors, truly believes in learning as a lifelong source of motivation and fulfillment, specifically in corporate settings."

—**Roland Acra**, Senior Vice President, Cisco Systems

"Finally a book that presents a full, integrated, and practical view of all the dynamics necessary to navigate the treacherous waters that determine winners and losers in today's business climate. The interlocking concepts between execution, governance, leadership, and culture lend final credibility to subjects that have for too long been treated as independent subjects to be studied one at a time. Exceptionally well done and useful book."

—**Marianne F. Jackson**, SVP and Chief Human Resource Officer, Palm, Inc.

"A uniquely different approach to describing and analyzing what it takes to succeed in these difficult and complex times. All business leaders can't help but improve their effectiveness by embracing some of the key leadership concepts so thoroughly and convincingly presented in this book."

—**John Radford**, Senior Vice President, Aon Consulting/Founder, Radford Surveys

"Mary has helped build countless startups, as well as consulted to large, established companies; Kevin has managed in one of America's most important scientific companies and has been an integral creator of one of the most dynamic cultures in American business. Together, they have written a clear, practical guide for management teams and board members to use day in and day out. It stands head and shoulders above the kind of overly theoretical books, distanced from business realities, that we've all become used to. As a venture capitalist, I was naturally drawn to the book's sage advice on warning signs and best practices for startups. But my real mission is to build lasting, great companies, so the authors' advice for large companies may be even more invaluable."

—**Tom Rosch**, General Partner, InterWest Partners

"I love this book. Kennedy and Moore's insightful commentary, brilliant stories and compelling evidence make this a must read for anyone in business wanting to stay ahead of the curve. This book rocks!"

—**Jason Jennings**, worldwide bestselling author of *It's Not the Big That Eat the Small—It's the Fast That Eat the Slow* and *Less Is More*

Going
the
Distance

ISBN 0-13-046120-2

9 780130 461209   92495

In an increasingly competitive world, it is quality
of thinking that gives an edge. an idea that opens new
doors, a technique that solves a problem, or an insight
that simply helps make sense of it all.

We work with leading authors in the various arenas
of business and finance to bring cutting-edge thinking
and best learning practice to a global market.

It is our goal to create world-class print publications
and electronic products that gives readers
knowledge and understanding which can then be
applied, whether studying or at work.

To find out more about our business
products, you can visit us at www.ft-ph.com

Going the Distance

Why Some Companies Dominate and Others Fail

Kevin Kennedy
Mary Moore

 **FT** Prentice Hall

FINANCIAL TIMES

An Imprint of PEARSON EDUCATION
Upper Saddle River, NJ • New York • San Francisco • Toronto • Sydney
Tokyo • Singapore • Hong Kong • Cape Town • Madrid
Paris • Milan • Munich • Amsterdam

www.ft-ph.com

A Cataloging-in-Publication Data record for this book
can be obtained from the Library of Congress.

Editorial/Production Supervision: Faye Gemmellaro
Executive Editor: Tim Moore
Editorial Assistant: Richard Winkler
Marketing Manager: John Pierce
Manufacturing Buyer: Maura Zaldivar
Cover Design Director: Jerry Votta
Composition: Daly Graphics

©2003 by Pearson Education, Inc.
Publishing as Financial Times Prentice Hall
Upper Saddle River, New Jersey 07458

Financial Times Prentice Hall books are widely used by corporations and
government agencies for training, marketing, and resale.

For information regarding corporate and government bulk discounts,
please contact Corporate and Government Sales at (800) 382-3419 or
corpsales@pearsontechgroup.com

Printed in the United States of America

10 9 8 7 6 5 4 3 2 1

ISBN 0-13-046120-2

Pearson Education Ltd.
Pearson Education Australia Pty., Ltd.
Pearson Education Singapore, Pte. Ltd.
Pearson Education North Asia, Ltd.
Pearson Education Canada, Ltd.
Pearson Educación de Mexico, S.A. de C.V.
Pearson Education—Japan
Pearson Education Malaysia, Pte. Ltd.

FINANCIAL TIMES PRENTICE HALL BOOKS

For more information, please go to www.ft-ph.com

Business and Technology

Sarv Devaraj and Rajiv Kohli
> *The IT Payoff: Measuring the Business Value of Information Technology Investments*

Nicholas D. Evans
> *Business Agility: Strategies for Gaining Competitive Advantage through Mobile Business Solutions*

Nicholas D. Evans
> *Business Innovation and Disruptive Technology: Harnessing the Power of Breakthrough Technology…for Competitive Advantage*

Nicholas D. Evans
> *Consumer Gadgets: 50 Ways to Have Fun and Simplify Your Life with Today's Technology…and Tomorrow's*

Faisal Hoque
> *The Alignment Effect: How to Get Real Business Value Out of Technology*

Thomas Kern, Mary Cecelia Lacity, and Leslie P. Willcocks
> *Netsourcing: Renting Business Applications and Services Over a Network*

Ecommerce

Dale Neef
> *E-procurement: From Strategy to Implementation*

Economics

David Dranove
> *What's Your Life Worth? Health Care Rationing…Who Lives? Who Dies? Who Decides?*

David R. Henderson
> *The Joy of Freedom: An Economist's Odyssey*

Jonathan Wight
> *Saving Adam Smith: A Tale of Wealth, Transformation, and Virtue*

Entrepreneurship

Oren Fuerst and Uri Geiger
> *From Concept to Wall Street*

David Gladstone and Laura Gladstone
> *Venture Capital Handbook: An Entrepreneur's Guide to Raising Venture Capital, Revised and Updated*

Erica Orloff and Kathy Levinson, Ph.D.
> *The 60-Second Commute: A Guide to Your 24/7 Home Office Life*

Jeff Saperstein and Daniel Rouach
> *Creating Regional Wealth in the Innovation Economy: Models, Perspectives, and Best Practices*

Finance

Aswath Damodaran
The Dark Side of Valuation: Valuing Old Tech, New Tech, and New Economy Companies

Kenneth R. Ferris and Barbara S. Pécherot Petitt
Valuation: Avoiding the Winner's Curse

International Business

Fernando Robles, Françoise Simon, and Jerry Haar
Winning Strategies for the New Latin Markets

Investments

Harry Domash
Fire Your Stock Analyst! Analyzing Stocks on Your Own

Philip Jenks and Stephen Eckett, Editors
The Global-Investor Book of Investing Rules: Invaluable Advice from 150 Master Investors

Charles P. Jones
Mutual Funds: Your Money, Your Choice. Take Control Now and Build Wealth Wisely

D. Quinn Mills
Buy, Lie, and Sell High: How Investors Lost Out on Enron and the Internet Bubble

John Nofsinger and Kenneth Kim
Infectious Greed: Restoring Confidence in America's Companies

John R. Nofsinger
Investment Blunders (of the Rich and Famous)…And What You Can Learn from Them

John R. Nofsinger
Investment Madness: How Psychology Affects Your Investing…And What to Do About It

Leadership

Jim Despain and Jane Bodman Converse
And Dignity for All: Unlocking Greatness through Values-Based Leadership

Marshall Goldsmith, Vijay Govindarajan, Beverly Kaye, and Albert A. Vicere
The Many Facets of Leadership

Frederick C. Militello, Jr., and Michael D. Schwalberg
Leverage Competencies: What Financial Executives Need to Lead

Eric G. Stephan and Wayne R. Pace
Powerful Leadership: How to Unleash the Potential in Others and Simplify Your Own Life

Management

Marketing

Michael Basch
CustomerCulture: How FedEx and Other Great Companies Put the Customer First Every Day

Deirdre Breakenridge
Cyberbranding: Brand Building in the Digital Economy

Jonathan Cagan and Craig M. Vogel
Creating Breakthrough Products: Innovation from Product Planning to Program Approval

James W. Cortada
21st Century Business: Managing and Working in the New Digital Economy

Al Lieberman, with Patricia Esgate
The Entertainment Marketing Revolution: Bringing the Moguls, the Media, and the Magic to the World

Tom Osenton
Customer Share Marketing: How the World's Great Marketers Unlock Profits from Customer Loyalty

Yoram J. Wind and Vijay Mahajan, with Robert Gunther
Convergence Marketing: Strategies for Reaching the New Hybrid Consumer

Public Relations

Gerald R. Baron
Now Is Too Late: Survival in an Era of Instant News

Deirdre Breakenridge and Thomas J. DeLoughry
The New PR Toolkit: Strategies for Successful Media Relations

Strategy

Thomas L. Barton, William G. Shenkir, and Paul L. Walker
Making Enterprise Risk Management Pay Off: How Leading Companies Implement Risk Management

Henry A. Davis and William W. Sihler
Financial Turnarounds: Preserving Enterprise Value

Contents

Foreword

Where was this book when I needed it? In 1977 when we started Apple? In 1982 when we started 3Com? In 1983 when we financed Oracle? In 1982 when we started Electronic Arts in our office? In 1989 when we took control of Microchip from General Instruments? In 1994 when we financed Network Appliance? In 1987 when we started Cisco? In 1995 when we started Yahoo?

This book is an ideal distillation of the lessons of company success and failure, many of which I have learned the hard way, in more than 30 years of nurturing venture-backed companies. As I read it, I found myself wishing that such a handbook had been available to help me diagnose and repair problems so many of our promising companies and founders faced over the years.

I've had the wonderful opportunity of watching the evolution of Silicon Valley, almost since its inception—1960. Despite an ever-increasing number of motivated, talented, and entrepreneurial managers, high-tech companies have a mixed history of commercial success, with only a few reaching the state of dominance enjoyed by Intel, Cisco, and Oracle. The majority fail to "go the distance." Not only does conventional wisdom tend to distill the lessons of success and failure into over-simplified premises—the choice of a particular CEO or a late product transition or a failed merger, for instance—but it also appears to blame the symptoms rather than the causes. What underlies these failures? What early signs might be read before the last straw breaks the camel's back? How can management do a better job of learning from the past to improve the future?

In a meeting some time ago with one of the authors, I posed this question: "Why do great companies fail?" This was at the beginning of the current economic downturn, and given the graveyard of historical failures, it seemed to me none too soon to pose the question. Imagine my surprise when I received an email almost two years later, requesting that I review a book that offers real answers to that very question.

A distinguishing feature of *Going the Distance* is that it avoids the oversimplification of offering a single principle that promises salvation. In fact, this book effectively organizes the experience and observations of two people who have collectively logged more than

50 years in complex organizations. The complexity that gradually develops in a successful company brings with it both opportunity and peril—it is a double-edged sword that can make the difference between winning and losing. The authors describe two categories of challenge—governance and execution—that provide guideposts to longevity or, if neglected, become the fault lines of eventual failure. These two categories encompass eight critical challenges in all. This presentation makes it clear that it is seldom a single occurrence or characteristic that brings a company to its knees; rather, the book makes clear that it is the buildup of unmet challenges that choke a company over time.

A second distinguishing feature of this book is its description of stages of evolution of companies, contrasting the nature of challenges experienced in startups, in companies on the rise, and in well-established, multibillion-dollar companies. These challenges are possible during all stages of a company's evolution, but some are far more likely to present themselves at certain stages than at others. Just as important, some challenges, such as establishing a learning culture and a bias for constant innovation, are critical to meet early, as they are very difficult to address once the wrong DNA culture is formed. In fact, it is notable that throughout this book, the authors emphasize the importance of a learning organization as central to the adaptability necessary to survive quickly changing markets at any stage of a company's life.

Third among this book's distinctions, I particularly appreciate the authors' awareness that success depends on attending carefully to what's really going on in a company—facing the harsh facts as they are. One of my jobs as a board member has been to counsel management to avoid distraction and to execute with constructive paranoia. *Going the Distance* provides detailed practical application of these ideas.

The unique and pragmatic insights necessary for success are here—for new and experienced CEOs, for other executives, for venture capitalists, for students of business, and for anyone interested in the dynamics of corporate success and failure.

This handbook is so fundamental to the process of creating world-class companies that I may continue in the venture capital business another 30 years!

Don Valentine,
Sequoia Capital

Preface

All companies are organisms. They are born; they grow and develop in complexity; and they eventually diminish in energy, become absorbed into another company, or expire. To think otherwise ignores the realities of corporate competition and the physics of life itself. Complexity and demise are part of life. No one is guaranteed indefinite success or long-lasting youthful vigor.

However, this does not mean that excellent health—or, for a company, dominance—has to be fleeting. Some people and some companies are healthier, live longer, and find greater success than most of their peers. Moreover, companies such as GE and IBM, which have dominated in one era, can, under transformational leadership, create new windows of dominance, adding new meaning to "going the distance."

Some books imply that corporate decline is shocking and tend to blame the leadership in place when the demise occurs. This book is different from most texts on the subject; our premise is that challenges to corporate health are inevitable—that they are part of the natural life of a company. Some companies, however, like some people, are more able to rise to the inevitable challenges of life. Our book seeks to explain this phenomenon and to help your company live a longer, brighter life.

In a complex company there are many factors vying for attention, and the danger signs have to be sorted out. Agents of demise emerge, but they are not necessarily obvious. Companies must learn to navigate their own evolving complexity, just as aging people must monitor their fitness. This book describes the predictable challenges to a company's health, the sources of those challenges, and the internal vital signs that signal the condition of the corporate patient. *Sustained* success hinges on proactive response to these vital signs.

Although the framework of beliefs defined in this book includes concepts that might appear self-evident to most company leaders, the discipline of assessment that we propose is unusual. It requires ownership of new metrics, which we call *vital signs*, which are typically obscured or ignored. Our predisposition toward operational considerations is backed by a belief that execution is paramount for long-term success.

The initial thinking about this topic began in the mid 1980s, as the previously undisputed momentum of a great company, AT&T, was hit hard by deregulation and divestiture. This disruption ultimately caused the breakup and restructuring of what was then a company of over one million people.

As a result of that breakup, an imposing new set of competitors relentlessly pursued AT&T with new telephone equipment and services. "Ma Bell" responded with a "ready, fire, aim" approach. Product development grew too rapidly, challenging the ability of manufacturing, logistical support, and sales channels to align and compete in new and now competitive markets.

Unable to succeed at this new level of complexity and speed, AT&T acquired NCR in a last-ditch effort to succeed in the new environment. Later, insiders and outsiders alike saw the move as a debacle. The challenges of complexity and alignment overwhelmed and ultimately choked the living, thriving organism that had once been a great company.

The thinking in this book was also stimulated by experience at Cisco Systems. We both became involved with Cisco—one of us internally and one of us externally—when it was a small company, albeit one growing in scale and complexity at great speed. Unlike AT&T, Cisco used complexity to gain competitive advantage. During its time of rapid growth, the leadership team realigned the company many times, from a functional organization to business units, then to lines of business, and then to other structures that fit the changing state of Cisco's markets.

Like all of high-tech, Cisco hit the wall of economic downturn at the end of the year 2000. In the Introduction, we tell the story of venture capitalist Don Valentine's January 2001 invitation to study Cisco's position in this new economic world. That story is the birth of the book you're now holding.

We have both worked for many years in high-tech, with many large and small companies, both inside and outside Silicon Valley. We've participated in dozens of mergers and acquisitions in which the inevitable differences in culture, leadership styles, product life-cycle management, customer management, and so on have challenged companies to completely reinvent themselves. Through this participation, we witnessed and acted in events with signatures of both excellence and failure.

We are inspired by two main passions: to study growing organizations as they currently operate and to find ways to make improvements. We wrote this book as an attempt to define the nature of *the double-edged sword of complexity*, which contains the potential for greatness as well as for demise.

This book is based on our personal experiences and observations in high-tech over the last 25 years. We are proposing an operational framework distilled from that experience. With it, we hope to help organizations prepare for the future. We hope our words will resonate with your own experience, stimulate insights into the nature of the challenges your company faces, and provide new motivation to meet these challenges as well as the tools with which to surmount them.

We wish you much success in creating and sustaining the next generation of great companies that *go the distance*.

Kevin Kennedy
Mary Moore

Acknowledgments

Writing this book together has given us a chance to expand our relationship from one of client and consultant to one of partnership. It has been rewarding on many levels for both of us. We have long since recognized our alignment on leadership values and philosophy, and writing this book has given us both a chance to learn more from each other.

This has been an extremely humbling experience for us both. First and foremost, we want to acknowledge our families. On the Kennedy home front, I am grateful for the patience, encouragement, and inspiration that my wife Barb, daughter Kate, and son Patrick provide day after day and year after year. Family has simply been a blessing. In the Moore family, I am glad for the opportunity to acknowledge my mother and father, Ella and Jim Moore, and my brothers and sister, Webb, Kris, Steve, and Ben—my essential history.

Professionally, a number of people helped us generate this manuscript. Without their hard work and perseverance, this book would not have completed. Jackie Landsman, Tamie Zrecny, Deb Dahl, and Linda Fairchild have borne the brunt of the logistics and managed them exceptionally well. We received a significant amount of editorial help from Kim Bostrom and Jordan Bass, who have made the difference in this book being of use to its readers. In addition, thanks to Sean Korba and Bryan Hoyas for helping us keep our tight travel on schedule. We also thank our publisher, Tim Moore, for bringing the support of Prentice Hall.

We would like to specifically mention the following people for their mid-course reviews of the materials and their very helpful feedback: Roland Acra, Ron Bernal, Alan Black, David Bradford, Michael Brown, George Clark, Donny Closson, Bill Elmore, Rob Faw, Jerry Fiddler, David Gudmundson, Russ Hall, Marianne Jackson, Ed Kozel, Deborah Lacy, Don Listwin, Kay Lovegrove, Geoffrey Moore, Art Schnitzer, Jon Shantz, Jozef Strauss, Don Valentine, and Rich Wong.

Of course, the learning depicted in this book evolved from the insights and techniques of many strong leaders we have worked with and observed over many years. We can only thank them collectively, with a special thank you to the Cisco team that created a great culture and sought to do what others had not yet achieved.

Introduction

In January 2001, Don Valentine, the renowned Silicon Valley venture capitalist, called a meeting of leaders at the networking giant, Cisco Systems. He posed two simple questions:

1. Why do great companies fail?
2. Will Cisco continue its momentum as a dominant company?

The discussion began with a review of two charts. One, shown in Figure I–1, listed the leading computer and component companies in their particular markets over the last half century. Each had held a uniquely recognizable "signature" position in its market at one time. As the chart shows, very few maintained this position over decades. In most cases, their dominance was fleeting, and new, relatively unknown companies ascended.

The other chart, shown in Figure I–2, was a similar list of companies, this time ordered by technology segment or specialty. All of these companies grew relatively large, and most were recognized during their high-growth phases as desirable workplaces. Again, it is apparent that few maintained their position of dominance for very long.

1950				→ 2000
Computer Companies	**Mainframes**	**Minis**	**Personal Computers**	**Workstations**	**Mainframes**

	Mainframes	**Minis**	**Personal Computers**	**Workstations**	**Mainframes**
Computer Companies	IBM	DEC	Apple	Sun	IBM
	Burroughs	Data General	Microsoft	HP	Fujitsu/
	Control Data	Prime	IBM	Compaq	Amdahl
	Honeywell	IBM	Compaq	Dell	
	NCR	Comp Auto	Dell		
	Univac	HP	Microsoft		
Components Companies	**Vacuum Tubes**	**Semiconductors**	**Semiconductors**	**Microprocessors**	**Silicon**
	GE	Texas Instruments	Intel	Sun	Intel
	RCA Philco	Transitron	Motorola	Intel	LSI Logic
	Sylvania	Fairchild	Texas Instruments	Motorola	AMD
		Motorola	AMD		Micron
			NSM		Motorola
			Rockwell		

Figure I-1 Computer and Component Markets, 1950–2000.

	1980	1995	2000
Network Companies	**Data Networks** 3Com IBM SynOptics Wellfleet Cisco	**Data Networks** Cisco	**Data and Voice Networks** Nortel Lucent Cisco Alcatel Siemens
Components Companies	**Standard, ASIC, ASSP** Intel Motorola Texas Instruments LSI Logic	**Silicon** Intel ATT Semi AMCC PMCs Texas Instruments Broadcom	**ICs** Intel Lucent Semi AMCC PMCs Broadcom

Figure I-2   Computers and Components by Segment, 1980–2000.

In the world of high-tech, intense competition and fast change are endemic. Risks are high. Yet extraordinary contribution and wealth have emerged out of this world. We believe the lessons of success and failure in high-tech have application to other industries. Don Valentine's questions are important for venture capitalists, consultants, boards of directors, company leaders, students of business, and market analysts in all industries. We believe that if answers can be codified, they can be used as a model for maintaining long-term success. With such a model, key *vital signs* can be identified by which a company's health can be constantly assessed and from which appropriate prevention or correction strategies can be formulated.

What Constitutes a Great Company?

When we say "great company," we are thinking of those that have achieved dominance in a relatively large market over a period of 5 to 10 years. We can assume that these companies have created a culture, affected the technology in their market, expanded with new product generations into new markets, and built some degree of governance systems. In other words, great companies have faced and responded well to increasing business complexity.

We're interested in helping great companies—those that have achieved this level of dominance to go *the distance*—that is, to achieve dominance over the long term, to transcend the barrier to sustained greatness and be among the companies that the rest will learn from in the future. We urge those of you now leading or working with great companies to look at the lists in Figures I–1 and I–2. At the time of their dominance, did any one of these companies see the fall coming?

Eight Challenges, Eight Opportunities

We believe that it is possible to recognize eight challenges that leaders predictably encounter in building great companies. Each of these challenges has the potential to become a thread of failure or an element of competitive advantage. A company's response to these challenges brings about a future of either failure or success.

If a single challenge is left unmet and develops into a thread of failure—a trace of things starting to go wrong—it is not likely to cause the demise of a dominant company. However, if one thread is not dealt with when it appears, several threads may become active simultaneously. This will weaken even great companies and allow competitors to unseat them from their pinnacles.

Complexity—A Double-Edged Sword

Complexity, an inherent feature of organizational growth and success, is a double-edged sword. When it is well understood—its challenges monitored and the antidotes well applied—complexity can become a competitive advantage that creates *barriers to entry* by competitors. On the other hand, complexity contains the threads of failure that constrict the momentum of otherwise great companies.

An apt metaphor is the day-to-day fires of execution. If they aren't kept under control, they will overwhelm any hope of keeping up with market changes. Great organizations, however, anticipate fires and have plans in place to prevent them or snuff them out. Unhealthy companies wait too long to act while the fires rage on, uncontrolled.

With growth comes complexity; with complexity comes the potential for failure—and the potential for competitive advantage. That is our basic proposition. There are *predictable challenges* of complexity that will inevitably appear in a successful company's life cycle. With the right tools and strategies, complexity can be exploited and the life of the company prolonged. How routinely corporate leaders check their company's vital signs and how effectively they take appropriate action are what determine the long-term success of a great company.

Related Literature

While preparing to write this book, we reviewed other books on success and failure in companies. We found that many tend to focus on one kind of problem or solution or on applying a given solution in the same way at every point in a company's life. These books are excellent in their focus. However, they don't address the different stages of company complexity. We hope to add to these ideas and refine them into a more comprehensive, flexible, and practical approach.

Books that we believe have relevance to ours include the following:

- *Who Moved My Cheese* by Spencer Johnson (New York: Putnam, 2000), which shows how complexity causes change, for better or worse, and evokes emotional responses and discernible behavior patterns
- *The Innovator's Dilemma* by Clayton Christensen (Boston: Harvard Business School Press, 1997), which demonstrates how product or company success often threatens to make a company a prisoner of its own successful past
- *Crossing the Chasm* by Geoffrey Moore (New York: Harper Business, 2002), which discusses the complexity of high-tech markets and the idea that great companies must embrace customer intimacy, fulfillment, and satisfaction
- *Fit, Failure, and the Hall of Fame* by Raymond Miles and Charles Snow (New York: The Free Press, 1994), which shows how misalignment in complex systems causes failure
- *Good to Great* by Jim Collins (New York: Harper Collins, 2001), which discusses common leadership and operational elements among companies with exceptionally high financial returns over a protracted period of time

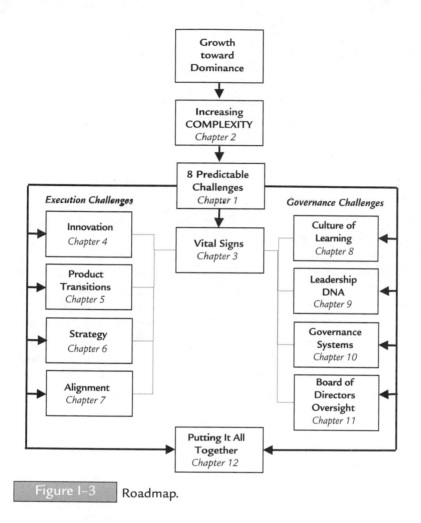

Figure 1-3 Roadmap.

The Organization of This Book

The book is organized around the middle eight chapters (Chapters 4–11), which focus on each of the eight predictable challenges. In each of these chapters, we explore the origins and features of each challenge, identify the vital signs indicating its emergence, and suggest relevant antidotes that can turn the potential for failure into an advantage. First, however, Chapter 1 introduces all eight of the challenges and describes their relationship to the evolving nature of successful companies. Chapter 2 sets the stage with a discussion of complexity and corporate evolution, and Chapter 3 defines the idea of vital signs and suggests how they can be put to good use.

The succeeding eight chapters cite real-life examples of failure and success for each of the eight challenges. In each chapter we suggest "Things to Think About," offering methods of monitoring the critical vital signs and preventing or mitigating the threads of failure. Finally, Chapter 12 discusses the interdependency of the eight challenges and poses a methodology for routine company health assessment.

Figure I–3 maps the organization of the book to allow you at a glance to access any chapter. We encourage you to use our book as a manual as you navigate through your company's growth.

A Call to Action

We want to challenge you with this book to do more than intermittently place your finger on the pulse of your company. We hope this book will help you learn to use your intuition to read a company's vital signs and to balance that intuition with routine analytical assessment. The real challenge is to face the tough task of listening to what will at times be news you don't want to hear. Without courage and perseverance, your ship will be subject to the unpredictable sea of complexity rather than being carefully steered by your vigilance through any storms that arise.

The threads of failure can be seen if you look. You can anticipate where they are going to appear in a company by observing the right vital signs longitudinally. The potential dangers are real; they are not avoidable, but they are manageable. Have the courage to face reality, and live by what you learn. This goes for all leaders, not just for the CEO. A great company's susceptibility to threads of failure is *every* leader's problem, *every day*.

1
The Predictable Challenges Faced by Dominant Companies

Overview

- Success means growth, and growth results in complexity.

- *Eight predictable challenges* emerge out of complexity, which we organize into two groups:

  - *Execution*
    - innovation
    - product transitions
    - strategy
    - alignment

  - *Governance*
    - culture of learning
    - leadership DNA
    - governance systems
    - board of directors oversight

- The threads of failure for a great company lie in ignoring or responding poorly to these challenges.

- At the same time, these challenges represent opportunities to achieve a powerful competitive advantage.

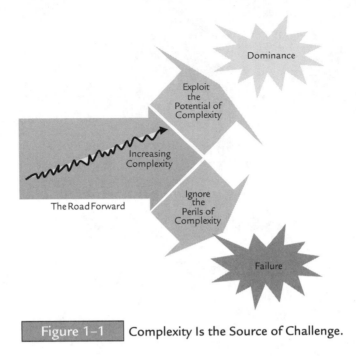

Complexity Is the Source of Challenge.

Long-term dominance, the goal of many companies, is achieved by few. To understand the difference between the winners and the losers, the great companies and the "also-rans," it is necessary to understand complexity, a natural by-product of success.

Success in an enterprise necessarily means growth, and growth means new technology, more complicated structures, new processes, more customers and employees, new locations, and so on. This complexity brings with it inevitable but predictable challenges, and these challenges can be met in two ways:

- They can be exploited, to increase competitive advantage.
- They can be ignored and allowed to drag the company into failure (see Figure 1–1).

Eight Predictable Challenges

The intrinsic challenges of complexity faced by all growing companies can be organized into two groups: four *execution* challenges and four *governance* challenges (see Figure 1–2).

Going the Distance: Why Some Companies Dominate and Others Fail

Execution Challenges	Governance Challenges
• innovation	• culture of learning
• product transitions	• leadership DNA
• strategy	• governance systems
• alignment	• board of directors oversight

Figure 1–2 Eight Predictable Challenges Faced by Great Companies.

Challenges Can Become Threads of Failure

Each of the eight challenges has the potential to become a *thread of failure*. Seldom will any one thread derail a great company. However, sustained periods of ignoring any one of them can mean that several will become active simultaneously and eventually threaten a great company's success, if not its very survival. Let's look at a couple of examples.

Imagine an organization where technology inertia has been allowed to develop—that is, the company has continued to focus on its existing products while the competition routinely disrupts the market with technology innovation (Chapter 4). In its weakened position, if that company also manages its product transitions poorly (Chapter 5), it might not only stagger but could actually fall to its knees.

Or take a large company that is well established as a disruptor and good at product transitions. Imagine that its initial cultural underpinnings have calcified with age and now reinforce the leaders' tendency to believe that they already know all that they need to know. As the company encounters the normal rough weather of doing business, it can find itself flying blind for lack of the active feedback that a strong learning culture would assure (Chapter 8). Experience can guide the company's leadership for a while, but if this same company imposes rigid and centralized governing systems

Recommended Reading
Robert Sobel, *When Giants Stumble* (Paramus, NJ: Prentice Hall, 1999).
Donald Sull, "Why Good Companies Go Bad," *Harvard Business Review*, July–August 1999, pp. 42–52.

(Chapter 10) or selects a strategy suited to the past rather than the future (Chapter 6), its ability to navigate bad weather will be lost.

Threads of Failure ... or of Opportunity?

Beyond their potential to erode the strength of a great company, the eight challenges also represent *opportunities for competitive advantage*. Each predictable thread of failure can be monitored, identified, and turned into an opportunity. An organization that monitors these threads of failure and takes advantage of the resulting information can create a competitive advantage. Exhibit 1–1 explores this idea further and suggests a model for understanding the nature of complexity as a double-edged sword and how that complexity can be exploited to a company's advantage.

Following that model, our focus in this book is to explore the double-edged nature of the eight challenges—to understand them both as threads of failure *and* as opportunities. An organization's ability to *leverage* the challenges of complexity into a competitive advantage is the mark of a great company. The also-rans lack the rigor and courage to monitor themselves and take necessary action.

Figure 1–3 suggests how each of the eight challenges we address in this book can be seen as a thread of failure and as an opportunity for competitive advantage.

	Challenges as Perils	Challenges as Opportunities
Execution Challenges	• technology inertia • poor product transitions • misguided strategy • misalignment	• market disruption • effective product transitions • differentiating strategy • effective alignment
Governance Challenges	• weak cultural underpinnings • undeveloped leadership DNA • ineffective governance systems • weak board of directors oversight	• culture of learning • strong leadership DNA • effective governance systems • strong board of directors oversight

Figure 1-3   Eight Predictable Challenges, as Perils and as Opportunities.

Exhibit 1–1: Complexity as a Double-Edged Sword

As we describe in detail in Chapter 2, a company's success breeds complexity. Growth inevitably brings with it a greater quantity and variety of people, products, and processes to be managed. Distribution channels must be expanded and new markets must be cultivated, even as competitive pressures are intensified by other companies seeking to take advantage of the potential for success. If handled correctly, this increasing complexity can be a competitive advantage.

Let's visualize complexity in three dimensions and see how it might be used to advantage (see Figure E1–1).

Each axis in Figure E1–1 represents a separate dimension of complexity—and of competitive advantage:

• technology/products and their positioning

• distribution—the reach, mix, and productivity of channels

• operational scale and size

Companies can take advantage of complexity and sustain growth by *simultaneously* innovating or disrupting, relative to the competition, on *two of the*

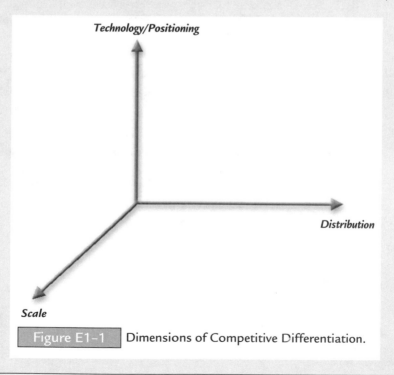

Figure E1–1   Dimensions of Competitive Differentiation.

three dimensions of this model—that is, on any one *plane*, where a plane represents the combination of any two dimensions.[1] Further, we pose that the most common and reliable successes result from disrupting on either of the following two planes:

• technology/market *and* distribution channel mix
• distribution channel mix and economies of scale

Before we illustrate these two means of disrupting for dominance, let's look at two alternatives—disrupting on the basis of the plane of technology/market and scale, and disrupting on all *three* dimensions. We believe more fleeting success is found in the combination of technology/market and economies of scale. This plane has the highest risk of losing invested capital, as disruption on the technology/market dimension usually requires sustained periods of economic and industry stability to enable dominance. In the Information Age, most markets move too fast to be able to rely on such stability. In addition, in the rare cases when a company differentiates on all three dimensions simultaneously, such as Intel and Microsoft, it can achieve a virtual monopoly. This especially strong condition of competitive power carries its own risk.

Early-stage companies naturally focus on a marketing or technology position to create a change in the patterns of purchasing. This competitive differentiation lasts for a while. But to achieve sustained dominance, a company must not only continue to differentiate itself on the marketing/technology dimension but also establish a level of reach (distribution) or economic scale that cannot easily be achieved by others. This can happen by overt strategy or by simple iterative execution toward that end.

To see these dynamics in a non–high-tech environment, consider Longaberger, the maker of premium handwoven baskets. To break out of the pack of its competition, the company decided to redefine its baskets from a commodity to a collectible, upgrading its market appeal. Its success in this transition is illustrated by the fact that a Longaberger basket purchased several years ago for $50 to $100 is worth the same or more today.

At the same time, the company reorganized sales and distribution, embracing a lower cost, more viral approach, using home sales associates, as do Avon, Tupperware, and Mary Kay. Through disrupting on both the technology/market

---

[1] Relative to Geoffrey Moore's CAP and GAP, the vertical axis translates into GAP (product differentiation), and the combination of the other two axes (scale and distribution) translates into CAP market power. See his book *Crossing the Chasm: Marketing and Selling High-Tech Products to Mainstream Customers* (New York: HarperBusiness, 2002).

and distribution channel dimensions, Longaberger created a high-margin business in a market with seemingly poor margins and too much competition.

Longaberger is an excellent example of our theory of "planar" (two-dimensional) disruption. Given its transformation from a family business that began in Dresden, Ohio, to a highly renowned public company, it represents a great American success story of sustained dominance.

Turning to the high-tech world, in the early 1990s, Cisco Systems innovated on the technology/market dimension by consolidating low-bandwidth data traffic that traveled over widespread, large company intranets, establishing itself as a data communications supplier to 80 percent of worldwide enterprise customers. Simultaneously, Cisco created three complementary distribution channels—direct sales, Tier 1 integrators (big systems integrators such as EDS), and Tier 2 channels (fulfillment houses such as Tech Data)—at a time when competitors were using one or, at most, two channels well.

Conventional wisdom said that channel conflict would foil Cisco; the result was quite the opposite, as we explain in some detail in Chapter 5. Again, this is an example of successful disruption on the plane of technology/market and channel distribution, rather than on a single dimension only.

To demonstrate disruption on a different plane, let's look at Dell Computer Corporation and Compaq. Dell created a new business based on direct distribution of PCs, establishing customer intimacy while achieving an economy of scale that dramatically lowered costs. Compaq similarly took on scale and distribution as its dual focus. It employed economies of manufacturing as a weapon, thus lowering cost. At the same time, through many thousands of channel partners, Compaq expanded its channel structure more smoothly and more swiftly than any other company. Both Compaq and Dell disrupted on two dimensions—not one, and not three.

In contrast, Ascend is an example of a company that disrupted in only one dimension and could not sustain its success for more than five years. At first, Ascend boosted its strong technology position by creating a new product category, concentrating modem (asynchronous dial-up) and ISDN dial-up communications onto one hardware platform for Internet Service Providers like America Online (AOL), UUNet, and PSINet.

However, disrupting on only one dimension was insufficient to ensure Ascend's continued competitive advantage. Without creating a second dimension of differentiation, the company was vulnerable to Cisco's strength in the market and ultimately was absorbed by a company with stronger distribution—Lucent

Technologies. Before it was absorbed, by the second quarter of 2001, Ascend's market share fell below 30 percent, when at one point it had exceeded 60 percent. Creation of a competitive gap on only one dimension leaves a company vulnerable to a new disruptor or a company that has much greater market power on another dimension. In other words, dominance tends to be short-lived with only one dimension of competitive differentiation.

Figure E1–2 suggests a few more examples, and there are many more that demonstrate the same point: A *plane* of competitive advantage can be exploited that *creates greater complexity* relative to the current way of doing things, thus creating greater complexity for the competition. When managed in this way, this higher level of complexity can propel a company's growth while creating barriers to entry for the competition over a sustained period of time.

Complexity, then, while a breeding ground for difficulties, is also desirable for differentiation. The body of this book builds on this theme of complexity as a double-edged sword—an agent of peril and of opportunity. We examine this dual nature for each of the eight challenges created by growth and success. Each of Chapters 4 through 11 addresses one of the eight challenges; in each chapter, we suggest specific actions to take as complexity shows itself to be both friend and foe.

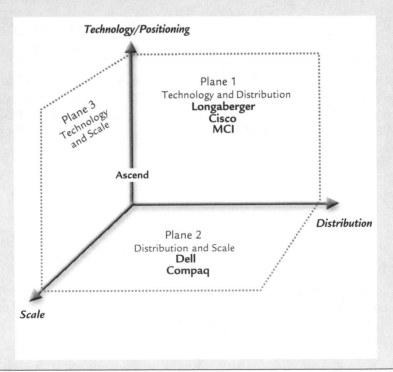

Execution Challenges

As introduced earlier in this chapter, we organize the eight challenges into two groups: execution challenges and governance challenges. The execution challenges follow:

- innovation
- product transitions
- strategy
- alignment

Innovation

All markets reach turning points that require new directions; some markets do this more frequently than others. A high level of competition, which drives a high level of innovation, means more frequent points of market disruption. However, companies that have established some success based on past innovation often see themselves as dependent on that past success—usually a function of their original technology—and often ignore the inevitability of change. It's not the technology they are dependent on, however; it's the *market* in which that technology was successful. The market *will change,* whether a company is part of that change or not.

Technology *inertia* means leaving the unavoidable disruption of the market on which a company is dependent in the hands of competitors. Technology disruption, however, is an advantage to a company and can put its *competitors in peril.* Disruption, which creates strong competitive differentiation, often brings great rewards to those who do the disrupting. Although it is true that the strategy of being a *fast follower* can also bring success, doing neither is the road to mediocrity, if not failure.

Market or technology disruption, which we discuss in depth in Chapter 4, results in permanent change in buyers' preferences and therefore in the size and segmentation of a market. With this level of change, the winners of the past, who served the former market, are often no longer the winners of the future.

As we discussed in Exhibit 1-1, market disruption occurs on one of three dimensions (Figure E1–1), so managing market disruption means meeting the challenge ideally on two of the following three dimensions:

- **technology/products and their positioning.** The functionality of the technology and the way it is brought to market change a buyer's preferences.

- **distribution.** The way products are made available to buyers affects a buyer's preferences and the means of delivery.

- **operational scale or size.** Economies of scale that are great enough to affect the cost at which products can be brought to market (and thus the price) change a buyer's preferences.

In Silicon Valley, market disruption often occurs based on technology. Steve Jobs and Steve Wozniak, for example, like others at that time, envisioned a *personal* computer; unlike others, however, they had the energy and intelligence to invent one that worked. In one of Silicon Valley's most famous stories of a great product emerging out of a garage, Wozniak and Jobs invented a user interface for a PC that has become a long-term success and that assisted in the disruption of the then-enormous mainframe computer market. We look at many more examples like this in Chapter 4.

Product Transitions

Customer demand drives innovation, and innovation requires product transitions. Yet introducing new products into a market in which a company is already earning revenues is always a risk to those revenues. As a company's revenues grow and the company becomes more complex, the risk grows simply by virtue of the amount of revenue involved. The ability to take calculated risks in product introductions is an art and is essential to long-term success. No company survives well in a competitive environment without successfully conquering this challenge.

The natural tendency for market-driven product improvements to cannibalize revenues of existing products creates the risk inherent in product transitions. Paradoxically, cannibalization is necessary for progress but is also a thread of failure if the risks are poorly managed. Either a company cannibalizes its own revenues—strategically—or it leaves itself open to the competition.

While product transitions are predictably complicated, they are nonetheless often undertaken with too little strategic and operational planning. Typically, a product manager will assume that in introducing a new product to replace an existing one, the distribution channel and the customer will quickly absorb the new product.

There are many examples of the negative results of this naïve assumption.

In Chapter 5 we pursue these ideas in greater detail, telling the story of a successful and complicated product transition to illustrate a set of axioms we believe can help companies meet this challenge.

Strategy

There are many different moments in a great company's growth cycle during which it faces critical strategic decisions. Selecting and implementing the strategy that provides sufficient thrust in the right direction—and reviewing this on an ongoing basis—is essential to building and sustaining a dominant position.

There are many ways, however, that companies fail to identify the vector with the direction and power to hit the mark. They select, for example, weak strategies that don't compete well; strategies that double back and are self-defeating; or strategies that don't take into account the complexities of the market and go straight for the target when more subtle, flanking moves are required.

Strategy defines *direction*. A successful company defines the key vectors by which it will approach the vision or destination that it has set. That destination might never be fully reached. In fact, as a company realizes its destination *can* be reached, it must set its sights on a new one, as driven by the needs of the markets it serves. At any one time, strategy defines the roadmap by which a successful company makes its way to its desired future. Misguided choices about strategy result in missing the long-term target and meeting failure rather than success.

As a company grows and succeeds, the risk inherent in its choice of strategies increases. The stakes get higher, and complexity tends to obscure the organization's eyesight. Leaders often become over-whelmed with operational challenges. Their ability to see what's wrong, what's possible, and how to get there becomes obscured. We call this condition *glare*. As companies get more complex, glare builds, and decision makers often adapt to and accept it. This lack of being able to see the right direction leads to weak or misguided strategies.

For example, consider the case of a fast-paced company that makes software for wireless telephone handsets and has grown exceptionally fast to exploit the potential of the market. In achieving its growth, the company has made numerous acquisitions without developing an organizing infrastructure, having put all its effort into meeting the next customer demand. Suppose the market shifts, however, slowing down or adapting to a new technology. A new strategy is required—one that involves, for example, a more thoughtful solutions approach that mandates the coordinated effort of functions that previously operated almost autonomously. In this example, not only is it important to recognize the need for a new strategy and select the right one, but such a significant change in strategy necessarily causes other significant execution challenges. In the case of this software company, for instance, the missing infrastructure and lack of a common culture create real risks to the success of an integrated solutions strategy. In the next section, we will discuss this kind of problem—alignment, a key element in executing strategy.

Differentiating strategies—defined, implemented, and redefined on an ongoing basis—separate the great companies from the also-rans. Such strategies overcome the competition and facilitate a company's domination of the market. In Chapter 6, we look further at the challenge of strategy and examine in detail how Cisco used acquisitions to differentiate itself and maintain momentum in the accelerated market of the 1990s. As for many other great companies, of particular importance was the *alignment* of the differentiated strategy with Cisco's execution engine.

Alignment

Alignment is an essential ingredient in assuring execution of the right strategy. Alignment is evident when the flow of work, from the source of a company's products or services through to the customer, is efficient in a way that achieves sustained customer satisfaction. When companies are large and complex, maintaining such an efficient flow can be very difficult. It means smooth operations flowing from Engineering, where products are born, through Manufacturing and Marketing, and on through Sales and Service, while being capably supported by corporate functions like Finance and Human Resources. Misalignment can occur anywhere in the flow from a product idea to product maintenance. It can be found in disconnects between strategy and structure, structure and processes, and so on. In Chapter 7, we discuss many examples of misalignment.

Even if a company achieves alignment, it must constantly adjust to maintain it across the critical dimensions of the company, given the shifts and changes of growth and adaptation. When done well, this frequent realignment of goals and structure will exploit the fact that *structure biases results*. In other words, the results of any effort are heavily influenced by how that effort is structured.

One result of misalignment is organization *thrash*—organization energy bounding from one focus to another with little or no productive output. This kind of unresolved conflict arises out of misaligned goals, priorities, or assumptions about roles. If Sales and Service are misaligned about roles, for instance, customers can get mixed or even competing messages. If Marketing and Engineering get out of sync on priorities, they can end up working toward different schedule objectives, again with the likelihood of confusing or disappointing the customer.

Meeting these four execution challenges is the most essential element of achieving dominance and going the distance. However, as a company grows, complexity drives a need for more and more sophisticated governance to ensure the execution challenges will be met. In the next section, we look at what we consider to be the four predictable governance challenges required for going the distance.

Governance Challenges

In addition to the four execution challenges, there are four governance challenges:

- culture of learning
- leadership DNA
- governance systems
- board of directors oversight

Culture of Learning

A learning culture, marked by openness to information and the willingness to change that information, encourages and provides the foundation for success. A learning culture is built on active, useful feedback loops by which leaders can regularly obtain information from markets, customers, employees, competitors, and shareholders. These feedback loops are the "infrastructure" of learning and good decision making. Using that feedback to spur dialogue, experimentation, and coaching will result in a learning culture that consistently renews itself.

The evidence of culture (as with the other predictable challenges we discuss in this book) can be found in various internal indicators we call *vital signs*. For instance, lack of learning in the culture can be diagnosed by signs of slow decision making or frantic activity without focus. These kinds of vital signs indicate problems long before those problems affect the more public, lagging measures of success, like revenue growth and customer satisfaction.

Let's illustrate this with a comparison of two executive teams operating under (and shaping) two different cultural imperatives. One team meets weekly to keep the business on target, but it spends little time exchanging views and focuses almost entirely on monologue status reports. There is no evaluation or comment, except possibly by the leader, and this often occurs after the meeting is over. In time, this pattern becomes an implicit norm for the team: We don't critique each other's piece of the business. The other team, however, operates with a lot of discussion. The team members share status reports, but their purpose is as much to get reactions and ideas—to learn—as it is to inform. The first team is missing valuable opportunities not only to learn from each other but to establish a culture of openness and mutual critique that can sharpen their thinking, lower resistance to change, and model learning for others in the organization.

Early behaviors on a team readily become *patterns* of behavior (culture) and then are hard to break. Thus, it is essential to establish the roots of a learning culture in the earliest stage of a company's life. The key to assuring this, as we discuss in Chapter 8, is the attitude of the leaders. Learning leaders breed a learning culture.

Leadership DNA

Leaders who are more concerned about personal success than company success can build great companies, but these companies are not likely to thrive after the leaders depart. When leaders are more concerned about their own reputations than their companies', the focus is on the short term, not the long term.

Authenticity, an orientation to serving others, and a bias for learning are the ingredients of leadership that build companies for the long term. These ingredients in a company's DNA mean that company will attract and grow leaders with these qualities. These kinds of leaders grow other leaders, build learning into the culture, and focus on building for success long after their own tenures. A company whose leadership DNA—its ability to grow leaders for the future—includes these qualities will meet a key challenge in building a dominant company. In addition to authenticity, service orientation, and a bias for learning, leadership DNA must generate leaders who are suited to the requirements of the markets they serve. Large companies serving slow-moving markets need leaders who are skilled at building and maintaining a stable workforce and making thoughtful decisions that help the organization grow carefully, often with appropriate risk aversion, given the inherent scale of the company. The characteristics of such leaders are very different from those of leaders working in fast-paced markets where change is endemic, job security is not expected, and boldness wins the day.

In Chapter 9, we look further at how leadership DNA works and how it can be nurtured.

Governance Systems

At a certain size, the informal processes of culture and leadership can no longer provide sufficient guidance to assure good decision making and execution in a company. With more employees located in more places, with many more customers, and with many complex tasks to accomplish, informal mechanisms of governance can't do enough. Successful companies need formal methods of data collection, review, and problem solving.

However, as small companies grow and feel the need for infrastructure or formal governance systems, they often resist developing them. Too often, governance systems are equated with bureaucracy. Bureaucracy means systems for their own sake. Effective governance systems, on the other hand, are useful tools to ensure a company executes on target, sees the road ahead, and makes the turns it needs to make. Fundamentally, they accomplish this by institutionalizing the flow of useful information and the constructive use of that information for good decision making. At their best, they are a formal representation of a learning culture.

When companies grow exceptionally fast, as did many companies associated with the Internet in the late 1990s, the development of governance systems lags behind the need for them. Cisco addressed this challenge as it grew from a few thousand employees to over 30,000. In this effort, Cisco developed a system of operations reviews that drove a constant, healthy process of measurement and self-critique. At the same time, it built decentralized information systems, which both helped and hurt—they facilitated local growth and measurement but they lacked a common architecture. Eventually, these disparate systems had to be unified, an expensive and necessary step in growth and adaptation. This is not an example of doing it the wrong way, but rather of adapting to new needs over time. IBM and General Electric are also examples of companies that have found ways to restructure their governance systems to facilitate new business goals. We discuss several examples when we delve into governance systems in detail in Chapter 10.

Board of Directors Oversight

A board of directors provides a backstop to management's ability to assess the terrain and make good calls regarding strategy and alignment. When a board is sufficiently attentive to key vital signs, raises tough issues, and makes the necessary tough calls, it contributes to momentum and success.

However, too often boards are weak instruments of governance, having become the proverbial rubber stamp to the CEO's ideas or often seeming to fall asleep at the wheel while important problems are arising in the company. The year 2002 saw debacles at Enron, Global Crossing, and WorldCom, to name only three. In these companies, internal governance was not capable or trustworthy enough to protect stockholders and employees, and the boards were too weak to prevent the cataclysmic results.

The solution to the problem of weak board of directors oversight is linked to the other governance challenges. If a company has developed a culture of learning, for instance, it is not likely to be interested in a rubber-stamp board of directors, but will instead build a board that challenges management and provokes learning. Leaders bred by strong leadership DNA will similarly look for strong partners at the board level, not subordinates. In the same way, a company with effective governance systems will see the board as an important governing element; it will establish systematic means of guaranteeing that the board has the information it needs to test management's thinking, raise tough issues, provoke learning, prevent failure, and propagate long-term success.

We look at these and other means of assuring strong board of directors oversight in Chapter 11.

Summary of the Eight Challenges

The eight challenges introduced by this chapter, and summarized in Figure 1–4, are the focus of this book. Each is discussed at length in Chapters 4 through 11.

Execution Challenges	
Innovation	Maintaining a sustained pace of innovation to lead the competition or be a successful fast follower is critical for long-term success. Technology inertia—getting stuck in thinking that past innovations are enough—is a significant peril. Using disruption to advantage, however, a company can put its competitors in peril. Disruption, resulting in strong competitive differentiation, often brings great rewards to those who do the disrupting.
Product Transitions	Customer demand drives innovation, and innovation requires product transitions. Yet introducing new products into a market in which a company is already earning revenues is always a risk to those revenues. As a company's revenues grow and the company becomes more complex, the risk grows simply by virtue of the amount of revenue involved. The ability to take calculated risks in product introductions is an essential art of long-term success. No company survives well in a competitive environment without successfully conquering this challenge.
Differentiated Strategy	Strategy defines direction. Successful companies have a vision or long-term goal and define the key vectors by which they will approach that destination. At any one time, strategy defines the roadmap by which a successful company makes its way to its desired future. Misguided choices about strategy result in missing the long-term target and meeting failure rather than success.
Alignment	Alignment is an essential ingredient in assuring execution of the right strategy. Alignment is evident when the flow of work, from the source of a company's products or services through to the customer, is efficient in a way that achieves sustained customer satisfaction. When companies are large and complex, maintaining such an efficient flow can be very difficult. It means smooth operations flowing from Engineering, where products are born, through Manufacturing and Marketing, and on through Sales and Service, while being capably supported by corporate functions like Finance and Human Resources. Misalignment can occur anywhere among these various functions, as well as between other organizational elements, such as strategy and structure or structure and processes.

Figure 1–4   Summary of the Eight Predictable Challenges Faced by Great Companies.

Governance Challenges

Culture of Learning	A learning culture, marked by openness to information and the willingness to change that information, provides the foundation for success. A learning culture is built on active, useful feedback loops by which leaders can regularly obtain information from markets, customers, employees, competitors, and shareholders. These feedback loops are the "infrastructure" of learning and good decision making. Using feedback to spur dialogue, experimentation, and coaching will result in a learning culture that consistently renews itself.
Leadership DNA	Leaders who are more concerned about personal success than company success can build great companies, but those companies are not likely to thrive after the leaders depart. When leaders are more concerned about their own reputations than the company's, the focus is on the short term, not the long term. Authenticity, an orientation to serving others, and a bias for learning are the ingredients of leadership that build companies for the long term. These ingredients in a company's DNA mean that company will attract and grow leaders with these qualities. These kinds of leaders grow other leaders, build learning into the culture, and focus on building for success long after their own tenures.
Effective Governance Systems	At a certain size, culture, leadership, and informal processes can no longer provide sufficient guidance to ensure good decision making. With more people, with more locations, with many more customers and many complex tasks to accomplish, informal mechanisms of governance can't do enough. With growth, successful companies use formal methods of data collection, review, and problem solving. Institutionalizing feedback loops that promote both local decision making and company-wide coordination ensures learning, effective execution, and ongoing growth as a company increases its size and complexity.
Board of Directors Oversight	A board of directors provides a backstop to management's ability to assess the terrain and make good calls regarding strategy and alignment. When the board is sufficiently attentive to key vital signs, raises tough issues, and makes the necessary tough calls, it contributes to momentum and to success. Too often, though, boards are weak instruments of governance, having become the proverbial rubber stamp to the CEO's ideas and seeming to fall asleep at the wheel while important problems are arising in the company.

Figure 1-4   continued

In the next chapter, we address how these eight predictable challenges emerge out of the complexity that naturally develops as successful companies grow. In Chapter 3, we discuss the notion of vital signs—early internal indicators of these challenges beginning to grow into threads of failure. From there we proceed to dedicate a chapter to each challenge, delving into each in detail and citing examples that show how each challenge can develop into either a thread of failure or an opportunity to sustain greatness in real companies.

2
How Complexity Develops

Overview

- Organizational growth can be seen as occurring in the following four stages:

  - **Stage 1**—single product, single market focus

  - **Stage 2**—new products, additional market segments, expanded distribution

  - **Stage 3**—multiple product lines, new markets, global reach

  - **Stage 4**—multiple lines of business, global presence

- A company faces *predictable* challenges throughout its existence, and some challenges are more likely to appear at certain stages of growth.

- Each challenge represents an opportunity for competitive advantage as well as potential for failure.

- Momentum is an important factor in moving through the four stages successfully.

The eight challenges presented in Chapter 1 can threaten a company's health at any point during its life. However, in the same way that certain health problems are more likely to arise at certain ages during a person's life, each of the eight challenges is more likely to emerge at a particular stage in a company's growth. When a person falls ill, physicians use that person's age as an indicator of likely causes. Similarly, in examining organizations it can be useful to consider a company's developmental stage to anticipate likely threads of failure—traces of things starting to go wrong.

To illustrate this, let's imagine a great company, one that has dominated its market for five years or more. The company begins as a startup: a great idea, some smart people, new money. From such modest beginnings, successful startups evolve into larger organizations through the intense effort and sacrifice of their employees and the passion of their leaders. This was the genesis of many companies that have changed the world. Think of the first Wells Fargo stagecoach, or more recent examples like Bob Noyce and his colleagues miniaturizing circuitry on silicon and William Hewlett and David Packard working in a Palo Alto garage.

As they grow, successful companies on their way to dominance can be seen as developing through the following four stages:

- Stage 1—single product, single market focus
- Stage 2—new products, additional market segments, expanded distribution
- Stage 3—multiple product lines, new markets, global reach
- Stage 4—multiple lines of business, global presence

Stage 1: Single Focus

During Stage 1, a startup is tightly focused—a single product, one type of customer within a single market segment, and one sales channel. The company has a simple, early-stage value chain serving the customer, as shown in Figure 2–1.

At the center of the company is the Research and Development (R&D) "engine"—a group of smart engineers, eager to produce something tangible out of an idea. In addition, the company has a skeletal sales force and few people to manage operations informally—all energetic and hungry for recognition through customer response. Support is handled by whoever gets there first. The

Going the Distance: Why Some Companies Dominate and Others Fail

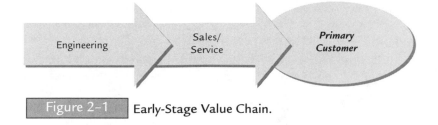

Figure 2–1
Early-Stage Value Chain.

internal alignment of the company's structure, from CEO to individual contributor, is simple, and internal unity is maintained by the collective focus on a single product. Communication occurs naturally through getting the day-to-day job done. "Cool" technology gives birth to solutions to real problems. Entrepreneurial spirit fuels the fledgling organization.

A Mindset for Change and Disruption

Success in Stage 1 brings challenges, primarily in the form of growing competition. Competition breeds innovation, and innovation disrupts markets. The greater the competitive pressures in a given market, the more frequent the moments of market disruption. The companies that stay ahead and are able to compete in a changing market don't rest on the laurels of their past success. Introducing new products based on new technology is essential.

New products accomplish a number of things: They replace the company's first-generation product, which has by now attracted competition; they extend the company's market reach, possibly into new markets; and, at best, they *disrupt* the market, which allows the company to maintain control in the market. This is how successful companies pursue dominance.

Too often, though, the leaders of successful ventures are unprepared for the next market disruption and its inevitable effect on what they have just created. New players come along and change the world. Ray Kroc, the expansive leader of the McDonald's hamburger chain, changed the world of fast food forever with his inventive notion of franchising the hamburger stand. How many local, successful hamburger stands survived this disruption?

Once an invention succeeds, *inertia*—a company's propensity to continue to conduct business as it has in the past—tends to set in. The company feels dependent on the success of its first innovation and is likely to develop assumptions based on this success. Future decisions are then hampered by increasingly outdated assumptions. Still it can seem logical to maintain a commitment to the company's initial successful thrust.[1]

Kaufman Footwear of Ontario is an example of a company caught in the inertia of its own success. In 1995,

> Kaufman enjoyed its best year ever, selling three million pairs of boots and ringing up sales of C$170 million. But perhaps the company was too successful.
>
> "With things going so well, it almost seemed the company could do no wrong," remarked Tony Dowling, a Kaufman veteran who now runs a brand consulting business. "That may have created some complacency."
>
> He notes that the company gave up market share to competitors because it was slow to respond to changes in the market. It continued to focus on heavy, functional boots when people were buying stylish, lightweight boots.[2]

This inertia was amplified by management's resistance to moving manufacturing offshore and by its lack of response to long-term weather changes. Eventually, a U.S. firm bought the company.

The crucial point is that early in a great company's life, its leaders need to both *drive* and *prepare* for market disruption—in fact, they need to make the company a *disruptor*. Complacency derails companies. A company must be willing to strategically *cannibalize* its own revenue streams, both to grow and to preempt the competition. If a company doesn't disrupt its own market—if it doesn't vary from its initial successful direction and thereby create new barriers to entry by its competitors—other companies will. Countless stories bear this out, as we explore in greater depth in Chapter 4.

In an example of planned cannibalization, the leadership at Cisco Systems engaged in a major internal debate in 1993–94 over the question of technology development: Should the company expand beyond its currently successful business in large routers—the boxes that facilitated data transmission over corporate intranets and gave companies access to the Internet? These products provided Cisco with a high average selling price (ASP) and the industry's best gross margins. The debate centered on the size of this new market

[1] Clayton Christensen's book *The Innovator's Dilemma* (Harvard Business, 1997) describes this dynamic in detail.

[2] Ron DeRuyter, "The Boot Stopped Here," *Hemispheres* magazine, October 2001, pp. 25–28.

and the impact of lower gross margins, given the likelihood of a lower ASP for smaller routers and cannibalization of demand for the more profitable high-end products. Thus, diversification could cause a reduction in sales and the loss of profits.

However, the visionaries at the company saw the emerging market for smaller routers, which would be important for enterprise branch offices, and argued for the move.

Eventually, based on the estimate of the growth of both intranets and the Internet and a sense of expanding customer demand, Cisco moved forward into the smaller router market. Although the new product ASP did turn out to be half that of the larger routers, the sales force was able to sell the new products at a volume *six times* higher. The competition could not keep pace, and Cisco's business grew to an annual revenue of billions per year. This development catalyzed the evolution of the router market and disrupted the enterprise information systems market, which IBM had dominated until then.

Constant Vigilance and Adaptation— A Culture of Learning

Effective management of disruption and competitive pressures demands an extraordinary learning curve in Stage 1. Everything's new and everyone's learning—about the customer, about the market, about the solutions, and about each other. Because success wakes competitive sleeping giants and entices new entrepreneurs to the opportunity, constant vigilance and adaptation are essential.

Adaptation to the market and to the competition requires constant learning. If an openness to change grounded in a culture of learning is not established at the earliest stage of a company's growth, it is very hard to develop later. The story of MCI's impact on AT&T illustrates this. As an upstart service provider, MCI decided not to offer the full gamut of long-distance services. Instead, it attacked AT&T on its flank, competing in high-margin business-to-business communication first, thereby skimming the profit cream of long-distance service. To compete successfully, MCI used "guerilla" marketing to pick away at AT&T's deeply entrenched position. AT&T had never encountered aggressive competition and did not have the adaptive culture that would have allowed it to respond quickly. As a result, AT&T soon found itself in the position of adapting to catch up rather than adapting to lead.

In establishing the roots of a learning culture, successful companies must avoid a tendency toward *learning inertia*. Once a team achieves some success, a sense of "we get it" can develop. Mistaking success for the idea that there is now less to learn is a profound error. Recognition that the next moment brings change and that change requires constant learning is crucial for ongoing success. It is not just the learning but also the *valuing* of learning—promoting it and establishing it as a basis for company culture—that results in competitive advantage. It is in Stage 1 that the seeds of a learning culture are planted, a topic discussed at length in Chapter 8.

Leadership for the Future

Similarly, it is in this first stage that the roots of leadership DNA develop (Chapter 9). Leadership DNA is the ability of a company to grow the right kind of leaders for the future.

In a startup's earliest days the venture capitalists on the board of directors often take a strong role in assessing the founders' leadership skills and appointing or hiring the first CEO. As the company releases its first products and gains traction in the market, the board assesses the ability of the CEO to take the company public. If the individual in place is not suitable, he or she is replaced to ensure the company's success in dealing with a more sophisticated set of demands—new customers, new sales issues, and Wall Street. This type of transition often results in the painful but necessary replacement of founding leaders with seasoned CEOs.

A company's leadership DNA is affected by these early surgical maneuvers—for good or for ill. It is the sophisticated, experienced venture capitalists who understand the importance of developing early leadership and that leadership's ability to replace itself in the future, instead of focusing only on the immediate concerns of delivering on customer commitments and establishing profitability. Similarly, leaders who gain profitability at this stage *and* who cultivate other leaders as they succeed are the ones who establish leadership DNA for the long term. In this way, a company's leadership DNA transcends its early leaders, but it is nevertheless established by the most influential of them.

To summarize Stage 1 of a company's life, evidence of a company's ability to exploit market disruption, foster a learning culture, and establish sound leadership DNA are the hallmarks of this stage. It is not too early at this point to check for vital signs (Chapter 3) in all of these areas. The complexity developing even in Stage 1 provides both the opportunity to establish a foundation for long-term success and the potential for the first threads of failure.

Stage 2: Adding Products

As a company succeeds and moves into Stage 2, its markets grow and customer expectations expand. The company introduces new products to extend market reach and sustain competitive advantage. The growing number of new products requires new sales channels, which must be established without stalling existing sales. Quality is of increasing concern, and customer loyalty is subject to pressures from competitors. Operational excellence takes on growing importance and must be established in each of the corporate functions that emerge to handle the larger set of tasks.

Figure 2–2 suggests this emerging complexity across time.

Product Transitions

The ability to insert new products successfully into markets in ways that preclude unplanned cannibalization of existing revenues is an art form (as we discuss in greater detail in Chapter 5). New products,

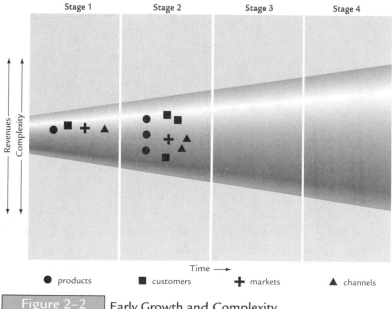

Figure 2-2 Early Growth and Complexity.

whether derivative or disruptive, are essential for success, but they naturally compete with existing products, possibly endangering revenues that are essential to the company's survival. Changes in buying patterns are difficult to predict. Some customers will be attracted to a new product, whereas many will hesitate to buy an unproven choice. Customers who are not "early adopters" will wait until early design flaws are fixed.

Sometimes, in an attempt to gain an advantage over competitors, a company will announce a new product well before it is actually available. This strategy can backfire if the company isn't able to meet its announced release date. What's more, existing revenue can also be impacted if customers stop buying the old product in favor of the promised "better" technology. If new releases are held up for too long, customers will even migrate to a competing company with an available product, regardless of the relative quality of that product.

The timing of product transitions is a delicate thing. A company must take reasonable risks in responding to the demands of the market to generate quality products and expand its customer base without abandoning existing products. Cisco has struggled with this challenge countless times, and it has both won and lost these battles. For example, in an effort to reinvent its operating system software, Cisco's development process bogged down, fostering a reputation for nondelivery both inside the company and out in the market. This delay created challenges and frustration for Cisco's sales force, which was working hard to stay ahead of the spawning competition.

This challenge was minimized, eventually, by separating Cisco's software development organization into two parts—one focusing on delivering capabilities for products not yet in existence and the other on improving the existing operating system for markets currently served. A common cost center was thus split in two so that parallel initiatives could focus on completely different goals.

When organizations are profit centers instead of cost centers, however, splitting them to manage complexity can also cause new problems. The classic error is structuring separate organizations, one for the "old" product and one for the new, but with both attempting to solve the same problem for the same customer. Without ensuring a separate focus for the two organizations, internal competition develops. In addition, the best talent often migrates to the new work, leaving the original organization depleted. The faulty structure fuels a vicious cycle—quality and morale decline among those responsible for the existing products, and employee turnover increases. Worst of all, both sales and market share of the existing product are impacted, and pressure on the new organization to deliver can become overwhelming. Competitors will take full advantage of a company's inability to deliver new products in time to salvage its losses.

Let's look at a company that handled this successfully—Microsoft when it split its development organization to manage the introduction of Windows NT. Microsoft established an NT organization, separate from the existing Windows organization, to position NT as a server-oriented, high-end operating system and exploit the new potential of the Internet. The separate structure distinguished NT from Windows, which was targeted as a single-user product. As it turned out, this focus on differentiated positioning was crucial in allowing NT to be born without stalling sales of Windows.

Because *structure biases results*, a concept we discuss in depth in Chapter 7, it is predictable that two organizations will act differently from a united one that produces both products. Split organizations might be important to ensure incubation of new ideas or to manage results in cost centers, but they are inherently dangerous when revenue streams for both old and new products exist and compete for the same customers. On the other hand, a single organization risks unsuccessful incubation of the new product. This is an example of the kind of complex structural issues that emerge with company growth.

The challenge of product transitions and structuring to manage them remains throughout a company's life. In addition, in Stage 2 and on into Stage 3, the challenges of strategy and governance mechanisms arise. Before we examine them, let's look further at the way complexity grows as a company enters what can be called Stage 3.

Stage 3: Multiple Product Lines

By Stage 3, a successful company has dominated its market for at least five years. But to continue to do so, that company must still overcome new challenges produced by the increasing complexity that accompanies success. Opportunities for growth and growing competition at this stage drive new products into new markets or market segments. New products and legacy products coexist. The company's organizational structure becomes complicated by the need to focus on many products in many markets with many different market drivers.

Microsoft's expansion from Windows to Windows and Windows NT is, again, an example of two competing technologies developing within one company, each with a different market focus. The competing priorities of these two products pressured their shared support functions, adding to internal complexity. The entire company—from Marketing to Engineering to Support—had to respond with a more complex structure and processes to manage both products and ensure an organized focus. As indicated earlier, managing the engineering of both Microsoft products was a complex organizational issue of its own, further complicated by the need to motivate some engineers to continue to work on an existing product while inviting others to invent the new.

Thus, as opportunities expand and become more diverse, so too does a company's internal set of responses. The growing complexity of demands drives functional organizations to become more complex to handle the multitude of competing demands from both internal and end-use customers. Manufacturing, for example, is now charged with reducing costs, whereas Support is pushed to drive new revenues. These changes lead to new positions, new functions, and a new set of power dynamics, all adding to the larger organizational complexity.

With these internal organizational changes, new leaders with greater market expertise are brought in to manage the company's growing complexity. As they do so, they also begin to influence existing corporate culture. With many disparate leadership backgrounds in the management ranks in Stage 3, a company's culture can become diluted. Some, if not many, of the new leaders come from acquisitions, where they might have had only small company experience. Some will resist a large company environment yet are essential players for market credibility. Some may stay, however, only because of contractual obligations.

A Differentiating Strategy

At Stage 3, a company's size and complexity tends to obstruct an organization's eyesight. Leaders become overwhelmed with operational issues. This can result in glare—like the glare off the face of a compass in the sun—a condition making it difficult to read the direction you are going. As a company grows in complexity, glare increases, and it gets harder and harder to see where the company is headed.

Because glare builds gradually, decision makers tend to adapt to and accept it, even more so if other threads of failure have developed. For instance, if a nonlearning culture is established, it can act like hardening glue, resulting in rigidity even as flexibility is required. The company could be stumbling from poor product transitions—when a new product results in unplanned lost revenues from the old—or from competitive market disruptions. Leaders can fall into passive acceptance of outside influences or select a misguided strategy (discussed further in Chapter 6).

In Stage 3, those companies that can design and adopt strategies that successfully reduce glare and provide a differentiating direction are the companies that will become great; those that can't, won't. Furthermore, differentiating strategies are grown in the soil of a learning culture. If the organization is bred to listen, if the channels of communication encourage differing points of view and creative input, strong leaders are likely to find the right path. Without open feedback loops—systems for collecting information from customers, the market, the competition, and employees—a company is dependent on what it already knows, on what has worked in the past, or on what is politically palatable.

In the 1980s, for example, DEC—a great company with an unusually strong reputation for being a great place to work—reached the deadly strategic conclusion that PCs were not going to be relevant. Furthermore, as the internal communications of the growing company became more complex, DEC chose proprietary inter-networking approaches as opposed to the open standards necessary in the emerging and ultimately dominant client/server industry. The company had stopped listening and, as a result, developed an obsolete view of the world. A learning orientation was missing, and overconfident decision makers never received the information that would have pushed them to change their ways. Their misguided strategy led the company into steep decline and ultimate failure.

Effective Governance Systems

By Stage 3, corporate culture and effective leadership are insufficient by themselves to govern the level of complexity a company faces. At this point, companies often fall victim to *Brownian motion*—

expending lots of energy without consistent direction. Systematic tools of governance are needed to ensure basic governing processes, like inspection of progress against goals. Governance systems include forecasting systems, operations reviews, design reviews, delegated budget accountability, and customer account reviews and accountability, all discussed further in Chapter 10. The increasing risk of multibillion dollar revenues requires reliable systems to ensure focused governance, to enhance a company's culture of learning, and to assist in the integration of new leaders.

Although these systems can be in place before Stage 3, they are usually informal until then. If formalized, these early governance systems often operate weakly—that is, in ways that do not provide new information, learning, and follow-through. To succeed, governance systems need to be built on a culture of fact-finding, free exchange of opinions, and rigorous follow-through.

The various governance challenges that organizations face by Stage 3—culture, leadership DNA, and governance systems—are interdependent. If these challenges are poorly met, the resulting weaknesses can *reinforce* each other in endangering organizational health. The good news is that if culture, leadership, and governance systems are strong, they will collectively provide a powerful thrust for competitive advantage. In addition, the concurrent *execution* challenges of managing market disruption, product transitions, and strategic shifts in the middle stages of a company's life are more likely to be met successfully with the help of effective governing systems. We discuss these interdependencies further in Chapter 12.

With the day-to-day pressures of more complicated delivery, resistance to the changes required to meet all of these challenges is common. For example, attention to culture is too often considered either extraneous to the current demands for delivery or, worse, a sign of the bureaucracy that drove many leaders to leave previous employers. Resistance to governance systems is common as well, for similar reasons. Leaders must be able to distinguish between the drag of bureaucracy and sterile programs for cultural and leadership development and the benefit of day-to-day, real-time actions that build culture and cultivate the right leadership DNA. With the pragmatic use of systematic feedback loops, for instance, leaders can actually empower employees: Information, decision making, and accountability are placed in the hands of those best positioned to affect critical business outcomes. We look at this further in Chapter 10.

Stage 4: Multiple Lines of Business

With continued success comes more and more organizational complexity that must be managed. The dimensions of this complexity in Stage 4 can be staggering:

- hundreds to thousands of customers, many far more sophisticated than those in earlier stages

- thousands of employees in myriad organizational layers

- multiple markets with fast-changing business imperatives

- hundreds, if not thousands, of products, with expanding technology about which no one salesperson can be fully knowledgeable

- multiple partners and suppliers with whom healthy relationships are critical

- new types of channels in global markets

- enormous financial risks: revenues, investments, and public accountability

The depiction of this complexity in Figure 2–3 cannot communicate the sense of barely controlled chaos and conflict that is typical behind the front doors of a large company that is succeeding in a fast-paced market. Managing high complexity at high speed is extremely difficult, yet essential. Natural barriers to further growth emerge at every turn unless problems are monitored, subdivided, and managed to allow for further expansion.

If a company reaches Stage 4, it has developed multiple lines of business as it grew to meet its opportunities and competitive threats. Effective execution depends on complete understanding of the market and a clear vision—not always possible when a market is emerging. As an example, let's look once again at Cisco.

In 1995, Cisco established four lines of business, each with separate units managing engineering and product marketing to meet the changing markets the company served. In that era, the Service Provider business was expanding. It required not only products different from those produced for Cisco's established Enterprise market but also a different approach to sales and distribution. Meanwhile, Cisco was experimenting in the small-to-medium business world as well as exploring the consumer market.

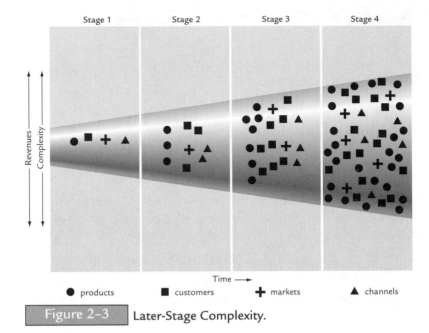

Stage 1   Stage 2   Stage 3   Stage 4

Revenues — Complexity

Time →

● products   ■ customers   ✚ markets   ▲ channels

Figure 2–3 | Later-Stage Complexity.

It took some time for the company to sort out the mission of the consumer organization. The central issue was whether Cisco should be making products for consumers or focusing on promoting consumer demand for Internet appliance products, which would then drive demand by Service Providers for Cisco's existing product line. Should the consumer line of business be conceived of as a profit center or strictly as a business development venture? If Cisco did choose to sell directly to consumers, what expertise could it offer to succeed in that market? How would the company manage the very different business model for a consumer business involving significantly lower margins? Should manufacturing prepare for an explosion of demand?

These questions were eventually sorted out, well ahead of failure, and much was learned in the process. At the same time, the experiment was expensive insofar as the answers were found through jumping right into the fray rather than from a differentiated strategy up front.

Alignment

At Stage 4, various types of complexity develop. The number of product offerings may expand to the point that distribution channels are seriously strained. The expanding product portfolio can also make it difficult for salespeople to maintain a sufficient depth of knowledge. In addition, diverse business models can develop within the company. Multiple products compete for priority with specialized functional organizations, such as Manufacturing and Support. In these kinds of ways, natural disparities develop, resulting in misalignment. Misalignment is a serious problem, as it drives inefficiencies, loss of competitive advantage, and ultimately failure.

Success at Stage 4 depends on alignment of the organization to the realities of the market and customers. This means alignment across the company's value chain—from Marketing to Engineering to Operations to Support, and through multiple customer segments to each individual customer. Complexity naturally creates stress in achieving that alignment (see Figure 2–4). When several points in the value chain are misaligned, the results can include decreased productivity (which translates into decreased revenue per employee), cultural dissolution (e.g., departments operating to different cultural norms), and outright failure to achieve results. Organizational structure always biases results, so alignment facilitates desired outcomes, whereas misalignment interferes with them.

In Stage 4, misalignment often manifests as *silo organizations*— organizations within one company working independently from each other. The pressures for cost containment and economies of scale in a large, complex company drive the development of large, functional units with an inward—or silo—mentality. The likelihood of a silo mentality emerging is even greater if one functional unit feels heavy pressure to produce outcomes for which other units do not share accountability. A typical example is a manufacturing organization charged with reducing costs while the rest of the company is focused on inventing and selling new products.

These local pressures tend to build a bias toward local thinking, which, in turn, tends to encourage polarized attitudes. This progression precludes easy alignment when changes in the organization are required, such as when customers demand a new technology. Resorting to a silo mentality is a kind of coping mechanism to preserve some sense of local order in larger chaos, but organizations that engage in it only create order on the local level, not on an enterprise level.

The misalignment caused by silo organizations also generates glare. Two siloed organizations may be unable to solve a mutual problem because each is committed to its own way of operating and ends up working at cross-purposes with the other. Both groups lose

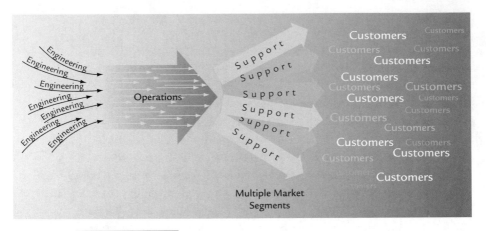

Multiple Market
Segments

Figure 2-4 The Challenge of Alignment in Later Stages.

sight of the real focus of their business, the common focus—customer satisfaction. This condition can be camouflaged and thereby prolonged by high-growth market conditions and develop into *glare longevity*. Glare is highly typical in Stage 4 organizations.

The good news is that although misalignment is a peril in highly complex organizations, if it is recognized and corrected, alignment is then a powerful tool to both create and exploit positive momentum and ongoing success. The bad news is that resistance to organizational change is common. As the organization's size grows, reorganizing is not only a sizable administrative task; it inevitably disrupts emerging or well-established power bases and disturbs job security. The results of realigning organizational structure are uncertain, and those in control of realignment decisions are often reluctant to risk costly errors and take the heat for unpopular outcomes. The company's ability to overcome these natural barriers and its willingness to realign organizational structure to fit changing markets is essential. We explore these issues in further detail in Chapter 10.

Stage 4 is when resistance to change in the company is at its highest—when successful companies are most readily seduced by their own success. After all, they have sailed safely around many rocky shoals already. Leaders' previous thinking is naturally reinforced by the successes of the past, even though the future requires new strategies, methods, and people. Elements of the culture may be calcifying, even as they seem sacred.

To break away from old ways of thinking that have influenced company success and personal wealth is a difficult task. Many leaders miss the need to change altogether; others see the risk as too great, especially if change requires overcoming popular political forces. In the case of the very old, seriously entrenched companies in the tobacco industry, they had every reason to believe that they could continue to do business as they always had. They had won every court case brought against them, they had the plight of tobacco farmers to wield with politicians, and their addicted customers guaranteed a future market. Furthermore, the non-U.S. market for tobacco products is growing. Still, despite much resistance, fundamental change is occurring in regulation and in the market, causing significantly different behavior on the part of tobacco company leaders in terms of investments, product development, and marketing and public relations.

More typically, companies less entrenched than those in the tobacco industry still miss the signs of change. We look at a number of such stories in future chapters, including AT&T's response to the disruption brought on by deregulation and IBM's mistake in believing it could win with proprietary software in the mainframe-to-mainframe communication market in the early to mid 1990s.

Board of Directors Oversight

One of the governing forces in a company that can help reduce its resistance to change is the group of "outsiders" who make up its board of directors (discussed more fully in Chapter 11). Unfortunately, by Stage 4, new board members are often invited to join only as high-profile "window dressing." Although individual board members might provide confidential counsel to the CEO and dutifully review the company's key metrics, as a group they often fail to provide a robust governing function.

We can hope that the high-profile business failures that have occurred in the downturn of 2001–2002 will result in significantly increased board oversight in U.S. businesses. Up to now, however, oversight has tended to be weak. Board members' attention to the business of a company is typically overcome by full-time job obligations elsewhere or, for venture capitalists, by the distractions of fund raising, investment decisions, and multiple board obligations. Thus, boards are often *reactive* when they most need to be *proactive*—that is, they wait for a crisis instead of anticipating and preparing for it. In addition, professional CEOs, who have the most influence over the composition of their company's boards, too often select members who are "friendly," whom they can manage, and who see the world in essentially the same way that they do. CEOs rarely choose board members who will regularly challenge their own views.

Companies that fall into trouble in Stage 4 badly need a strong board of directors—one that can see through the glare that may be blinding executives internally. A strong board can help ensure alignment, revitalize a great culture, and demonstrate "healthy paranoia." This kind of heightened awareness can be essential in guaranteeing that hard decisions and new strategies are openly addressed.

The Eight Inevitable Challenges and Stages of Growth

Figure 2–5 locates each of the eight challenges by the four stages of company growth described in this chapter. Across the top of the figure are the governance challenges. Across the bottom are the challenges of execution. The horizontal axis represents time, and the vertical axis represents complexity. As before, the various symbols suggest elements of complexity, such as products, customers, classes of customer segments, and distribution channel types.

As we said at the start of this chapter, the placement of the challenges by stage is not intended to suggest their precise timing or sequence; rather, it implies a general sense of what to look for and when.

Figure 2–6 summarizes the typical events of successful companies as they grow through the four stages and the threads of failure that are most likely to appear in those stages. Again, any thread can be found in any stage. But in managing complexity, it helps to have even a rough roadmap for assessing problems and prioritizing actions.

The length of the growth stages varies, of course, depending primarily on the length of product design cycles—the somewhat predictable length of time it takes to design and introduce a new product into the market. In silicon and networking, for instance, a design cycle tends to last 18 months, give or take 6 months. A good rule of thumb is that a stage will last for approximately two design cycles. At the end of the 1990s, a high-tech company's first stage tended to be shorter than in former years, as the Internet market growth drove so much to happen so quickly. The bursting of the "Internet bubble," however, could return markets to past patterns.

Although we believe that a typical company that ultimately

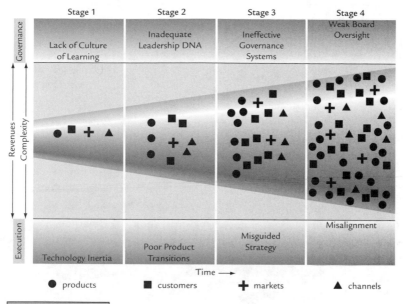

Figure 2-5 The Eight Threads of Failure by Growth Stage.

dominates its market moves through the stages we have described, we also believe that companies and units within companies *recycle* through earlier stages. For instance, new businesses within a larger company will in some form or another go through all four stages, replicating early-stage dynamics. Responding to new product introductions by the competition can also throw a company back to an earlier stage. This is just one reason why we believe that these execution and governance challenges are not just those of the CEO; they are every leader's problem, every day.

Momentum through the Four Stages

To move effectively through the four stages of growth, great companies read, create, and exploit market momentum. A new idea breeds a startup company and creates momentum. Disruption creates or renews momentum, as does the introduction of new channels. On the other hand, failure to anticipate disruption can mean that a company is riding a declining wave of momentum when the tide turns. Poor product transitions, misguided strategies, and misalignment all interrupt momentum and can result in Brownian motion and, ultimately, negative momentum.

Stage 1	Stage 2	Stage 3	Stage 4
• venture-driven • single product • single market • technology focus • informality • early customer reception • first product release • first revenue • new CEO • Q over Q revenue • IPO?	• established entity • professional management team • competition for customer loyalty • next-generation products • new sales channels • early infrastructure • IPO?	• new market entry • multiple sales channels • multiple strategies • acquired management talent for new markets—very small and very large company sources • worldwide presence • growing importance of PR	• multiple businesses • potential for mixed business models • complex functional organizations • high-risk dollar impact with each strategic shift • global presence
Most Likely Threads of Failure			
• insufficient culture of learning • weak leadership DNA	• poor product transitions • misguided strategy • insufficient culture of learning • weak leadership DNA • technology inertia	• poor governing mechanisms • poor product transitions • misguided strategy • insufficient culture of learning • weak leadership DNA • technology inertia	• misalignment • weak board • misguided strategy • poor governancy mechanisms • insufficient culture of learning • weak leadership DNA • technology inertia

Figure 2-6   Stages of Dominant Company Evolution and Their Challenges.

1. Identify the stage your company is in, according to Figure 2–6. The unique qualities of your company's history might not put you neatly into a stage according to the company's age. Growth, downsizing, and significant changes in leadership, strategy, and product offerings, as well as market shifts, can result in a company cycling back through earlier stages from time to time. With the stage of your company in mind, what threads of failure are you most likely to find? Does your intuition suggest which of these threads may be emerging?

2. What is your sense of the level of fresh air in the organization?

   • Does new information come in from the outside?

   • Is it solicited, well captured, assessed, and utilized?

   • Is there too much stale air—are decision makers breathing their own unhealthy exhaust?

3. What is the volume of open exchange in meetings?

   • Are meetings primarily status reports, with little or no exchange?

   • Do typical meetings include lively exchange about important issues, with various viewpoints?

4. If you draw a mental line from your key customers back through Support, Manufacturing, Sales, Marketing, and Engineering, would there be a true straight line? If not, where is the gap or eddy of confusion? What does this tell you?

5. How well linked are strategy and structure in the organization?

   • Is one more neglected than the other?

   • Do you attend to them separately or in tandem?

Momentum is something we are all familiar with, inside and outside of business. Anyone who reads a daily newspaper can feel the geographical shifts in momentum as different teams take the dominant position in college basketball. For years, John Wooden reigned over the UCLA dynasty. Through his leadership talent and university support, he created remarkable momentum by which he could attract the finest talent, and increase revenue and attract alumni contributions, which are then invested in sustaining that momentum.

However, even in college basketball, threads of failure inevitably appear as a result of natural internal and external forces and begin to create drag on momentum. Perhaps another team threatens the leadership spot, or the reigning team develops lethargy as a result of consistent success or the ego of a new star who won't play as a team member. Without constant vigilance to prevent and correct these emerging threads of failure, the negative pull against the momentum of one dynasty can create room for the next to take over.

Despite the obvious importance of reading, creating, and exploiting momentum, sports dynasties and great companies alike naturally tend toward inertia. Success breeds inertia, and fear of failure reinforces resistance to change. To battle these tendencies, a bias for learning in the culture and the company's leadership DNA is crucial. Constant learning is critical—learning about the momentum of the business, the number and strength of competitors in the market, and the level of organizational inertia. Learning starts with careful, studied attention to the vital signs that measure the emergence, strength, and decline of all the threads of failure. These vital signs are the topic of our next chapter.

3
Vital Signs for Monitoring Complexity

Overview

- Vital signs indicate emerging threads of failure before those threads develop into serious problems.

- Monitoring vital signs allows leaders to prevent problems from growing; if vital signs are ignored, problems may not be detected until they are externally apparent.

- Vital signs include such internal dynamics as the following:
  - speed of decision making
  - level of cross-functional coordination
  - clarity of priorities
  - complementary vs. competing goals
  - willingness to depart from past successes
  - organizational energy out of line with productive yield

- Vital signs can indicate bad news, which leaders too often avoid. Discovering bad news early, however, is an advantage, and the willingness to face it is a cultural strength.

Taking effective action when one or more of the eight predictable challenges is becoming a thread of failure requires early awareness. We believe that there are many internal indicators in a company that can provide that early awareness—indicators that enable leaders to recognize nascent problems before they become endemic and public, thus eroding success. We call these early warning signals *vital signs*. As a company's momentum increases, so must the rigor with which its vital signs are monitored. Methods and examples of measuring vital signs for particular threads of failure are discussed in future chapters; in this chapter, we address the general notion of vital signs.

Public, external indicators of success or failure, as opposed to internal vital signs, are obvious:

- revenue trends
- consistency of forecasts with actual performance (operating expense, revenue, production)
- rise or fall in customer satisfaction and critical accounts metrics and the company's ability or inability to improve them
- stock performance gain, stall, or loss
- ability or inability to maintain or establish partnerships
- public relations—good or bad

If a company's leadership gets its first inkling of problems from these *public* signs, it is as if they are discovering a full-blown cancer that could have been caught in its treatable stages by focusing on early *warning* signs. Once problems are public, it may be too late to take action and avoid further damage. Recognizing threads of failure before a real downturn occurs is essential to sustaining success. Questions that exemplify internal vital signs (and the challenges with which they are associated) include the following:

- Are active feedback loops in place? (culture of learning)
- Are structure and strategy aligned? Has the structure changed with shifts in strategy? (alignment)
- How active is cross-functional communication? (culture of learning, leadership DNA, alignment)
- Are internal priorities clear and in alignment? (differentiating strategy, governance systems, alignment)

- Is there a tendency to cite past successes rather than look to tomorrow's technology? (technology inertia, culture of learning)
- What is the trend in employees' sense of empowerment? (leadership DNA, culture of learning)

Vital signs are often first identifiable intuitively. With experience, leaders can sense problems in the earliest stages of their emergence, then look more specifically for evidence of those problems to determine if their intuition is right. Staying alert to the right questions, such as those mentioned previously and many others that we pose in each chapter of this book, is a way of developing intuition. As intuition develops, learning to trust it when it tells you that something is going wrong is critical; following up on that intuitive sense by collecting factual information is just as important.

Glare as a Vital Sign

Let's look at the specific case of the vital sign of glare—the growing inability to see both where you are going and what is going on around you in the organization—often manifest by the inability to resolve lingering problems. Glare is insidious because it can develop slowly; leaders often adapt to it and unwittingly make excuses for the situation rather than correcting the condition. By knowing that it develops in conditions of complexity, however, leaders can stay alert to the danger.

Glare often develops when different sections within a company are focused on different goals. Product managers may focus on features while engineers focus on quality and schedule, or one part of the organization may feel that selling to new customers should be the imperative while another part feels that servicing existing customers is more important. Excessive attention given to provincial concerns engenders a collective myopia—no one in the company concentrates on reaching long-term, company-wide goals. Growing complexity only exacerbates these tensions.

Let's consider two examples of driving blind in glare conditions and look at what intuition could have detected early.

The Example of Manufacturing and Engineering

Pressures to reduce costs and the growing complexity of multiple product strategies can result in glare conditions for Manufacturing.

In response, Manufacturing may focus more on its own concerns, such as inventory turns, than on time-to-market—a customer satisfaction metric and a measure of company success. With glare, the line of sight to the customer becomes obstructed.

Glare conditions can be resolved with the right kind of information. In this example, it is likely that the problem can be solved with more input from Engineering and Product Marketing, product-line decision makers who can better assess market risk and trending during high rates of change. "Owners" of manufacturing cost reduction must be able to transcend their local focus and maintain primary focus on the customer. As organizational structure grows more complex, it can obscure this broader accountability.

It is often too easy to dismiss conflict such as that between Manufacturing and Engineering as classic or typical, implying that it is inevitable and untreatable. If, however, leaders are alert to *trends* in conflict and recognize the potential problems of growing complexity, they are more likely to believe their own sense of concern— their intuition—when they perceive the growing conflict. They can then take control, using this intuitive "red flag" as a prompt to look at *measurable* vital signs:

- Are Manufacturing and Engineering measured only on the basis of functionally oriented measures of success?

- What common measures of success are being monitored by Manufacturing and Engineering? If none, why not? What common measures (e.g., time-to-market) should be in use? How customer oriented are these measures?

- Is the normal level of conflict between Manufacturing and Engineering growing? If so, why? What can be learned from it? How is it being addressed? Is there a clear place, process, and accountability for resolution?

The Example of Sales and Finance

Consider a situation in which sales transactions are facilitated by vendor financing. As Lucent and other telecommunications vendors realized at the end of 2000, this strategy can become problematic due to a lack of good data and inadequate risk assessment. The consequences are not only financial but also include reduction in customer and sales team morale and deterioration of cross-functional team relationships and learning. The solution lies in representatives of the various functions involved—Sales and Finance, in this case—joining forces, facing the facts unflinchingly, and using the right sources of knowledge to assess risk.

Again, trusting one's intuition when the trend of cross-functional conflict is upward can lead to looking at more measurable internal vital signs:

- What common measures of success are being employed by Sales and Finance? If none, why not? What common measures could be used effectively?

- Is Sales being rewarded only on the basis of near-term success? What is the balance of focus in the rewards process on bookings versus revenues versus margins versus customer success?

- Is the normal level of conflict between Sales and Finance growing? If so, why? What can be learned from it? How is it being addressed?

When Glare Is Likely to Occur

In general, we assert that glare occurs when one or several of the following situations arise:

- **polarization based on business unit or functional organizations optimizing locally, rather than for the enterprise.** For example, one organization drives decisions on a time-to-market basis, whereas an interdependent organization drives decisions on a quality-at-high-volume basis.

- **unclear accountability.** There is no single point of accountability for key results—for instance, no operational decision maker or decision body charged with resolving conflicts when polarization is occurring.

- **an absence of feedback, listening, or metrics.** The right information isn't flowing into the organization, no one is listening to what is coming in, or no one is using the information to measure company health and progress. In this case, organizations are unaware of real problems.

These three conditions associated with glare are the first things to look for when attempting to diagnose the situation.

Putting It All Together

Early detection provides the greatest potential to prevent emerging threads of failure and turn the situation to advantage. Yet leaders too often avoid examining real information to discover emerging problems. Responding to day-to-day demands distracts them from asking the questions that can affect the long term. The natural human bent to avoid bad news, which will require time, attention, and change, is always present.

One way to mitigate the tendency to avoid vital news you do not want to hear is to establish, in the earliest days of the company's life, a routine process for examining useful data—monthly operations reviews, for instance, or release postmortems. The use of consultant evaluation and reports at the right time is another way of making sure you are paying attention to early warning signs. Make it a firm part of the culture. Leaders can build a reputation on it.

We believe that precisely like careful examination of *outcome* metrics—revenues, expenses, and customer satisfaction information—routine examination of data that reveals the presence of *emerging* threads of failure is possible. Constructive paranoia is the engine for this effort—not a constant state of believing that the sky is falling but rather a constant state of listening, willingness to see what you hope is not there, and thinking soundly in response to what you see.

One measure of constructive paranoia is the time you spend looking at information that can reveal the threads. You might say to yourself, Yes, *of course* I'm interested in knowing the state of thread development in the company. But somehow there's never time to examine the data, to look closely at what might be an unwelcome reality. It is not your intention that counts, but real action. Unconscious avoidance, even with "good" excuses, is an early warning sign in and of itself. The courage to face unadorned reality is a core feature of strong leaders.

Another way to reduce the tendency to avoid unpleasant news is to engage others in the monitoring process so that you can keep each other honest (watch out, though: Your avoidance can also be reinforced by others). Again, *formalizing* your approach to checking vital signs at both the operational and board levels makes the process of exposing the data and creating accountability less avoidable.

On the other hand, responding to emerging threads of failure with knee-jerk reactions is of little value. This approach can be

Something to Think About

- First ask yourself the following:

  - Are you surprised to see any of the internal vital signs identified in this chapter?

  - How recently or routinely have you paid attention to these kinds of indicators?

  - If you have had concerns about these vital signs, what actions have you taken?

  - Are there effective feedback loops in place that can give you the information you need?

  - What trends do you see related to these issues?

  - Who is accountable for remediation or prevention?

  - What actions can you take if some are needed?

- Talk over the list of vital signs and identify solutions with your leadership team.

- Assign someone to get to the root of any problems you've identified.

tempting: It can feel like a way to speed up the elimination of the problem, get it out of the way, and get everyone back to the real work. Knee-jerk reactions, however, often signal a lack of appreciation for the insidious and deep-seated nature of the threads. Like deep-rooted weeds, they cannot be plucked out quickly; threads of failure require a thoughtful response and well-planned action.

Always deal with the issues, always have a plan, and always follow through. Measure what makes a difference. *Inspect* what you *expect*. Be willing to see what you don't expect and don't want to see. Use the results of your actions to understand the next set of challenges. Set and hold accountabilities. Keep listening; keep learning; and, most important, be cautious about believing your own publicity. The next challenge is surely on its way.

4
Innovation

Overview

- Great companies innovate continuously to stay ahead of the competition.

- However, even great companies can miss key market turning points that require a new direction in technology.

- Leaving control of market disruption to competitors is a significant peril to a company used to strategic advantage; market disruption is a key element of success.

- To avoid technology inertia and create competitive advantage, great companies need a strategic plan for managing market disruption.

- Tools like the five Laws of Disruption and a Checklist for Disruptors, both found in this chapter, can help.

Before the breakup of Ma Bell in the 1970s, Bell Labs designed and Western Electric manufactured the only phone available, the sturdy $50 black phone. It could be dropped from six feet and would bounce, unbroken. Voice quality was great, and if the dog chewed the cable, Bell would replace it for free.

In the wake of the company's breakup, however, just about anyone could build a telephone to attach to AT&T's network. Bell Labs engineers never suspected, however, that consumers might prefer a programmable phone for $300, a Mickey Mouse phone for $100, or a Princess phone for $15 to the familiar black model. But consumers did. In the 9 months after the court ruling opened up the telephone market to other manufacturers, AT&T lost 5 percent of its market share; in 18 months, it had lost 30 percent.

Fast-forward to the 1990s and the advent of wireless technology. Phone service in a car became the new rage. Large mobile units were installed in automobile trunks, and aerials sprouted off car rooftops, announcing the presence of the new device. For the next decade, competitive innovation drove increasing user adoption and one price drop after another. Eventually, growth in the wireless phone market eclipsed that of traditional, wired phone service; and in 2001, a new era of market disruption developed. That year saw long-distance services bundled with wireless mobility, mobile voice service enhanced with access to information like movie times and store sales, and Internet access through mobile phones.

Market Disruption or Technology Inertia

Figure 4–1 shows examples of these and other innovations that became disruptive technologies. Most of these major technological innovations are well known. For each of these examples, there are stories of companies that did not foresee the change and were brought down by *technology inertia*. They stagnated technologically while the world moved on, a common thread of failure, even for great companies.

Take IBM, for example. Once the world of business had adjusted to the wonders of mainframe computers, it became clear that customers needed to exchange information between those computers. IBM invented a proprietary mechanism, called systems network architecture (SNA), for accomplishing this exchange.

SNA was optimal for low-bandwidth transmission. It was also timing dependent, meaning that it required responses within a

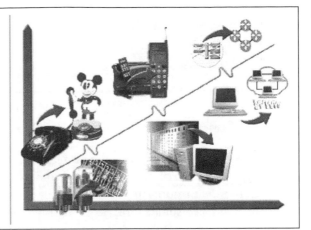

- tubes to transistors

- black phones to designer handsets

- wireless phones to cell phones

- mainframes to client server computing

Figure 4-1 Examples of Disruptive Technologies.

specific amount of time to work correctly. Because SNA, using IBM proprietary network protocols, was timing dependent and technically complex, the competition could be kept at bay, and customers were held hostage to the technology they had already bet on.

But with the advent of client/server technology, the market began to demand lower costs and easy transmission to multiple vendors. As a result, local area network (LAN) protocols and then Internet protocols swiftly overcame earlier proprietary implementations like SNA. IBM's basic SNA proposition lost its viability in the disrupted market.

Another example is Intergraph, a company that achieved $1 billion in revenue in just over four years, based on the sales of its proprietary product. Then the market disrupted, causing a backlash over proprietary software, and Intergraph's worth dropped drastically. Growth markets can exact a heavy toll from proprietary behavior.

Despite these well-known examples of the problems caused by technology inertia, such stagnation is nonetheless a common thread of failure. When a company is successful based on a given technology, its leaders often find it difficult to see the need for change. Why would they risk the company's margins to invest in changing what has made the company successful? Like the elephant in the proverbial cartoon, however, they can be oblivious to the hole they are about to fall into if they do not continually question the currency of today's business model.

A Closer Look at Market Disruption

In the first 40 years of the high-tech industry, markets moving at high speeds were new and not well understood. Companies raced to keep up with opportunity. They made mistakes, picked themselves up, and raced some more, or simply failed. A new, even faster generation of competition emerged in the 1980s and 1990s, as the demand for Internet products accelerated high-tech markets. Disruption occurred in the competitive fervor, but the physics of the process were not conceptualized or well understood until Clayton Christensen published his book *The Innovator's Dilemma*. In this chapter, we want to add to his thesis.

In Chapter 1, we introduced a three-dimensional model to demonstrate how complexity can be both friend and foe. That same model (Figure 4–2) is a tool for understanding disruption.

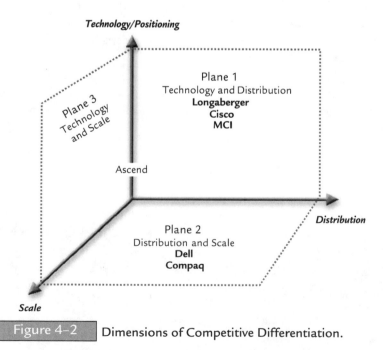

Figure 4–2   Dimensions of Competitive Differentiation.

Something to Think About

Look at the three-dimensional model of Figure 4–2. Compare your company with its top competitor:

- Does it have a disruption advantage in either technology or positioning?
- Can you find a difference in channel strategy with a significant benefit?
- Is there an important difference in economics of scale?

If you answered *yes* to two out of three of these questions, you have the basis for the two-dimensional differentiation that effective disruption requires. The next step is to complete a well-thought-out strategic plan for disruption.

Disruption can occur in relation to what is offered to the market (technology or products and how they are positioned), how it is offered and delivered (distribution), or at what price/cost structure it is offered (economies of scale). Disruptor companies use one, two, or even all three of these dimensions, although, as we argued in Chapter 1, there are sustainable advantages to disrupting on two. Let's look further into this phenomenon using the example of Dell Computer.

Although Dell has never been a technology leader, it has achieved extraordinary success and certainly changed the landscape of the PC market through disruption on the dimensions of distribution and economies of scale. Dell exploited the e-business opportunity at the onset of Internet retail commerce, establishing itself as the leading online computer distributor and using high-volume, low-cost production techniques to support low prices for customized PCs. Dell's enormous foothold in Internet distribution and its relentless drive to lower costs have made it the 500-pound gorilla of the PC retail world; the company grew from a zero share in 1984 to a top-ranked 13.5 percent share of the PC market by 2001.

Elements of Successful Disruption

To understand further how disruption works, we can ask how typical disruptor companies, such as those listed in Figure 4–3, have learned to exploit the changing waves of market momentum and thus succeed on two of the three disruptive dimensions.

• Amazon.com	• Compaq
• Longaberger	• Microsoft
• AOL	• Dell
• MCI	• Nokia
• Cisco	• Intel
• McDonald's	

Figure 4–3 Well-Known Disruptors.

To embrace disruption, as these companies have, means strategic planning—formal or otherwise—that maximizes the opportunities afforded by both market and competitor-caused disruption. Such plans contain the following elements:

- a clear sense of strategic position in relation to disruption, either causing disruption or anticipating and exploiting it

- an attitude that embraces change, with a balanced focus on customers' needs today *and* the realities of tomorrow

- an understanding of market physics in relation to disruption, including the five *Laws of Disruption*, which we discuss next

- a description of key actions designed to cause or anticipate disruption, including selecting the best two dimensions (market/technology, distribution, and/or scale) on which to differentiate the company

- product launch strategies that include accurate timing for the insertion of new products

- development of the right partners and acquisition of the right companies to assure migration to the future

Each of these elements is discussed further in the upcoming sections.

The Choice of Strategic Position

A great company knows whether it will create the next shift in momentum or ride the wave caused by a competitor or other external force (such as a government intervention). This self-image is not wishful thinking: It is based on a hard-boiled understanding of the company's core competencies, constant assessment of customer preferences and new technology, and aggressive competitive analysis.

Like Dell, Amazon.com established itself from the start as a disruptor in the retail bookseller business, on both the scale and distribution dimensions. As a result, it has permanently changed the book-buying market. It has driven the largest brick-and-mortar retail competition to the Internet and forced many small bookstores out of business. Where Amazon cannot compete—in the submarket of customers either who want to touch and feel the books and read a little before they buy or who want to take the book home right away—the brick-and-mortar sellers maintain a hold. As of 2002, Amazon has yet to prove its long-term viability, but the market disruption it caused by selling books online appears to be permanent, as demonstrated by traditional booksellers embracing Internet order fulfillment.

To identify a company's strategic position in relation to disruption, it is essential to understand the nature of change that disruption represents. Not all change is truly disruptive. Disruption causes *irreversible* change. Its leverage is enormous and permanent, which is why it is such a critical dynamic to embrace and exploit. Therefore, it is important to understand disruption in relation to other types of change. Consider the following three categories:

- **adjustment**—a small alteration of the existing state—for example, changing an existing manufacturing process to lower the cost of goods sold

- **transition**—a move from one approach to another within the same basic environment, such as restructuring an organization, where not only structure changes but also personnel and processes

- **disruption**—a change in the environment that is so large and significant that it results in irreversible differences. Figure 4–1, earlier in this chapter, contains several examples of technology disruption

In today's competitive environment, the question is not whether disruption will occur but rather whether a company will be *ready* for disruption and avoid the elephant trap. Furthermore, will it *lead* with disruption, take advantage of the opportunity to leapfrog the competition, and create barriers to entry, or will it be ready with a fast-follower strategy? Determining the kind of change that can be created and anticipating the change that others will cause are essential in the planning process.

An Attitude that Embraces Constant Change

Successful disruption requires critical self-assessment, a risk-taking stance, and in some cases counterintuitive thinking. Even apparently good management practices can lead to failure. Consider a well-managed company, with a track record of innovation, that listens astutely to customers, keeps close track of competitors, and invests aggressively in new technologies. Even this kind of company can fail if it listens only to its *current* customers—customers whose success is dependent on *today's* cost structure, which itself might soon be disrupted by the next wave of change.

Again, the retail book business provides an example. Listening to its best customers, it was unlikely that Barnes & Noble would hear that those customers wanted to buy some of their books online or that they would actually buy *more* if they could do so. Brick-and-mortar customers' buying patterns had yet to adjust to the Amazon.com phenomenon. Given its dominant position in book-selling, imagine the counterintuitive thinking the leaders at Barnes & Noble would have had to do to take on Amazon's unprofitable growth model. (Amazon sold books at a discount to attract new buyers to its unfamiliar distribution process.)

Anticipation of new customers and new markets is the key, and anticipation depends on keeping an open mind and an active flow of information about technology, the market, customers, and competitors—all key to decision making that is adaptive to change. To cultivate their ability both to be disruptors and to anticipate disruption by others, companies need to achieve a balance of focus along the following four dimensions:

- sustaining *and* disruptive technologies
- today's market demands *and* future technological progress
- today's *and* tomorrow's most profitable customers
- the realities of today's current financial structures *and* those of tomorrow

These four dimensions—technology, market demand, profitable customers, and financial structure—give companies four categories for self-examination and planning. Challenging the status quo, open-minded market research, and creative thinking in all four areas can produce exciting options in the planning process.

Understanding Market Physics

How can leaders identify when and where to cause disruption? Understanding the physics of disruption is the first step. When disruption occurs, four kinds of results emerge:

- Market size increases as new customers are reached and developed.

- Markets tend to segment based on price, customer intimacy, expectations, and technology features.

- Consumer purchase criteria change—that is, new and significant segments emerge with new purchase criteria.

- New competitors become winners—winners of the past are often not those of the future.

When new options are offered to the market through technological disruption, customers develop new tastes. The examples in Figure 4–1 illustrate this phenomenon. Whichever company accommodates these new consumer tastes gets more business. Yesterday's Number 1 vendor doesn't matter anymore; unless it can offer customers what they want *now*, that vendor becomes a historical footnote. We discuss this further when we talk about the predictable patterns of opportunity later in this chapter.

To further understand the physics of disruption, we pose five Laws of Market Disruption (Figure 4–4). Let's look at each one in turn, with some examples.

Law 1	Disruption Occurs When Driving Forces Align
Law 2	Disruption Drives Structural Change
Law 3	Kinetic Structures Prevail
Law 4	Patterns of Opportunity Are Predictable
Law 5	Entropy Will Occur

Figure 4-4 The Five Laws of Market Disruption.

Law 1: *Disruption Occurs When Driving Forces Align*

History shows that when certain key market forces align, disruption occurs. Examples of the forces to watch for include the following:

- fast technological development (PCs, wireless products)
- intense market competition (dot.coms)
- a prevailing investment direction (space exploration, silicon technology, the Internet)

Let's look at three examples of times when these forces aligned and changed the field of competition permanently:

- First, in the post–World War II era, the United States was alarmed by the advance of Soviet technology, as represented by Sputnik. In response, the Vannevar Bush article of 1945 called for new investment in science and technology in both the public and private sectors—silicon, education, the space program, and so forth.

  A new competitive intensity developed, fueled by the infusion of investment dollars. The competitive fervor took advantage of the discovery of the transistor and other current technology breakthroughs. Computing and the use of silicon are examples of the resulting innovation, which profoundly changed the way the world did business. Sputnik activated fears that drove national investment in science and technology and produced new inventions.

- A second example is the development of the backbone technology for transmission of information over the Internet, including packet-network and optics technologies. Simultaneously, a whole new market sector that came to be known as *dot.coms* intensified the field of existing Internet competition. Both the technology potential and the market opportunity were fueled by a new focus on investment in the Internet. In this confluence of forces, the invention of technologies, like optics, to speed the transmission of data and the capability to transmit voice over an Internet protocol created massive and permanent change to the growing Internet market and accelerated a drop in the pricing structure of voice communications.

- The transition from a mainframe computing model to a client/server model provides the third example. The architectural model was new, the competitors were new (Microsoft and Compaq vs. existing leaders like IBM, DEC, and Unisys), and the industry at large began to invest in applications that supported client/servers—computing based on servers. The market disruption that occurred caused new buying patterns and a new hierarchy of "power players" in the market. Moreover, the market, previously based on proprietary vendor implementation and a vertical cost structure, moved to open systems and a horizontal cost structure that encouraged innovation.

  It is important to realize, however, that by the year 2003, the massive loss of momentum in the consolidating telecommunications market may influence market behavior relative to open and proprietary systems. The next phase of that market's life is unclear as this book is being written.

In each of these three examples, all three conditions for disruption—fast technological development, intense market competition, and a prevailing investment direction—were present. In each case, market disruption occurred, permanently changing the relevant markets.

Law 2: *Disruption Drives Structural Change*

The shift to a client/server model also illustrates the second law: Disruption drives shifts in structure back and forth between vertical and horizontal market models. Up until the year 2000, the information economy accelerated itself through a set of volatile, high-tech horizontal and vertical markets. In the case of the computer industry, before the client/server model emerged, IBM represented the existing, vertical market. It made mainframes, the silicon that went into the mainframe, the operating system, and application software, and so competed with companies like DEC and Control Data at each layer of functionality.

With client/server technology, along came competitors who specialized in chips, others who made computing platforms, still others who made operating systems, and some who created applications. What had been vertical (DEC vs. IBM vs. Control Data) became horizontal—an industry in which there was competition at each layer of the architecture. Independent standards emerged for each layer, and those standards shaped competition. In this case, disruption drove a new focus on technology standards, which helped drive the emergence of a horizontal structure, which in turn helped drive more innovation.

Law 3: *Kinetic Structures Prevail*

Kinetic energy is energy of motion. An organization that is kinetic is constantly in motion; this allows it to sense, as well as adapt to, market conditions and imperatives. One could say that the Internet is a *kinetic* force in the market. In this economy, companies that profitably exploit the kinetic energy of the Internet are more successful than companies that do not. Today's Internet market, even after the economic slowdown at the close of the century, moves at such an accelerated pace that companies that do not evolve applications and introduce them to the market at a high speed will fall behind. It is this pace that has caused companies to partner with each other, thus providing more complete customer solutions faster and capturing more market opportunities.

However, because of kinetic energy, when disruptions occur it is not easy to predict which market positions will be safe and which will be dangerous. Markets emerge, and experienced competitors can guess at their overall dimensions, but the size of any aspect of the market at any point is harder to estimate.

Visualize an erupting volcano. An expert can predict to some extent which direction the lava will flow, yet new fissures can bring surprises. Staying in one spot can mean getting trapped. Similarly, if a business stays on the move when markets disrupt—and if leaders keep their eyes and ears open—the company is more likely to survive. Another way to look at kinetic energy is in terms of gas filling a spherical volume and pushing it outward. Following the expansion in only one direction will not lead to understanding the full set of possibilities. Maintaining mobility in several directions, however, can allow discovery of new boundaries and, ultimately, the best new direction.

Emerging industries have no established standards—they are tentative and supple. Providing technology that can navigate three-dimensionally, so to speak, through the uncertainties of an emerging market requires great agility. A great company cannot afford to wait and see which standards emerge. It has to lead where it can and be agile enough to keep up (fast-follower mode) where it cannot.

In the late 1980s at Cisco, engineers had to design to allow for 17 different networking protocols. A decade and a half later, the technology for routing data over the Internet involved standard protocols. Through the earlier, extraordinary period of uncertainty, Cisco's culture promoted constant movement—a high level of kinetic energy that allowed the company to stay in motion and prepare for a multitude of outcomes. As a result, Cisco maintained its position of strength and consumed the less flexible companies.

On the other hand, this particular kind of technical agility is not a core competency at Dell Computer. Although Dell has been *the* leader in computer distribution and scale, its operational model depends on a well-established market, one in which technology standards are set and focus can be placed on scale and margins. Despite this basis of success, Dell entered the data storage market early, *before* standards had developed and at a time in which multiple companies promoted multiple visions for the future of storage technology. As a result, Dell found that its model did not apply the leverage it was used to experiencing. The storage market was expanding, finding its way.

In an attempt to meet the new challenge, Dell acquired the storage company ConvergeNet in 1999—a purchase that was not initially well received in the market, unfortunately. As of 2002, Dell had not been able to build a dominant position in the storage market. As the storage market matures, however, Dell's probability for success is likely to increase.

Law 4: *Patterns of Opportunity Are Predictable*

Companies with kinetic energy can avoid the inevitable revenue decline that results from being unprepared for market changes. To achieve this, however, they must navigate well through the areas of opportunity. Leaders must make choices carefully, aided by predictable patterns.

Let's go back to the four results of market disruption that we identified earlier in this chapter to recognize the predictable patterns that can guide good planning. As we said in the section Understanding Market Physics, after disruption occurs, four kinds of results emerge:

- **market size increases.** Markets expand and are likely to become dramatically more productive as innovation takes hold, especially when markets are released from artificial constraints imposed by regulation. Innovation drives new possibilities and new buying patterns, attracting more customers.

- **markets segment.** As markets expand, they segment, based on choices previously unavailable, such as new and inventive functionality. Remember the Mickey Mouse phone? That is an example of a product serving a new market segment. Low-cost phones from the Pacific Rim that sold for $14—phones with a lamp, phones with clock radios—provided new options that customers wanted. Business phones, with their 200 programmable features, gave business customers useful functions that were previously unavailable.

- **purchase criteria change.** Purchase criteria of the past are not likely to predict the criteria of the future. The past was the black phone: one color, high structural integrity, $50 price tag, and excellent voice quality. The future was many different kinds of phones, with varying quality and features. The $14 phones from Asia captured 30 market share points in 18 months. They came in many colors, but quality standards were far below what would have been acceptable for a black phone. If dropped from six feet, the inexpensive phones broke, and customers rated voice quality (mean opinion scores) at 3.4, compared to 4.0 for the AT&T black phone. (Compare this to 2002 scores of 3.6 to 3.8 for cell phones.)

- **winners change.** Winners of the past do not tend to be the winners of the future. Winners of the past all too often continue to define success in terms of their past wins while the market is betting on new choices. When a company is measuring itself with yesterday's criteria and at the same time there are signs of market disruption, that company is faced with the innovator's dilemma.

The predictable patterns that result from disruption can be planned for and exploited. Sound predictions can be made that provide a basis for good decisions and help avoid planning based on past successes.

Law 5: *Entropy Will Occur*

As we have said, after a disruption there are winners and there are losers, and industry structure will respond for some period of time with disorder. For every company that rides market momentum and pulls ahead, there is a company that falls behind just as quickly. Agile companies have the greatest chance to overpower the tendency toward entropy.

When disruption occurs, old business models hemorrhage. Unless the change was anticipated and planned for, money is lost. Companies go into a decline, leading to takeovers, mergers, or acquisitions. Examples of losers in the high-tech disruption scenario include Unisys, Burroughs, Tandem, and DEC. At one time, these names exemplified success. Today, they are scarcely remembered. Even if once strong, the weak get acquired. In the case of startups, some do not develop enough momentum to survive; they simply go out of business.

The dot.com boom illustrated momentum in the absence of business fundamentals. The dynamics that might have precluded the forces of entropy were not there. Dot.com companies—in fact, the entire high-tech industry—moved from a state of emerging order to a state of disorder. In response, with the economic downturn, the industry began to consolidate.

Eventually, the decline reaches bottom and a new state of order and momentum arises. The winners will be either incumbent companies that are aggressive in transitioning or new companies that disrupt the market and scale their involvement in that market at the same time.

Action Planning

So far we have discussed how great companies must do the following:

- establish the right strategic position in relation to their industry and their core-technology competency

1. Do you routinely introduce new revenue streams with a deliberate cadence?
2. Can you introduce a new service in response to a competitor in three months or less?
3. Do you have a plan for strategically cannibalizing your existing revenues with new offerings rather than lose your position to competitors?
4. Does your team know where to create disruption?
5. Are you using disruption for competitive advantage? How can you?
6. Do your leaders lead with organizational kinetic energy—that is, do they see and use structure as a flexible device to adjust to and drive new strategies?

Figure 4–5 A Disruptor's Checklist.

- maintain an attitude of welcoming constant change to ensure a balance of focus on today and tomorrow
- understand the physics of the disruption

The next step is to identify actions to take advantage of internal strengths and external opportunities. Figure 4–5 lists a set of questions that can lead to successful action planning. We call it A Disruptor's Checklist. The questions are useful in evaluating a company's current plan and determining the right course of action when that plan is challenged by market disruption.

Insertion Strategies

To develop the right strategic plan for disruption, product insertion strategies, which can emerge from the answers to the first three questions on A Disruptor's Checklist, are critical. As we discuss in greater depth in Chapter 6, certain axioms apply when planning new product insertions. For instance, the *timing* for insertion of a new product is more important than the *size* of the initial offering. Market shifts occur as a result of what the new product offers, not as a function of scale. Another way to look at this is that the sooner an insertion is made, the greater the potential for shareholder value. Companies need to act when revenue streams *begin* to move, not when the new market expands as a result of technology.

Consider the questions on A Disruptor's Checklist in Figure 4–5.

- How many questions could you answer affirmatively for the company you are assessing?
- Where you had negative answers, can you see a way to get a positive answer?

Here are some further questions to help:

- Are you putting the time into market analysis and planning?
- Who is accountable to be sure this is done and done well?
- Are you riding too confidently on yesterday's success?
- Where do you see signs of inertia in the company?
- Is Finance too concerned about maintaining today's margin structure without having enough understanding of technology changes in the market?
- Are Marketing and Sales overly focused on what a few large customers say they want?

Another axiom, also explored in more depth in Chapter 6, is that because new technologies change buying patterns by introducing new purchase criteria, new products that *solve the right problem* for the customer win. In addition, it is often critical to introduce disruptive technologies as *new* propositions, not as *replacements* that are seen as competing with existing products that might be driving a valuable revenue stream. Avoiding unplanned cannibalization of exisiting products requires careful management of customer expectations. Obviously, the objective is to cannibalize competitors' products as much as possible and to do it before they strike.

The cardinal axiom is *do not lose profitable revenue _and_ customers*. If they are both lost, buying customers back means an even lower product price, thus further reducing existing margins.

Partnerships and Acquisitions

As we alluded to in the section on the third Law of Disruption—Kinetic Structures Prevail—no *one* company can keep up with the pace and variety of high-tech disruption by itself. Great companies rely on *partners* to ensure success. Therefore, it is important to develop the right partnerships and be ready to ride the next wave of opportunity. Finding and developing strong partners who can help capitalize on disruption is an essential element of a strategic plan.

In the mid 1990s, Cisco emerged as the market leader in routing technology, whereas Cabletron, SynOptics, and others emerged as leaders in LAN technologies. To hold its dominant position, Cisco realized that it needed to link more tightly with LAN technology. During this particular time period, LAN technology improved its speed from 10 Mbps to 100 Mbps. SynOptics' response to this market development was to merge with Wellfleet, thus betting on the market for the higher speed products. Cisco's strategy was to partner with incumbents of the 10 Mbps technology, while also acquiring the new 100 Mbps technology through a startup called Crescendo. The success of this dual strategy lay in its partnering with the past (legacy) while acquiring the competency of the future. As it turned out, Crescendo became Cisco's most successful acquisition.

Juniper Networks also demonstrated an effective partnering strategy by forging relationships with Nortel, Ericsson, Lucent Technologies, and other voice-network legacy equipment manufacturers. Like Cisco, Juniper partnered with the incumbents while acquiring technology for the future.

Vital Signs for Technology Inertia

Figure 4–6 provides a summary of the key issues and lists both the external indicators of failure due to technology inertia and the associated internal vital signs, which can help identify emerging inertia as a thread of failure. The time to act is when *any* of the internal vital signs appear, not after they grow into a more intractable and public problem.

Call to Action

Managing disruption is a complicated process, requiring careful analysis and healthy risk taking. It is not a matter of luck or of being

The Challenge	Managing Innovation to Exploit Disruption and Avoid Inertia
Key Points	• positioning for disruption • an attitude that embraces change • understanding of market physics • action planning to cause or anticipate disruption
External Indicators or Existing Problems	• falling behind the competition technologically • declining growth • loss of market share • negative customer feedback
Vital Signs Indicating Potential Peril	• lack of planning for disruption • being surprised by competitors' moves • inflexible market strategy in response to market changes • lack of common understanding of disruption methodology • company culture loathe to partnership • cultural resistance to change

Figure 4-6 Technology Inertia.

in the right place at the right time; it is a science. When great companies ride the waves of change, they make sure they are on top of the biggest of those waves.

Reading the market on all three dimensions depicted in Figure 4–2, knowing the company's strengths and weaknesses in each, and establishing a solid yet agile business model that relies on those strengths and builds more for the future are essential to success. The steps we outline in this chapter for setting a strategic plan—and renewing it regularly—can create the edge in managing the three dimensions of disruption.

New market waves occur at least once every two to three years. Great companies compete in multiple markets, so at any given time they are in the process of finding and entering a new market. Leaders cannot afford to say, "Oh, we entered a new market eight months ago, so we can sit awhile and reap the benefits." Great companies are *always* searching for the next opportunity to disrupt, and

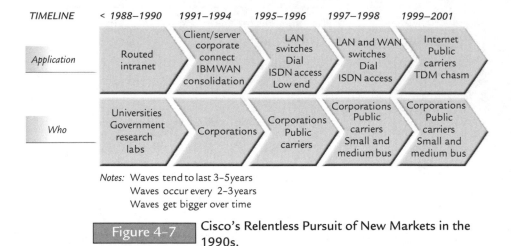

TIMELINE	< 1988–1990	1991–1994	1995–1996	1997–1998	1999–2001
Application	Routed intranet	Client/server corporate connect IBM WAN consolidation	LAN switches Dial ISDN access Low end	LAN and WAN switches Dial ISDN access	Internet Public carriers TDM chasm
Who	Universities Government research labs	Corporations	Corporations Public carriers	Corporations Public carriers Small and medium bus	Corporations Public carriers Small and medium bus

Notes: Waves tend to last 3–5 years
Waves occur every 2–3 years
Waves get bigger over time

Figure 4–7 Cisco's Relentless Pursuit of New Markets in the 1990s.

they are ready for disruption caused by outside forces. Disruption creates a point of entry, so readiness to capitalize on such openings is essential. As new markets are created, those that get there first with the right product can take the biggest share.

Is your company ready? Think about the kind of reputation you want your company to have in the market. Understand the leverage your technology has. Consider the partners you have now and could have in the future. What vision for disruption can your company create and achieve? How often do you take the pulse of the vital signs we have previously listed?

By way of example, Figure 4–7 is a timeline showing all the products that Cisco introduced over a 10-year period. In each case, Cisco moved forward, exploring new product possibilities before its current profitable products hit the end of their life cycles. Cisco's decision makers did not depend on a few "cash cows"—mature products that regularly sold large volumes. Rather, they constantly introduced new products and new versions of existing products, even while the old versions were selling well. Disruption was an *overt* strategy, backed by careful planning and constant learning.

Disruption provides the ingredients for success; inertia is a recipe for failure. The lessons are there.

5
Product Transitions

Overview

- Product transitions are both essential and difficult; they often threaten existing revenue streams.

- Effective product transitions require discipline, and counterintuitive thinking may be needed.

- Product transitions test a company's understanding of market physics and distribution channel properties.

- Axioms, derived from a detailed case study, which is included in this chapter, can help in preventing poor product transitions as a thread of failure.

At the West Coast Computer Faire in April 1981, Adam Osborne unveiled the "Osborne–1," a luggable computer with integrated word processing. It was the hit of the show. Not only was the inclusion of software an innovation, but the computer also sold for half the price of any competitive desktop. The sales pipeline filled immediately, and the Osborne Company had its first million-dollar month in September, just five months after product introduction. Osborne was aware, however, that he would need to continue to innovate. He immediately started planning for improvements and targeted their availability for 1983.

Meanwhile, the competition recognized the opportunity and began to come up to speed fast. IBM announced its PC, and although it was not transportable and sold for triple the cost of the Osborne–1, it *did* represent competition. Compaq and Apple soon arrived on the scene and quickly picked up market share. KayPro then introduced its own luggable, which included the same software as the Osborne–1 and sold for the same price. It also demonstrated improvement by adding a larger screen. Osborne's sales were immediately and negatively impacted.

To stave off further losses in market share, the company announced a new, more powerful machine, with its own larger screen. The price would go up, but so would the value. In anticipation of the improved product, however, customers stopped buying the Osborne–1. As a result, sales of the existing product dried up before the company could effectively introduce its new product. In what has become an archetypal story of product transition failure, the Osborne Company's premature announcement compromised its revenue stream. Worse, lack of execution ultimately prevented delivery of the promised next-generation version. Given the fragility of the company's financial structure at the time, it could not sustain this hard hit to its revenues. The Osborne Company ended up filing for bankruptcy. Adam Osborne and his computer became a verb in high-tech vernacular—*to Osborne*, meaning to inadvertently stall current product sales by prematurely announcing a new product and then not delivering.

A more recent example of product transition failure, also involving both poor strategy and poor execution, occurred in the telecommunications market. From 1998 to 2001, telecommunications equipment companies began to respond to the expanding influence of the Internet. The potential of voice transmission via the Internet, along with the larger data transmission market, spurred the entry of many communications equipment providers, new and old, into the Internet market.

To keep up with accelerating demand for transmission speed, however, service providers had to transition from their current telecommunications infrastructure technology—called time division multiplexing, or TDM—to packet network technology. This change was a significant risk for large companies like Nortel and Lucent, both of which had revenue streams worth tens of billions of dollars that were based on TDM technology. These companies would need to transition their primary sales focus from TDM to packet equipment, which at that time provided revenue streams of less than one billion dollars.

If this transition were to occur over five years, the growth of packet sales for each of the two companies would have to grow 100 percent to 200 percent year-over-year to overcome the decline of TDM sales and still maintain an expected net annual growth rate of 20 percent. These companies would have to do this while fighting off competition from packet network specialists like Cisco and Juniper. This would be a feat no company in the last century had accomplished. Not even Wall Street seemed to appreciate the risk these larger companies faced—until the Internet bubble burst and actual results were exposed.

A closer examination of this situation reveals that the same three product transition problems eventually occurred at both Nortel and Lucent. First, in both companies the strategy was to deliver packet technology *embedded* in TDM systems. Thus, each company was limiting itself to yesterday's technology. This was an appealing compromise to those who feared major change, but it was a weak strategy in competing with packet specialists. Second, both companies *failed to deliver* on their strategy—the embedded packet technology. And third, they *cross-subsidized profit sanctuaries* of their old products, meaning that they dropped prices on the old products to gain market favor for the new equipment, but then also dropped prices on the new equipment to drive the challengers' margins down.

It should go without saying that dropping prices on both past *and* future products is unsustainable in a multiquarter or multiyear transition. Such a strategy can only result in a drop in a company's overall margin structure. Add any product delivery problems or softening of the market, and the strategy, already precarious and unstable, will result in a negative revenue spiral.

Indeed, actual results for both Lucent and Nortel showed margin declines and financial woes that became epic. By the fourth quarter of 2001, both Lucent and Nortel experienced a peak-to-current revenue decline of 2.5 or greater—a drop of over 60 percent. Revenue continued to fall in 2002.

Product Transitions—The Inevitable Challenge

Let's go back to our basic model of great company growth and complexity, as described in Chapter 2. When companies reach Stage 2, during which new product generations emerge to drive new technology leadership, both the new *and* the current product generations require positioning. The primary focus of this positioning is to attract customers and thereby achieve, maintain, or extend the lead over the competition.

The challenge for a company at this stage is to introduce new products without driving itself out of business, because successful new products tend to cannibalize current revenue streams. A poor response to this challenge can mean bankruptcy for a small company whose revenues depend on one product line. For a larger company with other revenue streams, it can mean a significant loss of market share and a material drop in shareholder value and market capitalization.

Customer Demand—Faster, Better, Cheaper

Existing products inevitably become obsolete under the pressure of new product features and the price squeeze that occurs in maturing markets. Thus the term *cannibalization* is commonly used to refer to the situation in which sales of a company's next generation of products begin to eat away at its existing revenue streams. Why should customers continue to buy the old product if the new one is faster, better, or cheaper? Competitors enter markets based on the latest of these ever-changing demands, driving the companies who currently own the market to make their own transitions to keep pace.

An example of a successful product transition strategy can be found in the networking world. When popular demand drove modem speed from 28,600 bps to 56,000 bps, a transition strategy emerged by which the lower speed products were positioned with a reduced price, to appeal to the lower end consumer market, whereas the new technology was priced at a premium and aimed at the higher end enterprise market. This strategy, employed by many vendors including US Robotics, accelerated sales of the slower product, allowed introduction of the new product at a premium, and resulted in an effective product transition.

The Catch-22 of Product Transitions

Introducing new products into existing markets is always a risk, however, and as companies get bigger and more complex, the risk grows. The Catch-22 of product transitions is that cannibalization is *necessary* for progress and at the same time can be a serious *threat* to success if its risks are poorly managed. Either you cannibalize yourself—strategically—or you leave yourself to be eaten by the competition.

Although product transitions are predictably complicated, they are often undertaken with little strategic or operational planning. All too frequently, product managers introduce a new product as a replacement for old ones, assuming that the distribution channel and the customer will almost immediately absorb the new product. This can prove to be naïve. In addition, an inadequate level of attention to the process of insertion and a lack of understanding of market physics in response to product insertion both introduce increasing risk as companies grow.

In summary, the issues relevant to the challenge of product transitions are that they do the following:

- bring with them significant complexity and material risk
- rely on a mix of well-developed strategy and disciplined execution to achieve success
- require a clear positioning strategy and well-timed communication
- require detailed knowledge of market absorption dynamics, pricing barriers, and channel complexity
- must find a way to transfer the inevitable risk to the competition

The following true story of a complicated product transition challenge illustrates each of these issues. Further background and detail relevant to this case study is provided in the Appendix. Later in this chapter, we derive a set of axioms from this case study that we believe have application in any product transition planning. We also offer a tool for planning and managing transitions.

A Successful Product Transition and the Lessons Learned: A Case Study

In September 1997, the management team of one of Cisco's business units prepared a plan to launch the 3R, a new family of routers. The 3R routers were designed to be inserted between two current families of routers—the 2R and 4R. The plan was that the 3R routers would gradually cannibalize both of the existing product lines. The team prepared both positioning and pricing strategies and presented recommendations to the business unit vice president.

The VP had some doubts about these recommendations. It had been much easier to plan product transitions and cannibalize product lines when Cisco was a smaller company and its products produced revenues in the tens of millions. Now the revenues from the 2R and 4R products were over a billion dollars each; any plan involving cannibalizing current revenues held considerably more risk than in the past.

Developing and Positioning the 3R

Cisco had started development on this new family of routers in late 1995. The planned release date was in mid 1997. The 3R family would have the same functionality as the products in the 2R and 4R families. However, although the 2R and 4R product families primarily connected networks to networks, the 3R products would also allow an *individual* to connect to a network from outside the network's boundaries by dialing in. In addition, a user could plug a phone into this router and have a phone conversation. Thus, the new product would give Cisco entry into both the user-access market (dialing in) and the data telephony market (Internet phone service).

In considering the right strategy for the 3R product insertion, it was important to remember that customers typically make one of three buying decisions in relation to a given vendor, each with a distinctly different impact on that vendors' revenues:

- buy a new product
- continue to buy existing products
- wait and see what new products develop

Sellers have some influence over what customers do, and the one option sellers most want to steer customers away from is the third one—waiting. When customers do not buy anything, new *or* existing, revenue stall occurs—a serious drop in sales that could prematurely retire a product. Cisco's primary influence over its customers' buying decisions was greatest through its direct sales channel. However, Cisco's sales through this channel for both 4R and 2R products was less than 20 percent. So, it was questionable as to how much influence Cisco would have over customer choices. Consequently, it would be difficult to forecast the results of the proposed product transition.

It was also important to recognize the challenge of managing the transition in light of Cisco's growing complexity. When Cisco sold only its initial series of routers (the 7R series) *and* had relatively few customers—universities and large data centers—it was easier to keep track of where its routers were located and to communicate with all its customers. By 1997, however, Cisco had sold over one million units of just the 2R products alone, and the support and customer communication challenges were large.

The business unit VP anticipated that the current proliferation of customers would mean that a product transition would take longer than the two to three months normally required for a transition from one generation of large-scale routers to another. In addition, some new customers were very slow to make new equipment purchases. Telecommunications companies, for example, started their buying process by getting a purchase approved through Engineering, then proceeded to go to a procurement officer and then on to other approval points. Cisco or a Cisco reseller would have to negotiate a contract by communicating with each of these customer contacts. This long cycle gave Cisco even less influence over the outcome of product transitions.

The Options

Whatever the complexities, the business unit was in the fortunate position of having a product that exceeded expectations and had features that could not be found in any competing product. The 3R offered data telephony, user access, and high performance all in one solution. A miss in the product insertion process, however, could result in 6 to 12 months of pain and recovery. The winners, if Cisco blundered, would be the competition.

The options follow:

A. **Cannibalize the 4R and 2R families incrementally.** Introduce the 3R to incrementally cannibalize the 4R line and product 2R lines, using price/performance positioning to manage the cannibalization. This would require special care in the communication process. If the 3R performance numbers were announced, its superior capability would promote cannibalization of the 4R routers faster than was desirable.

B. **Aggressively replace the 4R family.** Replace the 4R family with the 3R family as quickly as possible, driving 4R sales to zero within nine months of 3R introduction. This was a particularly aggressive plan, given that 4R sales margins were higher than those of the 3R by about 5 percent and that nine months was an unusually short time to achieve product absorption.

C. **Communicate to the market that the 3R had only half its actual speed capability, while pricing it above the 2R line.** The 3R line could be introduced more precisely to compete with one of the low-end members of the 4R family. The goal of this strategy was for customers to buy a version of the 3R for its flexibility as a modular product, not for its speed (although improved speed was an actual feature). This way damage to the 4R product line could be limited to the one low-end 4R product. In addition, by pricing the introductory version of the 3R routers 20 percent higher than the high-end 2R product, those two lines could be kept distinct.

D. **Position the 3R as a completely new product classification.** Position the 3R as a network *server* and call it the *3S*. Market it for a distinct application (e.g., data telephony) in a relatively new market. This meant low cannibalization risk for the 4R and 2R families during the period the indirect sales channels would need to absorb the new product. Then, once the 3S was absorbed in the server market, the router version—the 3R—could be introduced and could begin to cannibalize the 2R and 4R families with the benefit of 3S revenues.

In evaluating these risks, the business unit VP was clear that, given the stakes involved, minimizing risk was the highest priority. Therefore, the following conclusions were drawn from Figure 5–1:

• Although Options A and B would likely be absorbed into the indirect sales channel the fastest, they would directly cannibalize existing products, and the risk of revenue stall in both cases was too high.

	Options					
Risks	**A**	**B**	**C**	**D**	**B + C**	**C + D**
Risk of channel stall	High	Very high	Medium	Low	High	Very low
Risk of stall affecting revenue	High	Very high	Medium high	Low	High	Very low
Level of cannibalization	Medium	Very high	Very high	Medium	Low	High
Rate of channel absorption	Medium	Medium	Low	Very low	Low	Very low
Margins	Low	Very low	Medium	Very high	Low	Very high
Revenue growth	Low	Very high	Medium	Very high	Medium	Very high

Figure 5–1 Risks of Options A, B, C, and D.

- Option B was also likely to dramatically hurt margins.

- Although the absorption of the 3R under Options C and D was likely to be slow, the lower risks of stall and of a negative impact on margin made these two choices seem most attractive.

- Combining C and D (C + D) appeared to offer the lowest risk.

Earlier, the business unit team had recommended a combination of Options B and C (B + C). However, considering the points made earlier, this configuration presented a potential "double whammy"—it had a high chance of hurting revenues as well as margins. Although this kind of cannibalization strategy had been successfully pursued when Cisco was smaller, the revenue streams from these products were now in excess of several billion dollars instead of tens of millions of dollars. The negative effects of any misstep would be greatly amplified.

Furthermore, although conventional wisdom suggested that Cisco could sufficiently differentiate the 3R product by using price/performance positioning, that wisdom was based on an era in which direct sales handled a significantly larger percentage of product sales. If customers realized that actual 3R performance exceeded that of the 4R and 2R families, the potential for cannibalization of Cisco's own revenues would be much greater.

Within the walls of a company known for strategically cannibalizing its own revenue streams, and given that it had done it successfully before, the team had recommended a business-as-usual approach. However, too many circumstances had changed.

The stakes were higher than ever before, given the size of the revenue streams. Furthermore, because margins on the 3R were lower than those of the older products, the risk was high for a decline in margins for the team's recommended alternative. The business unit VP estimated that a stall in the channels could cost approximately 10 percent of his unit's revenues within a quarter and thereby lower Cisco's earnings per share by several pennies per share. So, although the market opportunities for the 3R family were tremendous, the potential for damage was huge.

What to Do?

In the fall of 1997, the first 3R products were ready to be introduced. The time had come for a decision. The business unit VP's choice was to reduce risk in Cisco's current profit sanctuary (the existing profits on the 2R and 4R families) by choosing a combination of Options C and D, positioning the 3R as having only half of its actual performance and deploying the new product in a new market. With this option, the risk would be transferred to the *competitors'* profit sanctuary, and the new product would be differentiated from the existing router families. It would be called a server—the 3S—with modules optimized for the user-access market.

As it turns out, the strategy was a success. The performance of the 3S achieved a new performance benchmark for the server market, and cannibalization of the existing products was well managed.

Figure 5–2 shows the relative price/performance of the 2R, 3S, and 4R families, and Figure 5–3 shows the sales of the new 3S product and the continued sales of the 4R and 2R routers. Revenue from the 3S grew steadily, whereas revenues from the 4R declined gradually, and 2R revenues remained fairly constant. Although growth continued in the network-to-network applications (the larger routers), the 3S increased Cisco's market share in the network-to-user market.

Through sales of the new 3S product, Cisco also established itself as a competitor in the new data telephony market. By the end of 1999, Cisco had a 38 percent share. Even though Cisco had

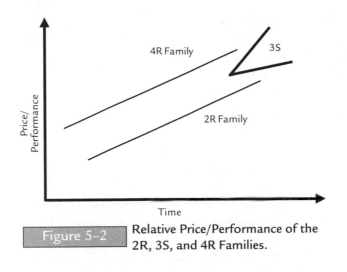

Figure 5-2   Relative Price/Performance of the 2R, 3S, and 4R Families.

	FY1993	FY1994	FY1995	FY1996
2R family revenue		$90.0M	$410M	$690.0M
4R family revenue	$90M	$240M	$420M	$660.0M
Total revenue from both families	$890M	$330M	$830M	$1,350M
Cisco total revenue	$649.0M	$1,243.0M	$1,978.9M	$4,096.0M
2R family—percentage of Cisco revenue		8%	21%	**17%**
4R family—percentage of Cisco revenue	13%	19%	21%	**16%**
Combined percentage of Cisco revenue	13%	27%	42%	**33%**

Figure 5-3   Sales of the 3S, 4R, and 2R Products.

stopped hardware development on the 4R and 2R families, demand for these products continued with the addition of new software releases. Cisco's share in all of the markets grew simultaneously, avoiding a stall in revenues.

Lessons Learned

The lessons learned from the 3S introduction experience can be summarized in a series of "axioms":

- **Axiom 1: Market-Leading Products Live On.** The 4R and 2R families of routers continued to be in demand by customers and distributors, even a year and a half after their announced end-of-life. For the reasons just discussed, Cisco could not assume that it could deterministically change buying preferences. It could no longer say to customers, "From this day on, the product you should buy is 3R instead of 2R or 4R," and assume that customers would comply. Any company would like to control customer engagement and disengagement from products, but in a case this complex, the rate of change in buying habits was not (and was not likely to be) as great as was desirable.

- **Axiom 2: Deliberate "Churning" Is Risky.** Deliberately "churning"—creating significant change—in a product portfolio in high-growth markets is risky, especially when the revenue streams are a significant proportion of the company's revenue. Cannibalizing existing revenues can stall revenue flow and confuse the customer. A vendor must think the way the customer will think.

- **Axiom 3: When Possible, Churn Your Competitors' Base.** It makes most sense to usurp competitors' profit sanctuaries or to target a new market with little competition. This minimizes the risk of upsetting your own current market and jeopardizing revenue flow and margins.

- **Axiom 4: Multiple Channels of Distribution Add a High Degree of Transition Complexity.** The distribution mix has a large impact on how product revenues taper off. Tier 1 integrators in particular have a high level of "channel memory"—attachment to existing products—which adds inertia when it is time for change. Cisco did not have the same influence over this channel as it did over its direct sales force. Direct sales people can be counted on to encourage customer adoption quickly, but if direct sales represents only a small portion of the product distribution, this influence is not sufficient.

- **Axiom 5: Risk Can Be Optimized by Surgical, Complementary Market Insertion.** Positioning a new product as a complement to an existing product and not as a direct alternative can reduce risk and enhance opportunity. In this case study, the business unit VP believed that price/performance factors were not strong enough to differentiate the 3R from the existing products. To minimize risk, the business unit had to position the new product as a server, the 3S, in a completely new market and then let it bleed into the existing router market. This required discipline in launching the product. It was essential to resist the urge to display the full strength of the product.

- **Axiom 6: Avoid Two-Border Product Transitions When Possible.** Because Cisco's new product bordered *both* the 2R and 4R product families, the transition was complicated by two transition borders. The new product threatened to cannibalize sales of an existing product family both "above" it (higher in performance) and "below" it (lower in performance), thus minimizing positioning flexibility during the absorption period. Customers could cross from either family to the new product, so Cisco had to worry about cannibalization of *both* higher-end and lower-end products. This is an exceptionally complex transition to make successfully, as the risk is essentially doubled.

- **Axiom 7: Make Sure the Decision Is Made at the Right Level.** Assessing the depth of knowledge of the team proposing a solution is critical. Ideally, probing is sufficient encouragement to stimulate a team's further consideration of options. In some cases, however, a leader has to make the call if too many elements of understanding are missing from the team's analysis.

Case Summary

In hindsight, the right decision was made. Margins and revenues grew for Cisco products in *all* of the markets—router, user-access, and IP telephony. A different decision might have been appropriate had the channel been dominated by direct sales, had it been a single-border product transition, had there been smaller revenue streams, or had Cisco had a smaller share in its various markets. Under the given circumstances, the consequences of the B + C option would have been catastrophic for Cisco. By approving the team's proposal without doing any analysis, the VP would have been responsible for lowering company earnings and damaging margin.

Two Tools for Planning Product Transitions

To take advantage of the axioms derived from this case study, consider the following two tools for planning product transitions.

The first is a checklist to use in product transitions (Figure 5–4).

The second tool is shown in Figure 5–5. As seen in the recommendations of Cisco's business unit management team, it is natural to think in terms of introducing new products into existing markets (Quadrant 2), where the sales force or channel has solid customer relationships and active lines of communication.

The assumption is that through positioning and customer management, the company can control the revenue churn caused by the new product introduction. Theoretically, then, the new product would be introduced into the company's existing market and, having gained traction there, could then be introduced into new markets (Quadrant 2 ➔ 1). However, the assumption of being able to control the revenue churn is suspect. The market forces driving the

---

- Is there a detailed launch plan?
- Is there a compelling case for positioning and differentiation that targets unserved needs rather than needs already served?
- Is there an analysis of how this product will be absorbed by each customer segment, distribution partner, and sales force?
- What levers exist for managing the transition?
  - pricing?
  - insertion?
  - competitive positioning?
- How will the marketing effort assist the transition?
- Are there detailed simulations on how the marketing effort will work?
- Are there detailed simulations on how the transition will evolve in terms of key measures?
- What measures can be employed to put things back on track, if help is needed?

Figure 5–4   Product-Transition Checklist.

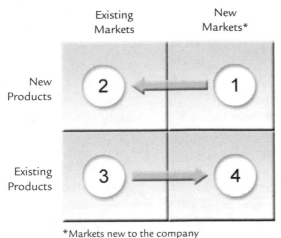

Existing Markets   New Markets*

New Products

2 ← 1

Existing Products

3 → 4

*Markets new to the company

Figure 5–5   Four-Square Product Planning Model.

success of a company's customers, who have customers and competitors of their own, far outweigh the forces of their existing relationships with a given vendor. If there is something better, faster, or cheaper to facilitate their own success, customers will find it, regardless of any vendor's effort to manage the timing of their choice.

To avoid the thread of failure that so commonly develops at the point of product transitions, a company must *use* market forces rather than try to *control* them. Often, then, this will mean introducing new products first into markets new to the company, then into existing markets (Quadrant 1 → 2). Introducing new products initially into markets new to the company allows two things to occur:

• Any impact in the new market is a threat only to the competition, not to the company's existing revenues.

• The company can establish and stabilize the new product in the new market while preparing to introduce it into existing markets.

A company can maintain momentum in current markets while it introduces new products into new markets. Later, the new products can bleed into current markets. At that point, a company can afford the cannibalization of its current products by the new because the replacement revenue stream has become reliable. Movement from Quadrant 1 to 2 works most effectively when a new product is specifically created for an incubating market where it can develop momentum and eventually be altered to serve an existing high growth market. A colleague reminded us of a military analogy: If the army is introducing new weaponry for which the field accuracy is uncertain and the potential for collateral damage is high, that system is initially placed on a battlefield located in enemy territory.

Conversely, Quadrant 3 represents introduction of derivative forms of existing products while awaiting the release of new products. These derivatives can then be expanded into new markets as they become established (Quadrant 3 ➔ 4). Movement from Quadrant 3 to Quadrant 4 allows managed expansion with high leverage.

Rather than trying to manage against natural market forces, even temporarily, use them to your advantage. And *always put the risk on the competition.* Using the model in Figure 5–5, always move from the upper right to the upper left, and not from the upper left to the upper right. Similarly, movement from lower left to lower right can work. A strategy that moves clockwise places insurmountable risk on the company itself, leading typically to failure.

<table>
<tr><td>

Something to Think About

</td><td>

Following are some questions to get you thinking more about product transitions in your own company and to help you assess your level of discipline:

</td></tr>
</table>

- Have you done a postmortem on the last three product transitions?

- Did your forecasts and actuals map?

- Were the risks and physics of absorption accurately modeled?

- Did you place your competitors in greater risk than yourself?

- Was the grid movement of Figure 5–5 counterclockwise?

- Is there a recognized authority and reviewer of transitions in your company?

- Does your team have a common understanding of how to make effective product transitions?

If the answer to one or more of these questions is no, it is time to add discipline—prepare a plan, identify responsibilities, and establish a process for monitoring and learning.

The Challenge	Making Product Transitions Profitably
Key Points	• plan carefully • use market forces; don't fight them • use strategies for today, not yesterday
External Indicators or Existing Problems	• unplanned loss of revenues • loss of customers • little impact on competition • revenue forecasts greater than actuals
Vital Signs Indicating Potential Perils	• lack of explicit product transition planning • no regular postmortems on product transitions • mismatch between actual and planned product absorption rate • inconsistent understanding among leaders of how to make effective product transitions • tendency to introduce new products only into existing markets • little product insertion expertise in the company

Figure 5-6   Product-Transition External Indicators and Vital Signs.

Vital Signs

Product transitions, like the other predictable challenges discussed in this book, can be assessed by their outward results (public, external indicators), but as always, we encourage looking for them much earlier, in a company's internal vital signs. Figure 5–6 summarizes the key points and lists the vital signs associated with poor product transitions. Remember, effective transitions require knowing what can be controlled and about optimally managing risks.

The Something to Think About section offers some questions that can help in identifying the risks inherent in product transitions.

6
Strategy

Overview

- Direction is defined by strategy.

- Strategy can be misguided in a number of ways, including being misdirected, weak, self-defeating, based on poor information, or inflexible.

- We examine various types of misguided strategy, using many specific examples.

- In addition, we look in depth at Cisco's acquisition and development (A&D) strategy—one that provided successful differentiation in a fast-growing market.

Between 1994 and 2001, Cisco became well known for making a remarkable series of successful acquisitions—more than 70 in all. This strategy is sometimes referred to as "the Cisco A&D strategy" (acquisition and development), in contrast to the long-standing term R&D (research and development.)

Cisco's success during this period has been widely referenced but only superficially understood. Various public comments on Cisco's aptitude in making acquisitions noted the company's attention to compatible chemistry, to balancing short- and long-term perspectives, to vision and alignment, and to geographic co-location with its various office centers.

Although these reasons for Cisco's success are valid, the list is incomplete. Cisco pioneered a *differentiating strategy* based on a powerful model, which was essential to its successful growth in the 1990s. We explore this strategy in detail in this chapter, starting with an overview of the strategy's components. Thus we begin this time with a success story, as we believe that the story of Cisco's successful acquisitions better introduces how to avoid misguided strategy than would a tale of failure.

Components of Cisco's Success

In 1994, Cisco's market reached an important transition point. The networking industry had come to believe that routing technology, Cisco's core business, would be replaced by high-speed LAN switching technology. Although this prediction was not unfounded, it assumed a significant technological shift. Such a shift would take years to develop, so the impact on revenues from Cisco's routing technology would be slow in coming. Still, the prediction could not be ignored.

The challenge was for Cisco to continue to beat the competition at satisfying current customers' needs while preparing for the major change required to meet the needs of future customers. To understand how Cisco set out to meet this dual challenge, let's start by looking at the particular beliefs, knowledge, and skill that characterized the company's leaders in the 1990s.

Both John Morgridge and John Chambers, successive Cisco CEOs during the period we are reviewing, had been executives at mini- and mainframe-computer companies when those companies and their industry hit points of decline and consolidation. Through those experiences, they both galvanized the following similar key beliefs:

- **Don't overinvest in prospective new markets before their time.** Too many companies met their demise in the 1980s by chasing markets that never developed.

- **Be "technology agnostic."** The days of vendors telling customers what they need are gone. Successful companies embrace technologies that solve customer problems.

- **Opt for open standards.** Open standards are crucial to the growth of big markets, as shown during the growth of the PC industry.

- **Focus with relentless intensity on the customer.** Focusing on customer success builds a successful company.

In addition to being led by these crucial precepts, Cisco had established a track record of understanding technology and how to leverage it for business results. It had developed a culture of self-measurement and self-critique that gave it a realistic understanding of its ability to execute. Through a few of its leaders, Cisco also had a reputation for understanding the intricate interdependencies of industry variables, both today and tomorrow.

Finally, Cisco demonstrated skill in both execution and continuous improvement of that execution, resulting in an industry record of more than 40 quarters of meeting or exceeding earnings expectations. In other words, Cisco had a unique expertise that allowed it to manage operating results in a highly consistent way. To maintain this kind of consistency for shareholders, the company had to maintain an intense commitment to minimizing operational disruption.

The Cisco A&D Strategy

Under the leadership of Morgridge and Chambers, a two-part strategy developed:

- Look *outside* the company for the development of new high-risk, capital-intensive, customer-driven solutions.

- Focus intensely *internally* on building products that customers are buying today.

The quest for both high growth *and* profit predictability drove Cisco to devise a growth model that allowed it to fund its future technology through equity markets. It accomplished this by investing in startups that had the technology it needed for the future, rather than risking operating capital by trying to develop that technology internally. At the same time, Cisco focused its internal efforts on incremental engineering of existing products that would beat the competition in satisfying current customers. This two-part strategy allowed the company to manage its operating expenses and yield greater profit predictability from its current technology, while gaining control over future technology developments that would secure Cisco's future.

External Investment

The focus for the external investment was to help manage risk where risks were high—the acquisition of startups with technology that was focused on new markets or new hardware. Acquiring companies focused on new markets was an obvious move for Cisco to make because it could purchase those companies after the market was more clearly in view, thus reducing risk. Acquiring companies that were focused on new hardware (rather than developing it internally) also helped reduce risk but not as obviously.

A high-technology hardware systems vendor typically spends 24 to 36 months developing a new product. In addition, in 2001, the average cost of hardware engineering, including prototypes, was $300,000 to $380,000 per engineer, per year. In contrast, software products in the same time period typically emerged in 9 to 18 months at a cost of $180,000 to $240,000 per engineer, per year. Large new hardware projects, then, represent twice the schedule *and* almost twice the cost per engineer, causing considerably greater uncertainty about a company's operating expenses. The risk would be exacerbated, of course, by any uncertainty as to when the new market will really emerge. Simply put, large hardware projects for new markets possess four times the financial risk of software-based programs. Thus, purchasing a company that had developed new hardware to a certain point represented less risk than investing operating capital in a complicated untried concept.

Internal Investment

The difference just described in hardware and software development guided Cisco's advantageous investment of its operating capital toward two areas:

- **incremental hardware development.** Cisco could invest more operating dollars in building customer satisfaction with today's products than its competitors could, who were spreading their operating dollars between today's products and tomorrow's.

- **software development—both incremental improvements and new development.** As with incremental hardware development, investing in incremental software development internally allowed Cisco to invest its operating dollars in building customer satisfaction. Software improvements were applicable to many of Cisco's products and could be leveraged across multiple product lines.

In addition, because new software development was four times less risky (half the schedule time and nearly half the cost per engineer) than new hardware development, it was clearly less risky than investments made by other companies in *combination* hardware and software programs that were chasing new markets where there was little predictability in the timing of those markets. Thus Cisco positioned itself with lower risk and could use its internally developed software to disrupt the markets in its specialty area—the handling of packetized information.

Implementing the Cisco A&D Strategy

Let's go back to 1994 and the challenge of the emergence of LAN switching technology, which some market watchers thought would cannibalize the revenues from routing technology. To respond to this challenge, Cisco made its first acquisition: a company that already had LAN switching capability. It could now define its future as a company that fused the technologies of routing *and* LAN switching. This and similar steps in the same direction eventually became a strategic pattern.

More than 70 other acquisitions followed, each based on the same strategy—using operating capital to improve today's technology and equity or risk capital to invest in tomorrow's. The results drove both predictable earnings performance and a growth strategy that beat all competitors.

Cisco's strategy helped navigate the fundamental dilemma of corporate expansion. The strategy ensured the right internal focus while enabling the company to scale beyond its competition. It proved that companies could manage customer satisfaction and operating expense, let equity markets manage creative risk taking, and enjoy the fruits of both types of investment.

This is not to suggest that this strategy is without its own set of risks. For this reason, Cisco's A&D model bears more detailed study, which we offer in Exhibit 6–1. Although this is a lengthy and detailed analysis of one success story, we recommend that you read it before proceeding to the rest of this chapter. It provides a basis for understanding some of the issues of misguided strategy, which we discuss later.

Exhibit 6–1: Analysis of Cisco's Acquisition Logic

In this section, we attempt to frame some conclusions that emerged from both a qualitative and quantitative assessment of the 31 Cisco acquisitions that we personally know best. The data represent our analysis and judgments. They span a population of acquisitions ranging from tens of millions of dollars to in excess of $6 billion.

Managing Risk—The Basics

By way of introduction, let's review some basics discussed at a summary level earlier in this chapter. There are two forms of capital: *operating capital* (used to invest in improvements in current operations) and *risk capital* (used to invest in new ventures). Large companies such as AT&T, GE, and HP have expertise in managing operating capital expense. By nature, these kinds of big companies are not as good at managing risk capital as are the venture capitalists in the equity markets. In fact, big companies often fail to pursue new developments. Or they may spend lots of money but lack sufficient technology expertise and sufficient customer intimacy. Instead, they are the experts in managing size and achieving stability.

Specialized technical depth and customer intimacy are typically the strengths of young companies pursuing new markets or changes in current markets. However, once these smaller, specialized companies succeed and expand (as we described in Chapter 1), they face the dilemma of transitioning to new products, which in and of itself introduces considerable uncertainty to their operating expense.

Consider the graph in Figure E6–1. The horizontal axis depicts operating capital, and the vertical axis depicts risk capital or the equity market. The diagonal vector is intended to show that through acquisitions, value that develops in the equity market can be acquired and become part of a company's operating capital. The "X" represents a startup developing new technology. The "O" represents incremental engineering in the acquiring company's R&D group. After an acquisition, the engineering cadre and technology of the startup become part of the acquiring company's R&D group.

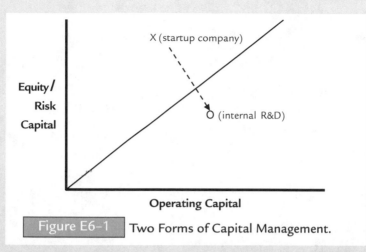

Figure E6–1 Two Forms of Capital Management.

Some companies have projects aimed at future technology in their operating expense portfolio. Figure E6–2 uses a dotted-line wedge to depict the envelope of risk that companies face as they invest in future products and markets internally. This envelope of risk becomes more difficult to manage as companies grow, face operationally complex challenges with legacy products, and develop increasingly higher levels of operating expense. The imprecise timing of new product absorption or the development of new markets means potential "jitter" in earnings per share (EPS).

There are several areas of difficulty that define the envelope of risk when investing in both today's and tomorrow's technology internally. These are summarized in the following list and explained shortly thereafter:

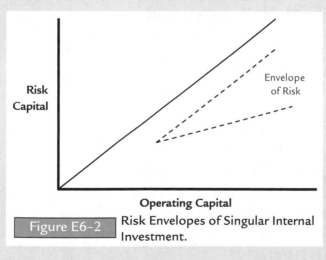

Figure E6–2 Risk Envelopes of Singular Internal Investment.

Customer Management
- managing current commitments, product lines, and customer satisfaction
- recognizing the opportunity cost of change for existing customers

R&D Challenges
- retaining specialized, best-of-breed talent while maintaining a flexible cadre of generic engineering
- managing for the future versus the past for the most important company asset: the people
- handling conflict between an acquisition strategy and internal R&D

Managing Financial Results
- investing operating capital wisely such that EPS jitter is minimized

Managing Customer Satisfaction

When competition was less intense than it is today, technology development was rarely customer driven. The normal course of business was for vendors to tell customers what they could have and for customers to accept it, lacking better choices. As we discussed in Chapter 4, growth in competition has changed this dynamic to one that is customer driven, in which vendors must listen to customers to find out what they want and then make investment choices accordingly. Companies no longer have the luxury of investing in future technology on its own merits and have reasonable predictability for its acceptance.

Opportunity Cost of Change for Customers

At the same time, managing disruption and investing in the future take money away from investing in products that customers are buying today. As products get old and pressure builds to keep up with the competition by investing in new products, companies often begin disinvesting in existing products too soon, thus disenfranchising their embedded customer base. They mistakenly believe their current customers are held hostage to the old product and won't forsake it, no matter how neglected it becomes.

New, Specialized Engineering Expertise Versus Current Skill Set

When the market calls for building new products with new technology, the less specialized engineering skill sets valued in larger companies cannot compete with the specialized knowledge found in smaller, newer companies. The less specialized model works well enough in a vendor-driven environment. In an intensely competitive, customer-driven environment, however, risk-funded companies that are founded on the specialized knowledge of their engineers and marketing leaders tend to win.

Product Versus People Orientation—Past Versus Future

When one company acquires another company for its people or intellectual capital first, it is focusing on what those people will create next, not what they have already created. The acquiring company buys the employees' ability to create the future. This contrasts with an acquisition based on a product that has already been produced. This approach values the product more than the people. It is less focused on future product creation and often results in lower employee retention after acquisition.

Competition Between R&D and M&A

Another element of risk is that mergers and acquisitions (M&A) leaders are sometimes placed in an adversarial position against R&D leaders. In companies focused on R&D for both today's *and* tomorrow's products, the M&A lead's role is to buy when R&D fails to deliver. Thus, the M&A thinking is to acquire *products* to fix problems, which is backward looking. Forward-thinking M&A acquires *people* to invent for the future. In this latter case, M&A becomes part of the aligned execution of a product plan.

Investment Timing

An anticipated market does not always emerge as expected. Here is where deep, specialized knowledge of the customer base and emerging markets is critical. Being able to read market momentum as it develops and changes is a crucial art in strategy management. Technology inertia is the danger to be avoided by this anticipation. As we discussed in Chapter 4, even great companies ignore new market shifts that can disrupt the company's existing successes.

Turning the Risks to Advantage

With these basics regarding investment risk in mind, consider Figure E6–3. Using the same framework shown in Figure E6–2, the envelope of risk here balances between operating capital and risk capital. What Cisco invented and executed was a model that used the equity market as a *technology* incubator.

Given its beliefs about the future of industry dynamics, Cisco invested a larger percentage of operating expense than any of its competitors in disruptive software technologies in new markets, such as SNA and voice-over-IP (voice exchange over the Internet). Both of these investment areas set Cisco apart; in

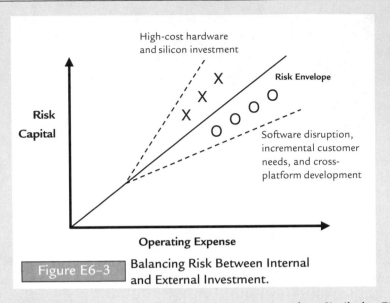

High-cost hardware
and silicon investment

Risk Envelope

Risk
Capital

Software disruption,
incremental customer
needs, and cross-
platform development

Operating Expense

Figure E6–3 Balancing Risk Between Internal and External Investment.

fact, Cisco has since dominated the SNA transport market. Similarly, Cisco has dominated the voice-over-IP market for years, providing the highest quality voice transport across the Internet and corporate IP networks.

First and foremost, Cisco's approach maximized risk investment *off balance sheet* and therefore rendered quarterly operating results more predictable and consistent, minimizing EPS jitter. Cisco's intense internal focus on products that customers were currently buying resulted in customer satisfaction and loyalty to Cisco's products, which outpaced all its competition from 1994 to 2000.

Furthermore, when Cisco acquired new companies, the engineers were specialists. Usually, potential teams were evaluated before one was chosen and assimilated into Cisco. In this model, the M&A agenda was an extension of the R&D agenda, including the assimilation of the acquired team into Cisco's R&D organization. A common rather than a competing strategy between the R&D and M&A groups was executed, resulting in collaboration and a forward-looking thrust.

Thus, Cisco's strategy turned to advantage each of the areas of difficulty in managing the risk of investments for today and tomorrow that were listed previously. Competitors that attempted to follow Cisco's acquisition behavior without a well-founded strategy did not match Cisco's success. In some cases, Cisco's competition tended to try larger mergers rather than smaller acquisitions.

In other cases, competitors executed catch-up acquisitions that were born out of execution problems and that tended to value products over people. None of Cisco's competitors seemed to have a coherent, differentiating strategy on which to base their acquisition choices.

A Tool for Analyzing Aquisitions

Let's look in more detail at Cisco's choices of acquisitions. First consider the tool shown in Figure E6–4, a two-by-two matrix that displays the potential *synergy* of an acquisition along the horizontal axis and the *growth* potential along the vertical axis. By synergy we mean the complementarity of an acquisition candidate's products to the acquiring company's distribution and support.

In the matrix in Figure E6–4, synergy suggests low operational disruption, low overlap, and distribution channel readiness. Maximum synergy is found to the right and maximum growth is toward the top. Consequently, the *most successful* and *lowest risk* acquisitions tend to reside in the upper right quadrant, Quadrant 1. Cisco's acquisition of Crescendo is an example of one that fits in this quadrant, where Cisco's sales channel and its manufacturing organization could quickly absorb a fledgling technology.

Quadrant 2 defines *lower growth* with *high synergy*. An example is when a company like Cisco, with its great networking products, acquires a company

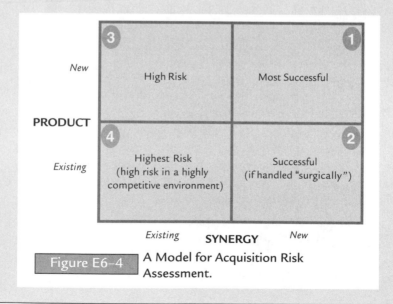

Figure E6–4 A Model for Acquisition Risk Assessment.

with new silicon technology to help make that networking product faster, cheaper, or more functional than the competition. The assimilation of such an "ingredient" technology is called *backward integration*. By acquiring silicon technology, Cisco could accelerate the momentum of its existing product. The improvement through better silicon technology did not drive vastly higher growth, but it *did* improve momentum and focus.

These ingredient acquisitions improve cost, performance, or function of existing products. Furthermore, when an acquisition is an ingredient technology, it is likely that only the R&D team will be involved in absorbing the new entity, thereby reducing the complexity of the integration of talent. Examples of such acquisitions by Cisco include Skystone, Growth Networks, and Telebit, all representing backwards integration with device-level ingredients that were added to product lines for specific competitive advantage. They provided the advantage of synergy more than of growth potential and are examples of *surgical acquisitions*—ones with a precise (or at least a more predictable) effect on the organization and therefore one with lower risk.

Quadrant 3 in Figure E6–4 represents *high growth potential* but greater risk due to *lower synergy*. If the alignment of the acquired product with existing products is poor, the value of the acquisition will not be exploitable. Or if synergy is lacking between the acquired product and the existing distribution and support systems, then timing will be an issue. If such gaps in the ability of the channel and the support organization to handle the acquired product are not closed within 6 to 12 months, for instance, there will likely be a negative impact on revenue and profitability.

The high growth/low synergy acquisitions of Quadrant 3 need great planning and preparation. When the acquired company is large, the need for planning is even greater, and the acquirer must be prepared for true metamorphosis to optimize the synergistic advantage.

Quadrant 4, *low synergy* and *low growth*, is an option in mature markets, where less intense pressures of competition allow time to develop the economies of scale and to consolidate operational expense. This choice requires a long-term horizon. Consequently, it is a higher-risk investment in highly competitive equipment markets.

Consider a merger of two large hardware companies in which the growth of both companies is slow and the synergies are low because there is, say, a 50 percent overlap in their product capabilities. In a case like this, the inevitable integration challenges can stall the already slow growth, even to the point of a decline in revenues. Sometimes rumors of discontinuing a product emerge in such an acquisition, driving customers to delay purchasing until certainty returns. Further, in the case of a large merger like this, the structures are *so* large that some systems have to be terminated rather than merged, which means even more adjustment for people, which can cause more delay. The low growth/low synergy merger scenario can work in markets with little competition in which 5 to 10 years to achieve synergy is manageable. An example might be the merger of two telecom giants such as SBC and Pacific Bell.

At the same time, two high-tech companies whose technology life cycles are typically short are ill advised to operate in this quadrant. The HP/Compaq acquisition of 2002 fits into this higher-risk category, as the exploitation of their potential synergy requires a relatively long time horizon, whereas the synergy of the merger must be exploited in a short time to be of value. At the time of this book's publication, it remains to be seen whether the advanced planning done to effect this merger can overcome the pressures against near-term synergy.

Analyzing Cisco's Acquisitions

Turning to some analytical data, Figure E6–5 displays several attributes in its column headings and includes data for a subset of Cisco's acquisitions. Specific names of acquired companies are withheld to enable focus on the trends rather than the specific transactions.

As can be seen in the figure, each of the acquisitions under study are evaluated in terms of the following attributes:

- **quadrant of strategy**—synergy and growth, as discussed earlier
- **stage of the market**—premarket (before a market is defined and monitored for share or revenue), tornado (t), and post-tornado
- **proximity (geographical)**—how close the acquisition was to a major Cisco development center—high, medium, or low
- **chemistry**—the potential of the acquired culture and Cisco's culture to meld—high, medium, or low
- **leadership DNA consistency**—how likely the acquired leadership team would be to fit, and remain, at Cisco—high, medium, or low
- **speed of integration**—how quickly the acquired company was actually integrated into Cisco's standard processes—high, medium, or low
- **customer momentum**—the volume of customer franchise wins in place in the acquired company at the time of acquisition—high, medium, or low

- **class of acquisition**—one of three: (1) ingredient technology, such as an Application Specific Integrated Circuit (ASIC) or silicon; (2) product-in-a-box, such as a switch, router, or modem; (3) system-level component, such as network management of an older generation of product that allows for the integration of internally developed primary products

- **goal achievement**—the extent to which the acquisition achieved at least 60 percent of its internally targeted goal of share and profit

- **resulting changes in market share**—up, same, or down

With some examination of the data in Figure E6–5, we can make a number of initial observations:

- **All ingredient acquisitions were successful.** These are the acquisitions that provided technology to products that were already selling. Sales channel momentum and knowledge already existed, so risk was relatively low. Four out of four ingredient acquisitions succeeded, and four out of six of the most successful acquisitions fell into this realm.

- **In general, buying in the tornado period led to a higher probability for success than buying pre- or post-tornado.** The tornado period of the market is when momentum exists. The market potential is real, customer momentum is most visible, and the acquiring company has the greatest emotional commitment across all organization functions that have to integrate the new entity.

- **Just under half of the acquisitions underachieved their goals.** All of these were in Quadrants 3 and 4, where synergy was low—that is, achieving when momentum was the greatest challenge.

- **Over half the acquisitions achieved what they attempted.** Over 60 percent of these were in Quadrant 1 or Quadrant 2, and almost the same percentage were timed in the tornado period of the market, fortifying the points made earlier.

- **Strong chemistry, proximity, and leadership DNA consistency all correlated positively with strong results.** These elements can be seen as important, although not sufficient to success.

Exploitability Assessment

To build on this theme of synergy and momentum alignment, Figure E6–6 depicts these acquisitions in another two-by-two matrix. This figure uses the horizontal axis to display the level at which the acquisition was complementary

Acquisition	Quadrant	Market Stage	Proximity	Cultural Chemistry	LDRSP DNA	Speed of Integration	Customer Wine	Class of ACQ	> 60% Goal	Market Change
1	1	t	h	m-h	l	m	h	prod/sys	h	up
2	2	t	h	m-h	m	m	h	ingred	h	up
3	3	post	l	l	l	m	l	sys	l	same
4										
5	3	pre	l	h	m	m	l	prod	l	no
6	4	post	l	l	l	m	l	prod	l	no
7	1	t	m	m	h	m-h	h	prod	m-h	up
8	4	pre	h	m	m	m	l	prod	l	no
9	1	pre	l	m	l	l	l	prod	m	no
10	3	t	m	m	h	m	m	prod	l	no
11										
12	3	pre	l	l	l	m	l	prod	l	no
13	3	t	l	m	m	l	m	prod	m	no
14	3	pre	l	m	l	l	l	prod	l	up
15	3	pre	l	h	m	m	m	prod	m	up
16	3	pre	h	m	m	m	l	prod	m	no
17	1	t	l	h	h	h	h	ingred	h	up
18	1	t	h	h	h	h	h	ingred	h	up
19	1	pre	m	h	h	h	m	ingred	m	up
20	3	post	h	m	m	l	m	prod	m	up
21	3	pre	l	l	l	l	l	prod	l	down
22	4	pre	h	l	m	m	l	prod	l	no
23	4	pre	l	m	l	l	l	prod	l	no
24										
25	1	t	l	m	l	h	m	other	m	no
26	3	pre	h	m	m	h	m	prod	l	no
27	3	pre	m	m	m	m	m	prod	l	down
28	3	pre	m	m	l	l	l	prod	l	down
29	3	t	m	l	m	m	m	prod	m	no
30	1	t	m	l	m	m	m	prod	m	no
31	3	pre	h	m	m	h	h	prod	l-m	down
32	1	t	h	h	h	h	h	ingred	h	up
33	1	t	h	h	h	h	h	prod	m	up
34	3	pre	h	m	l	l	l	prod	l	down

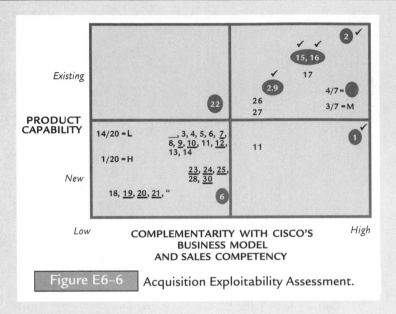

| Figure E6-6 | Acquisition Exploitability Assessment. |

with Cisco's business model and sales competence (low to high) and the vertical axis to show new versus existing product capability.

Correlating this with Figure E6–5, it is clear that the acquisitions that collect in the lower-left quadrant, where new products are offered when the business model and sales competence is not in place to accept the new product, show underwhelming results. Although this makes intuitive sense, using a matrix like this and like the one in Figure E6–4 can help make visible the risks of a potential acquisition. If the US Robotics and 3Com merger, for instance, which ended up being a point of no return for 3Com, had been analyzed in this way, the outcome might have been predicted and thus avoided.

In a similar manner, we can see from Figures E6–5 and E6–6 that the best results were with those acquisitions that added momentum to *existing products* (where there was already market momentum) and were compatible with the current business model and sales competence.

Channel and Product Compatibility

Finally, Figure E6–7 provides another important tool for acquisition risk assessment. This is another two-by-two matrix that displays existing versus new *channel* (sales distribution) and existing versus new *product* capability.

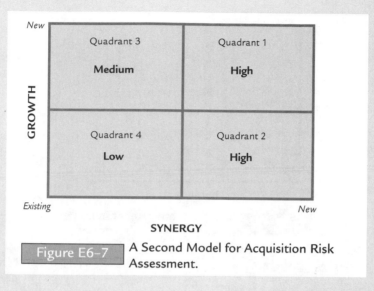

Figure E6-7 A Second Model for Acquisition Risk Assessment.

Risk is high anywhere on the left, where the go-to-market mechanisms (distribution) are inconsistent with the nature of the product. For example, a company that employs only a two-tier distribution model (optimal for a high-volume, low-touch product) would be ill advised to buy a company with a product requiring a very high touch sales approach (e.g., a super computer). Alignment of product and distribution is crucial to exploiting the value of an acquisition.

Tuning the Model for Bear and Bull Markets

Obviously, this model must be tuned for both bear and bull markets. In a bull market, the diagonal line in Figure E6–3 will rotate upward to above 45 degrees, driving more acquisitions into operating expense (Figure E6–8). As acquisitions become more expensive, this torque will tend to occur increasingly early. Acquisitions made in a bull market need to be highly exploitable, as the acquisition premiums tend to be the highest.

When conditions create a bear market, the diagonal line will fall below 45 degrees. In this case, the pace of acquisitions will slow and most likely be more focused on high synergies (backward integrations or larger acquisitions, in which acquired sales expertise can drive both growth and synergy).

No market—bull or bear—lasts forever. As the market turns either way, the approach to acquisitions must be tuned to the changing economic environment.

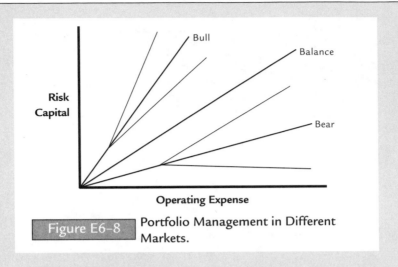

Risk Capital

Bull

Balance

Bear

Operating Expense

Figure E6–8 Portfolio Management in Different Markets.

Summary

In summary, it is important to recognize that the Cisco A&D model emerged out of intellectual depth and execution excellence. The approach was rooted in basic beliefs such as avoiding overinvestment in not-yet-existing markets, the value of financial predictability (growth with risk management), and the importance of responsiveness to the customer. These beliefs led to a differentiated strategy with an execution signature of sustained performance. It is a strategy that benefited from the minds of many and has proved difficult to replicate.

Successful Versus Misguided Strategies

Strategy defines *direction*. Once a vision or long-term goal is set, a company must define the key vectors by which it will approach that destination. The destination (vision) might never be fully reached. In fact, as a company realizes that it can reach its envisioned destination, it often sets its sights on a new one. At any one time, though, strategy defines the roadmap by which successful companies make their way to an envisioned future. Misguided choices about strategy, however, result in missing the long-term target and meeting failure rather than success.

Figure 6–1 suggests the simple yet crucial role of strategy in achieving success. By thinking of strategy as a set of critical *vectors*

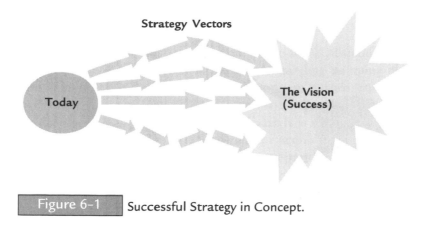

Strategy Vectors

Today

The Vision
(Success)

Figure 6-1   Successful Strategy in Concept.

that define the path to the company's vision, we can examine the various ways in which strategy can get off course and become a thread of failure.

Consider five possibilities for the vectors:

- **misdirected**—headed in the wrong direction
- **undersized**—too short to provide the thrust required
- **self-defeating**—headed toward an intermediate danger zone
- **shallowly rooted**—rooted in inadequate information
- **inflexible or fluid**—either too rigid or too subject to change

We examine each of these strategy weaknesses by illustrating them with examples.

Misdirected Strategic Vectors

Chosen strategies can be headed in the wrong direction, based on misreading the market (see Figure 6–2). This can be illustrated by examples of companies that position themselves in the wrong market and others that miscalculate their market value.

Positioning Error

The key to positioning is to understand market dynamics, competitors, and the value chain of the market. Probably the most common positioning error made by high-tech computing or networking companies is their decision to be proprietary (to build products that work

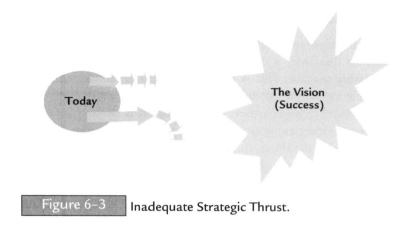

Today

The Vision
(Success)

Figure 6-3 Inadequate Strategic Thrust.

Make Versus Buy

Imagine an existing product that can be modified and used to enter a new market. If the modifications to this existing product take, say, 12 months, and the market inflection point (the point at which tornado growth begins, marked by expectations of 20 percent or greater growth quarter over quarter) has already hit, the product will be too late. In this case, *acquiring* the technology and product to get into the market earlier, rather than trying to develop it internally, is likely to be the better strategy.

However, if the internally developed product can be ready in 6 to 12 months, the question of make or buy is more debatable. The swing factor depends upon how much need there is for technical potency and customer intimacy by the particular customers who will determine the tornado growth. If the internal development organization has had minimal customer engagement and believes that simply running faster will beat the competition, beware. Winning the customer may well require more than winning at time-to-market. Believing in natural growth under heavily competitive conditions is especially suspect if the market will be very large, where the financial risks are very high.

A less obvious example of applying undersized vectors to achieve the desired thrust involves ignoring the rules of good acquisitions. The strategy to acquire may seem like a powerful (long) vector. But the value of an acquisition (the length of the vector) can be reduced if the merger has low synergy. In other words, its value may be miscalculated. A way of thinking about the growth and synergy in acquisitions is illustrated in Figure E6–6, in the exhibit on Cisco's

A&D strategy. Because the exhibit addresses acquisitions in depth, we only add a few more examples here and some final comments.

The Perils of Misguided Acquisition Strategy

When 3Com merged with US Robotics, the pundits predicted that this combination would beat the other established competitors, including Cisco. Together, the two companies had almost a monopoly on the dial concentrator market—the market for modem dial-up to the Internet—and a combined market cap equal to Cisco's. In combination, the new company could offer end-to-end solutions for data networks. There was little product overlap, and 3Com's corporate sales staff would complement US Robotics' retail distribution channels. According to management, the pricing of the acquisition would minimize earnings dilution.

Despite the appearance of high combined value, however, the lack of synergy was serious. The collective efforts of the two companies would not be able to improve customers' private intranets—a high-growth market—nor would the new company be able to offer large networks, high-end routing, or scalable carrier-class asynchronous transfer mode (ATM) for voice and data transfer over the Internet. In addition, the combined entities had distinctly different business models—one based on low-margin modems, one on high-margin systems. The two corporate cultures were likewise different. The results? Within two years, the new company's market cap was less than half of Cisco's.

A similar story can be told about the merger between Wellfleet and SynOptics, two companies that came together to combat Cisco and started out with a combined market cap larger than Cisco's. Again, two years later the value of the combined entity was cut by half. Not only did the envisioned growth not develop, but the new company also continued to lose market share and was eventually bought by Nortel.

Given the large risks and the spotty track record of large mergers and acquisitions, this particular approach to fast growth carries the potential for serious failure. Size alone exacerbates the risk inherent in any merger or acquisition, given the magnitude of the bet, the established nature of the existing cultures, and the steep challenge of integration. The changes required to become one company from two successfully can seriously disrupt operations in the short term, which can then influence the purchasing decisions of key customers.

Cisco's acquisition of Stratacom, although successful in the long run, caused problems when Stratacom's sales force was absorbed into the dominant Cisco router sales force, leading to an exodus of key Stratacom sales people, a severe blow in the short term. Successful management of acquisitions involves maintaining operational potency, especially the productivity of the sales force and engineering team. In general, the integration of an acquired sales force is the most complex and challenging of all staff integrations, which led to Cisco's strong bias toward acquiring early technology teams with small or nonexistent sales organizations.

In these smaller acquisitions, no one questions which culture and which set of operations will do the adapting. Adaptation by the people from the smaller company tends to be voluntary, as the logic for change is overwhelming. The choice to be acquired is often lucrative for those people, especially the most influential of them. Finally, the culture and methods of operation in a smaller firm are often more flexible or fluid than those of the acquiring company.

When the companies are of essentially equal size, however, the question of *who* and *what* has to change is often arguable, and much energy can be wasted in unconstructive conflict and resistance to the ultimate outcome. Mergers challenge established cultural practices and methods of operation, especially when business models and channels are different. The result is often increasing organizational thrash—indecisive and unproductive effort.

The choice to *buy* rather than *make*, then, should be based on several key conditions:

- If a company is late in terms of the market's development and does not have a team that has been intimate with customers and technology in the new market for at least nine months, it is likely to make more sense to buy a company with the customer relationships and the technology.

- Any acquisition should increase product potency, enhance time-to-market, or strengthen the acquiring company's current skills mix.

- Buying for growth and to get into new markets makes sense only if the acquiring company's distribution structure will be leveraged.

- If the merger is large, beware, unless the speed of growth of the market is slow enough to allow time for a highly complex integration.

Self-Defeating Strategic Vectors

Not infrequently, a company must go after its long-term vision in a circuitous fashion—for instance, to avoid creating significant intermediate problems (see Figure 6–4). Too often, companies go straight for the target, disregarding intermediate barriers.

Waking Sleeping Giants

A classic example of ignoring midterm barriers is a startup that positions itself against a gargantuan incumbent competitor. "Waking the sleeping giant" and provoking retaliation only raises the potential of war before the small company is properly armed.

An alternative strategy, which introduces a product into an ancillary market, however, operates in stealth mode and often proves successful. Once established, the new product can then begin to make headway into the incumbent's market, which tends to lead to greater success than an outright attack. Companies such as Juniper, Redback, Ascend, and Cascade all did this to Cisco, with varying degrees of early success.

Pricing Errors

Another example of going directly for the target despite intermediary barriers is making bad pricing decisions during product transitions. Pricing is critical for positioning and product transitions. As we discussed in Chapter 6, the misuse of pricing to gain or hold market share is a common peril. Pricing can be the wrong vehicle to achieve a competitive advantage, and it can deconstruct the very market in which a company is competing.

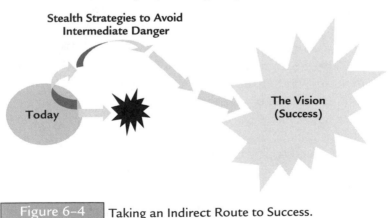

Stealth Strategies to Avoid Intermediate Danger

Today

The Vision (Success)

Figure 6–4   Taking an Indirect Route to Success.

Consider a hypothetical example in which a market leader such as Coca-Cola has 100 percent market share in a given country. A new participant, say Pepsi, considers entering the country with a low-price strategy. If Coke retaliates in kind, it can thwart the stability of one of its profit sanctuaries—a reliable source of profitability. Inserting an alternative product—for example, a generic product that is less expensive than the new competition—would be a more desirable tactic than dropping the price of the established product and cutting into a key source of profitability. This strategy presents a new product to the market, one that can compete with Pepsi's new price level while maintaining the profitability of its brand product, which many customers will continue to buy based on brand preference. Employing special incentives or product-bundling schemes that improve distributors' existing sales can also be prudent to combat insurgency while protecting the company's profit sanctuary.

In a real-life example, Cisco once found itself in a position similar to that of the hypothetical Pepsi. By the time Cisco finally decided to enter the dial-up market, it was far behind Ascend, the then-premier dial-up provider for ISPs. Like the hypothetical Pepsi, Cisco nevertheless developed the product that it needed to enter the market and inserted it in the market at half the price of Ascend's product. This strategy was based on market intelligence that showed that customers were looking for better pricing. Ascend responded by lowering its prices (surprisingly, in both new and existing accounts), which cut into its profit sanctuary. Its ASP dropped over 25 percent in two quarters, falling below that of Cisco's. The ASP drop resulted in a dramatically lower market cap and eventually led to the acquisition of Ascend by Lucent.

Although Ascend's response was exactly what Cisco's strategy was designed to cause, it was not necessary for Ascend to follow pricing down so quickly. It was not likely that its ISP customers would change installed products, as the cost of an ISP switching its operations support to a new product was too high.

Another example of pricing error occurred in 2000 and 2001, when the telecommunications equipment industry was in distress. The larger players, such as Lucent and Nortel, introduced new products at low prices, hoping to commoditize the new world of communications and hurt smaller companies, such as Cisco. At the same time, they dropped prices on their older products, bundling and cross-subsidizing—that is, subsidizing profits in one sector from those in another—to keep new entrants out of their accounts. In essence, by prematurely trying to commoditize their products of the future, they reduced the value of their present foothold, and there was no place to go for higher margin. A serious negative spiral resulted. Both players dropped their overall margin structures by 10 to 20 points during this period.

Competing with the Customer

A different kind of self-defeating strategic vector involves treating customers as the competition. This is one of the challenges that a vertically oriented company (e.g., telecommunications) can face when it attempts to serve a horizontal industry (networking). Lucent exemplified this when it announced an assault on Cisco while attempting to increase sales of Lucent microelectronics *to* Cisco. As a result, Cisco, now seeing itself in competition with Lucent, de-emphasized Lucent as a vendor, project by project. Other customers who were becoming competitors followed suit, and eventually Lucent's microelectronics unit was spun off as a separate entity (Agere) for this and other reasons.

Another version of competing with the customer can be seen in the area of channel conflict, when a company uses a direct sales force to sell its wares but also uses OEM (Original Equipment Manufacturer), integrator, or VAR (Value-Added Reseller) distribution. If the areas of cooperation cannot be easily articulated and are not simple to manage, it is easy to find oneself inadvertently competing with customers, resulting in revenue decline and a poor industry reputation. It is for this reason that a vertical company in a horizontal industry structure is inherently unstable.

Shallowly Rooted Strategic Vectors

Shallowly rooted strategic vectors are those based on inadequate information. Maintaining proprietary technology in the face of a market demanding open standards, which we addressed earlier as an example of a misdirected strategic vector, is also an example of one rooted in poor information. Another example is a company that stays committed to today's technology but thereby misses tomorrow's—that is, the company establishes a vision consistent with today's strategy, revenue streams, and comfort zone but not with those of the future.

In the telecommunications industry, behemoths such as Lucent and Nortel promoted the idea that the world would become an end-to-end fiber-optic circuit—that communications would continue to be circuit driven and that packet technology, the basic engine of Internet data transfer, would be consolidated into it. The reality has been that the Internet has continued to be a packet-oriented com-munications medium of which real-time voice is but one form. The passage of information between subscribers is done with blocks of information rather than two handsets and wires between. Both Lucent and Nortel announced plans to add packet switching to their circuit switches, but the price/performance of a circuit switch in the new world was so poor that few would buy this hybrid model. Eventually, both companies' programs were cancelled or downsized.

It is understandable for a company to be attached to what it understands and is good at, but when it uses the past to form its current vision for the future of technology, it tends to bend its sense of the future to fit its (successful) model of the past. Clues to the future lie *outside* the company—with customers, competitors, and industry trends. A constant flow of unfiltered information can assure well-rooted strategies for the future. (See Chapter 8.)

Inflexible or Fluid Strategic Vectors

Even if strategy vectors are directed well, of the right length, and rooted in good information, if they are *inflexible*, they cannot navigate the changing realities of the future. During technology transitions, for instance, the time it takes for new products to "harden"—that is, to be absorbed intellectually and operationally—varies from one to three years, or even longer. It is critical to have a realistic view of this time constant and a flexible model that allows for deviation and adaptation as the absorption period evolves.

To illustrate the advantage of timing flexibility, consider the competition between long-distance ISPs that emerged after the breakup of AT&T. As it happens, long-distance telephone service is much simpler than local phone service. Consequently, long-distance service was an area ripe for competition and technology disruption. The new ISPs led the advance of Internet Protocol (IP) telephony—voice

Going the Distance: Why Some Companies Dominate and Others Fail

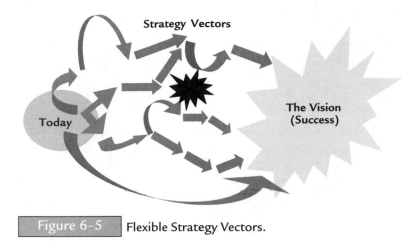

Strategy Vectors

Today

The Vision
(Success)

Figure 6-5 Flexible Strategy Vectors.

communication transmitted over the Internet—which allowed ISP customers to bypass charges from traditional long-distance carriers.

The adoption of IP telephony technology by the upstart ISPs occurred years in advance of its adoption by traditional telephone carriers because the infrastructure and operations of these larger, traditional telephone carriers were far more entrenched than those of the more nimble ISPs. The alternative carriers were in a position to be much quicker to operationalize the new technology.

In general, there is a critical balance to be struck between maintaining commitment to a strategy through rough times and having the flexibility to change it. As always, the key to a good strategic choice is in the source of data by which it is made—primarily *outside* the company, especially from customers, and then improved by healthy internal dialogue and collective consideration. (Again, see Chapter 8.)

In contrast with Figure 6–1, Figure 6–5 suggests how strategic vectors might actually look when a company has had the flexibility to make it through tough challenges and a changing world.

Recommended Reading

Geoffrey Moore, *The Gorilla Game: Picking Winners in High Technology* (HarperBusiness, 1999).

More on Timing

The old adage that "timing is everything" is clearly the rule in successful businesses. Here are four additional suggestions about using timing well:

- **Be first (or no worse than second) in a new market.** The early stage of a market is when the gorillas are made and disproportionate shareholder value emerges. For example, being Number One in market share at Cisco meant a 5 percent share advantage. Each share point yielded somewhere between a 0.5- to 2-point increase in gross margin. If Cisco waited a year to enter the new market, its opportunity cost could be as high as 5 share points per quarter, or 20 points of gross margin. Cisco found that playing the acquisition game—Cisco's particular method of getting in quick—was essential.

- **Don't invest too much too soon.** This is not to say that early bets are to be avoided—quite the opposite. Make bets, but do it carefully—insert surgically; build on earlier technology; avoid the "god box syndrome" (the product that does everything for everybody) in new, speculative markets. A god box approach results in huge expense burn rates and customer uncertainty and disappointment. Examples of overinvestment in a technology before the market was ready include AT&T's investment in Picture Phone in the 1960s, ISDN in the United States, and more recently Soft Switch Technologies for the telecommunications market as it experienced a massive slowdown.

- **When markets disrupt, don't wait to change with them.** Waiting means losing market share, margin, and customers. Even if the product used to enter the disrupted market cannibalizes existing products, find a way to manage the revenue transition and introduce the new technology in a way that customers, with their new purchase criteria, will want (see Chapter 5). On the other hand, if the time until disruption is long, waiting has its benefits. In these cases, waiting is a calculated risk that should be closely monitored and managed with specific sales channel strategies.

- **Pair strategy with execution.** A strategy without execution goes nowhere. It's vapor, an idea never acted on. Of course, this can make a team doubt the value of strategy altogether. Just as bad is *good execution of a weak strategy*. Always think of strategy and execution as two essential parts of one whole. Pursue excellence in both to win.

How would you rate yourself, your team, and your organization on the causes of misguided strategy?

Lack of a clear compass	1	2	3	4	5
A tendency to hubris	1	2	3	4	5
Avoiding unwelcome news	1	2	3	4	5
A tendency to react versus anticipate	1	2	3	4	5
Sticking too long with a structure of the past	1	2	3	4	5
Not listening, especially to customers	1	2	3	4	5
Lack of scenario assessment	1	2	3	4	5
Lack of contingency planning	1	2	3	4	5

How Does Misguided Strategy Occur?

So far, we have described misguided strategies and given several examples. But why does this particular thread of failure occur in the first place? We see several causes:

- lack of a clear compass—a vision or sense of true North—by which to determine the right strategy
- a tendency to hubris—believing that the leaders in the company know best and ignoring the limitations of current core competencies
- avoiding unwelcome news from the external world
- a tendency to *react* to rather than *anticipate* the future
- sticking with a way of doing business past its relevancy—one that optimized last year's operations, which can be limiting for the future

The Challenge	Developing a Differentiating Strategy
Key Points	• good market information • flexibility • sufficient thrust • avoiding early collision
External Indicators or Existing Problems	• falling behind the competition technologically • missing market windows • loss of customers/market share • declining revenues • loss of key acquisition opportunities to the competition
Vital Signs Indicating Potential Perils	• glare conditions—the inability to see problems and get them solved • organization thrash—decisions made inefficiently or made and remade • lack of consistent, shared understanding of strategic direction by key leaders • strategic decisions made without critical assessment • lack of multistep strategic plans, including contingency plans • technology "religion"

Figure 6-6 Strategy External Indicators and Vital Signs.

- ignoring crucial dimensions of strategy such as clearing up product/technology glare or factoring in distribution issues

- lack of scenario assessment in the process of strategy formation

- lack of contingency planning when confronted with risks

Each of these pitfalls can be avoided by applying the antidotes introduced in this and other chapters. The right kind of leadership DNA, for instance, which develops learning leaders, can prevent the

Consider the list of vital signs shown in Figure 6–6 and use it as a discussion agenda for the management team in your unit or company.

- Which of these vital signs do you notice in the company?

- How much agreement or disagreement is there on the team?

- For those vital signs that are apparent, what should you and the team do about them?

tendency to hubris. A culture of learning with active feedback loops in the company's governing processes can assure valid, useful information. Such a culture with open, candid, and active dialogue can develop and deepen not only the quality of the strategic decisions but also the capability of the organization to continue to make them. Governance systems that drive anticipation are essential. And continued *alignment*, the subject of the next chapter, is crucial to assuring reliable execution of strategy.

Vital Signs

External indicators of misguided strategy are obvious (Figure 6–6). However, as always, we encourage you to look sooner for *internal vital signs*, also shown in Figure 6–6, that will help you to identify the potential thread of failure of misguided strategy *before* it becomes public.

7
Alignment

Overview

- Alignment is an exceptionally potent tool for success, while misalignment is an exceptionally dangerous thread of failure.

- Organizational structure, the backbone of alignment, always biases results, and when that structure is misaligned, it leads to negative results.

- When achieved, alignment creates and exploits positive momentum.

- Natural disparities develop as companies grow, such as competing goals and internal priorities, which drive misalignment.

- These disparities must be managed and brought into alignment to ensure success.

In 1981, in a Western Electric factory in Aurora, Illinois, the father of the System 75 PBX—the product that allowed enterprise companies to manage the flow of telephone calls efficiently—walked into the factory to check on the production of a new packet-switched-data PBX, called the VCS. It was a new product, with unusual characteristics for this plant. For the prior 10 years, the plant had specialized in making very high volume stand-alone modems and systems, turning out hundreds of thousands of units per year. Now it was producing this new product that would sell as a low-volume (less than 10,000 per year), high-touch, and highly configurable product.

The VCS was adopted into this factory as an orphan to the mainstream business, so the process flow was hard to decode. At the end of the day, it was obvious that the PBX inventor was unnerved by something, as he held his head in what appeared to be pain. Asked what was wrong, he replied, "You know, in the world of engineering, any time you cannot follow how the inputs flow to deliver an output, you must realize you're in trouble."

This vignette is a story about *alignment*—how essential it is to a company's success and how evident its absence can be. Along with strategy and a culture of learning, alignment is the most potent and crucial tool to help great companies live longer. Like culture, alignment is not well understood, although we experience its presence—or absence—in everyday life.

Consider a pair of friends going on a vacation together. If the two of them have different goals, they will need to align those goals so that they can both accomplish what they want with their time off. Individual interests, options, and schedules must align to make a vacation pleasurable. The goals of the vacation and the vacation budget have to be aligned as well, or the travelers will end up with financial problems.

Despite the average person's daily experience of arranging things to achieve alignment, however, misalignment within organizations is not uncommon. The more complex the organization, the more complex the challenge of achieving and maintaining alignment. And although alignment is more difficult to achieve as complexity increases, it is also more important—there is more at risk.

Recommended Reading

R. E. Miles and C. C. Snow, *Fit, Failure and the Hall of Fame* (New York: The Free Press, 1994).

Five Tenets of Alignment

Let's start with some basics. To help explain alignment, we pose five tenets, each of which is discussed in the following text:

- You know when alignment is there.
- Achieving alignment becomes more difficult with growth.
- Alignment starts with clear goals and a clear leadership model.
- Alignment maps the value chain, which exploits momentum.
- Structure biases results.

You Know It When It Is There . . . and When It Is Not

We think it is essential to gain both an intuitive feel for and an analytical understanding of alignment to comprehend when it is there and when it is not. In the story of the Western Electric factory, it was obvious that the experienced PBX inventor knew that alignment was not there. This kind of "knowing" can be developed.

Start with the experience of alignment and misalignment in day-to-day life, like the earlier vacation analogy. Sometimes you experience alignment or the lack of it in a physical way. Anyone who has hit a softball squarely, driven a golf ball straight and true, or hit a tennis ball with pace, accuracy, and balance knows the feeling of alignment of body, ball, and instrument. You can sense it in your life and, with practice, in your company.

Consider a parallel experience in the realm of business. In the early 1990s, a company called Platinum Software ran into serious problems on a number of levels. Its appetite for growth through acquisitions had exceeded its leadership capability. The Chairman of the Board sensed the misalignment and called for help. Then even worse news emerged. Some of the leadership made questionable choices in accounting for revenue.

Suffice it to say, the outcomes were drastic. The company's stock fell from somewhere in the 40s to below 5 essentially overnight, the CEO and CFO left the company, and the Chairman of the Board took over as interim CEO. The company's survival was in serious question. The interim CEO was not in a position to attend to the company full time, so while he took care of Wall Street and the SEC, he appointed a small team of leaders to accomplish several things:

- stop the cash hemorrhage
- strategically cut programs to reduce the size of the company by 40 percent
- maintain critical customers
- retain key employees
- deliver critical products

Overall, the goal was to save the company so that the remaining employees could maintain their livelihoods and customers could get the products that they were counting on. The team worked 16 hours a day and more for six weeks, meeting every morning at 6 a.m. and every evening at 6 p.m. Between these twice-daily meetings, team members executed their agreed-to tasks with remarkable productivity. Issues were prioritized strategically: delivering on commitments to key customers, communicating honestly in those situations in which delivery could not happen, retaining key Sales and Engineering employees, establishing trust with both customers and employees by communicating unvarnished facts, and defining a strategic plan for cutting 40 percent of the programs.

During this turnaround crisis, the company's goals were highly meaningful, crystal clear, and shared among the leadership, employees, and key customers. Complexity was neutralized through this clear focus. The urgency, clarity, and common agreement drove alignment, demonstrated by the fact that a team of leaders who had not worked together before ended up achieving a monumental task in a short time. The overwhelming mission overcame individual desires for recognition or power, which might normally cause individual efforts to veer from a single direction. The company was re-righted and still thrives today, under a new name and new leadership. The experience of alignment was visceral, motivating, and highly satisfying.

A more typical example of team alignment can be seen in the early days of a startup, when complexity is low and alignment is easiest. Startup teams typically show great passion, energy, and innovation. There is a differentiating idea, a clear goal that unifies the team, one market, and a clear customer focus. The cleanness of the model can be seen in a depiction of the simplicity of the startup value chain (Figure 7–1).

When a company's value chain is aligned, you can feel it. And because the experience is very satisfying, as in the case of the

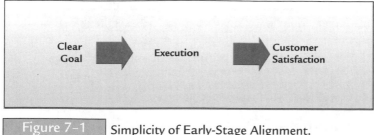

Figure 7–1 Simplicity of Early-Stage Alignment.

Platinum Software crisis team, people are motivated to maintain and regain that alignment once achieved. The learning and bonding are irreplaceable; employees and their leaders want this experience.

Alignment Is More Difficult with Growth

However, achieving and maintaining this same kind of alignment in a highly complex organization is much harder than in a startup. In addition, with increasing complexity, it is harder to have a clean sense of alignment's presence or absence.

Think of a child playing with dominoes. With a handful of dominoes, the child can make a standing row relatively easily—and then have the fun of knocking down the whole row by knocking down just the first one. However, the child's challenge grows as the number of dominoes grows. Setting up dominoes in a row over an extended area, with the additional complexity of curved shapes and branching sequences, makes a breakdown in the smooth, falling sequence more likely. Alignment is more difficult with the increased length and complex shape of the domino configuration.

A company in Stage 1 (startup) of its growth is like the handful of dominoes—alignment is relatively simple. At Stage 2—when new generations of products displace existing products, and new customers and new channels of distribution emerge—maintaining alignment is a bigger challenge. By Stage 4, with complexity at its maximum, the challenge is at its greatest. Goals are various, leaders are numerous, and alignment involves many variables.

In the Platinum Software example, we saw that complexity can be neutralized by clear focus. The most common way of achieving clear focus in a highly complex company is to break it down into manageable market components—that is, internal segmentation. Each segment can individually focus on maintaining technology potency and customer intimacy in its own specialized area, in a way that the larger, complex company cannot. The segments, often called business units, individually align with *market* segments to compete effectively with smaller competitors with singular technology and customer focus.

Alignment Starts with Clear Goals and a Clear Leadership Model

Let's look more closely at this idea of breaking down a complex structure to assure alignment of its parts. In adult sports, teams work well when it is clear who is calling the plays. Well-coached teams are disciplined, have a clear set of plays to work from, and rely on a clear leadership model. Now consider the opposite. Any of us with children who play soccer have witnessed misalignment in the typical version of "pee wee" soccer. Children from both teams all chase the soccer ball, no matter where it goes and no matter what their positions are supposed to be, furiously kicking their legs while the ball stays relatively stationary. This misalignment typically worsens, as the goalies ultimately leave their positions to "help." After some minutes, an inadvertent kick just might propel the ball into an unattended goal.

As much as we might find these cluster tactics amusing in children's play, it is not so amusing in companies to see *pee wee soccer dynamics*—a sure sign of organizational misalignment. In this dynamic, everyone jumps on a particular bandwagon but no one is accountable for a specific result. The sheer expenditure of human energy is expected to achieve the desired result. And as in kids' soccer, the organizational ball in play—the decision that needs to be made or the product that needs to be delivered—may well stay relatively stationary until enough expenditure of unaligned energy finally propels it in the right direction.

Let's look at an example in which alignment exists at first but then gets out of kilter. Consider the case of a software engineer who is responsible for the functionality of a specific product. Being a strong performer, he is assigned responsibility for several diverse objectives—fixing bugs on old releases, developing new functionality, and re-architecting the code for a new generation of the operating system, for example.

While a company is small and its focus relatively simple, this kind of setup is workable. But as that company becomes more successful, it grows in complexity, and the diverse set of goals the engineer is assigned are now set by different organizations—say, Support, Engineering, and an architecture committee. If the company does not restructure the engineer's job so he has a consistent leadership model to drive his priorities, he will begin to exhibit signs of *thrash*—the tendency to flip flop back and forth from one focus to another. Thrash, like the cluster tactics of the pee wee soccer teams, is an example of unproductive effort that can be *felt* in an organization.

If unproductive effort becomes common in a company, it can result in glare, that condition of poor visibility symptomized by a lack of progress and by people waiting for someone else to decide between competing priorities. *Do I optimize for schedule or quality? I can't tell. I'll wait until someone else makes the call.* Glare, then, is associated with a lack of action or focus in relation to a problem. Thrash and glare coexist in environments without clear goals or leadership to which roles and priorities can be aligned.

Alignment Maps the Value Chain

In sports, physical alignment maximizes the transfer of momentum (speed x mass) and minimizes strain. If you watch great tennis players serve, despite their different methods of winding up, tossing the ball, and raising their rackets, at the moment of impact they deliver the ball with powerful momentum into the court. A string held taut from the point of impact of the ball and racket and then down through the arm, shoulder, spinal column, and legs would form a straight line. This kind of alignment results in *momentum for maximum results*. In this scenario, alignment of the tennis ball, racquet, and player's body parts form the value chain of this activity.

A company's ability to serve the ball effectively is its ability to deliver better than the competition across its cross-functional value chain and achieve a consistent, straight line to customer satisfaction. (See Figure 7–2, a slightly expanded version of Figure 2–1.)

Imagine the following scenario—two people write business plans to go into the ice-making business. They both know that to do this, they will need water, freezers, forms to shape the ice, and so on. Actual execution, however, is very different between the two, by virtue of the businesses they individually conceive.

Big John goes into the business of producing block ice. It is sold wholesale and to retail stores. The blocks come in one size. Big John

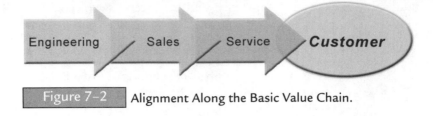

Figure 7-2
Alignment Along the Basic Value Chain.

uses cold water, large forms, central manufacturing, and refrigerated trucks for transport.

Little John goes into the specialty ice business, making little cubes in one of eight different shapes, for cocktails. Little John decides that the ice is best made at the customer's store site. He uses small trays and warm water to ensure that the ice freezes as quickly as possible (because of the Mpemba effect, whereby small, residual amounts of warm water will freeze faster than the same initial amount of cooler water), and invests in optimized freezers to sell to restaurants and grocery chains. No refrigerated trucks are needed.

Both Big and Little John make ice, but the value chains of their businesses are very different, and their raw material—water—takes a different form for each. The business models are quite different as well. To succeed, value chain alignment is crucial. Each ice-making company knows its own customers and what those customers want. Each establishes business goals, structure, and processes in alignment to deliver to the specifications of those needs.

Alignment of the Value Chain in Large Companies

Think about the many elements that make up the components of a large company's value chain, some visible, some not: employees, products, the channel, business units and functional organizations, processes, vision, values, goals, physical environment, and so on. For a company to build momentum and thrive, alignment across these different sets of elements is critical. One way to think about achieving alignment under such complex circumstances is that there are *various* axes along which alignment is essential for the central value chain to deliver effectively. Some of these are suggested in Figure 7-3. The greater the alignment along any one of these value chain axes, the greater the alignment of the value chain as a whole. And with value chain alignment comes positive momentum for the organization.

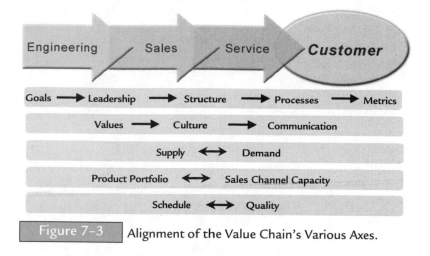

Figure 7-3 | Alignment of the Value Chain's Various Axes.

Mapping the Value Chain through Change

Any level of alignment of the value chain is subject to change because markets change constantly. So, to maintain value chain alignment, all its elements must evolve with the market and with company growth. In fast-paced markets like data networking, companies often feel the need to change organizational structure every 18 to 24 months to respond to market changes. Such flexibility requires an aligned culture—one that *thrives on change,* rather than resists it, and demonstrates this by constant sensing, preparation, and realignment to keep pace with the market.

Structure Biases Results

To clarify what we mean by saying that structure biases results, let's start with a classic engineering organization debate—should we organize functionally or on a project basis? For a Stage 1 startup, this question is typically moot. A startup usually comprises one product and one team. Moreover, because time is money and startup money is high-risk capital, the goal of beating the competition to market drives an intense focus on one product. A simple project structure, then, usually emerges.

As the team succeeds with one product and begins expanding the company's product offerings, however, competing goals develop. Growth and multiple goals require rethinking organizational structure. The original organization, which was biased toward a single project result, is not likely to be able to manage two or more competing goals. With growth and increasing complexity, a new structure will be required to *bias* efforts toward a new set of more complex results. A new structure must be developed—one that can enable concurrent and potentially competing goals, such as sustaining engineering, incremental development of first-generation products, development of new-generation products, and architectural rework.

Simply adding a second project organization is not likely to achieve the new and expanding results now required. At some point, a combined, functional organization might be needed. Although functional organizations are usually less adept at delivering projects on a tight schedule, they do minimize resource duplication and help homogenize process and quality performance. Sometimes a hybrid or matrix organization is needed. The organizational structure needed depends on *the results you want*.

To illustrate the issue of structure biasing results, we can look at an example on a small scale—how the structure of a training program influences its outcome. In this example, the structure of the program biased results in the wrong direction. In the 1980s, businesses zealously adopted a non-business-oriented program called Outward Bound. At AT&T it was called Project Miracles. During Project

Miracles, a several-hundred-person team would go to the desert of Sedona for three days to learn life balance and control of personal destiny. Activities such as scaling a wall or climbing a 30-foot telephone pole to a perch pushed individuals beyond their physical comfort zones. The goal was for each individual to take this expanded consciousness back to the office and apply it to the greater good.

Prior to the Project Miracles week, organizations would get excited. For the first week after the experience, the excitement continued. Project Miracles was a great success in terms of strengthening physical courage, building relationships, and providing a change of pace. Feelings of accomplishment ran high because of the experience of success. The program provided an environment where each activity was focused on a single goal. In attempting and completing the course, participants felt as if they had accomplished something.

Yet within four weeks of returning from the project, office morale dropped sharply. Work was not as simple as Project Miracles. In real life, rather than everyone having the same goal, they had many different goals. There was not just one leader, but many. The real environment was far more complex than could be rendered offsite in the Project Miracles version of reality. Most important, the exciting experience had not helped solve any real problems; it felt great, but its benefits were very short-lived in the workplace. The training was misaligned with the way organizational learning and change really occurs, ultimately biasing the results to the negative instead of to the positive.

There is no perfect structure for training or any other phenomenon. However, it is possible to bias results through a well-chosen structure that aligns *effort* with *purpose* and with the realities of the environment. When the right structure is put in place, results improve. When that same structure no longer serves a changed set of challenges, the result may be *Brownian motion*—the term used in physics to refer to a high rate of activity without common direction. Brownian motion is one of the dynamics in an organization that your intuition can sense, and if it is there, it is a sure sign of misalignment.

Alignment in Later Stage Companies

Now that we have examined the five tenets of alignment, let's look at some examples of predictable alignment challenges in a company at its maximum stage of complexity:

- "siloed" organizations and "billiard ball management"
- goals, metrics, and rewards
- product portfolio and sales channel capacity
- schedule and quality
- diverse business models in the same company

All of these challenges can appear at any stage in a company's growth, but they are most likely to appear and present the greatest difficulty in Stage 4 when size and complexity are at their greatest.

"Siloed" Organizations

In moving from Stage 1 to growing complexity at Stage 2, a company has typically delivered its first products and is responding to field problems and manufacturing quality issues for the first time. It is not unusual for the CEO to bring in strong functional leadership to handle Stage 2 issues and prepare for continued growth, both of which require specialized functional experience.

Stage 3, of course, only exacerbates these same challenges, with multiple products, customers, and distribution channels. In their efforts to stabilize the company's ability to deliver satisfaction by improving quality and process, leaders often get overly focused on building strong and independent functional organizations and end up demonstrating *silo* behavior. In fact, the coexistence of strong functional leadership at both the front end (Sales and Service) and the back end (Manufacturing, IT, and Support) of an organization's value chain results in conflicting functional pressure on Engineering teams, which are in the middle. Furthermore, the disconnected functional elements develop conflicts among themselves, and the value chain can begin to fragment.

This brings us to Stage 4 of company evolution, during which disparate markets must be managed simultaneously. Functional silos tend even more to focus inward in their drive toward stability and consistency. This drive is ultimately inertial, however. Functional silos, being specialized units, tend to follow the conventional observation that "when all you have is a hammer, everything looks like a nail." Their singular focus limits their flexibility and tends to impede speed and efficiency across multiple functions.

This tendency was evident in the postdivestiture era at AT&T (American Telephone & Telegraph). At that time, there was a legacy system for keeping track of internal orders for parts, called

DOSS, that was the bible for all orders. It had been built over many years and had become weighted down by a huge library of features, translations, mappings, attributes, and hand-offs. Its various elements had been initially and separately designed to record the increasingly complex details of what customers ordered; collectively, they presented an overwhelming tangle of detail. It could take 3 to 9 months just to get a new product accepted into the system, making it virtually impossible to get a product to market quickly. Furthermore, because Sales and Service were not likely to invest in product training until a product was ready for sale, it took as much as 18 months before the various siloed functional organizations were prepared to market or service a new product. Yet the divestiture of the company and resulting new competitive environment required fast action.

In the final analysis, individual efforts toward improving the existing system of parts order-tracking lost alignment with the larger purposes to which they owed allegiance—customer satisfaction. DOSS was no longer a tool that worked in the changed world.

Billiard Ball Management

Let's look at a more complicated set of issues, which emerge out of silo organizations, with their inward tendency. *Billiard ball management* refers to the dynamic that results from an organizational structure optimized for internal objectives rather than external ones. It ultimately leads to a breakdown in productivity or relatively inert operations, which may limit adaptation.

To clarify, let's start by comparing billiards to bowling. In bowling, the purpose of the game is to knock down the pins with the ball. The primary instrument (the ball) has a *direct* impact on the ultimate objective (the pins). In contrast, in the game of billiards, a player uses a cue stick to hit the white ball in order to hit other balls. In other words, the primary instrument in billiards (the cue stick) has an *indirect* impact on the ultimate objective (the colored balls).

To apply the bowling metaphor to organizations, the ball hitting the pins is the force of leadership achieving product delivery—direct and focused. This kind of leadership results from an organizational structure that is optimized to build a single product. With a simple alignment of focus from the leader through the people delivering the output, the organization can interpret customer needs, apply them in designing the product it is focused on, and continuously experiment to improve that output, learning from the results each time.

In the billiards metaphor, the cue stick hitting the white ball represents a different type of leadership impact, one that results from an organizational structure designed to manage a diversity of products and that includes large, specialized functional organizations, such as Manufacturing and Support. In a large company with many product lines, Manufacturing and Support develop as strong local organizations to help achieve consistency and cost control *across* product lines. However, in this setting, individual product leaders focused on a single product cannot impact the manufacturing or support of their products directly. They can (like the cue stick in billiards) only try to *influence the functional organizations* (hit the white ball) to do what is needed for a specific product (get a colored ball into a pocket).

Meanwhile, other individual product leaders are using *their* cue sticks on the *same* white ball, trying to get *different* colored balls in the pockets. The functional organizations (the white ball), then, are being hit with competing product priorities and, at the same time, are pressured by the corporation at large to reduce costs. They often believe that the only way they can respond to this is to apply similar processes to *all* the products and drive prioritization on the basis of cost containment. To them, the various colored balls become checkered—that is, indistinguishable.

To see this in further detail, let's consider a more specific situation in which there are three different lines of business, each with their own group of products. Let's give each line a color—*black* for the line serving Market 1, *gray* for the one serving Market 2, and *white* for the line involved with Market 3.

Because of the dynamics discussed previously, within the functions serving all three lines of business, people and processes are applied as uniformly as possible to all products, regardless of the line-of-business strategy or unique market conditions. Now picture this situation through the metaphor of billiard balls (Figure 7–4). The balls are tinted and grouped by functional organization, representing the way those organizations end up seeing the various products—indistinguishable, even though the products have different requirements for different customers.

Furthermore, the focus of the various functional organizations on uniform processes is represented by the orderliness of the balls, suggesting the functional effort to achieve efficiency and consistency in a

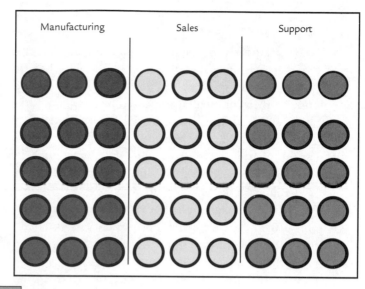

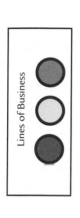

Lines of Business

Manufacturing   Sales   Support

| Figure 7–4 | Billiard-Ball Management. |

highly complex environment. Consider specifically the Manufacturing group of balls. In billiard ball management, the Manufacturing leader typically appoints a liaison to represent each line of business and drive its product needs *by influence* through the uniform manufacturing system. The single-colored black, gray, and white billiard balls at the top of each group represent the liaisons for their separate line of business interests—customer needs in Markets 1, 2, and 3.

Every liaison's job is to influence Manufacturing to respond to their particular line of business constituency. At the same time, the Manufacturing leader is the keeper of a single "Manufacturing Way," which has been able to achieve consistency and reduce costs. The liaison is therefore put into a no-win position—never able to exert enough influence to please its particular line of business and not able to adapt enough to fully support a consistent Manufacturing methodology. An extreme case of billiard ball management can even develop in which an organization has liaisons influencing *other* liaisons, who, in turn, influence the functional leads. The degrees of separation and the accountability gap in this situation can become extreme.

Where the rate of required change for a given market (and line of business) is high, and functional (in this case, Manufacturing) inward focus or inertia is also high, those in the liaison role are likely to get burned out. Product leaders can only *indirectly* influence their results because the manufacturing structure has been optimized for process and capacity management, not for delivery, market learning, and customer wins. The functional leaders feel caught in the pressure of competing priorities and the dissatisfaction of their internal customers. The stress on both sets of leaders is high. Furthermore, the potential for quality and customer satisfaction is reduced, and there is little chance of the product teams experimenting to improve their product, much less learning with each experiment.

Billiard ball management is one example of the dynamics resulting from misalignment. Specialized functional organizations drive process uniformity, scale, and functional excellence; however, they often become inertial and bias negative results when quick learning and change is required. Symptoms include low morale, an endless horizon of glare, unresolved issues due to this lack of visibility, and polarizing rhetoric (discussions of "them" vs. "us").

The solution is not simple. Organizing by divisions—for instance, creating individual P&L organizations, each with its own overhead functions—brings with it liabilities in redundancy and significant overhead cost. One way of minimizing the inertia of functional organizations while keeping the advantage of specialized expertise is to rethink the liaison position. Instead of giving primary decision-making responsibility to *functional* leads, who are not directly aligned through the value chain to the customer, consider making the functional leads responsible for rollup and process ownership within their individual learning organizations. Then, make the product-oriented liaisons, who represent the customer across the value chain, the *decision makers* for product prioritization, since they have clear customer-based criteria for that prioritization (see Figure 7–5). This can sometimes carry a transitional organization until it is ready for a larger scale, fully loaded divisional organization, aligned to markets.

Misaligned Goals, Metrics, and Rewards

Predictability in sales forecasting is, of course, desirable. However, predictability requires information on daily and weekly trending, changes in the demand mix, required configurations, differences by geography, and so on. The value of continuous data flow has led to today's efficient companies thinking in terms of a continuous process and pipeline analysis rather than monthly milestones. In

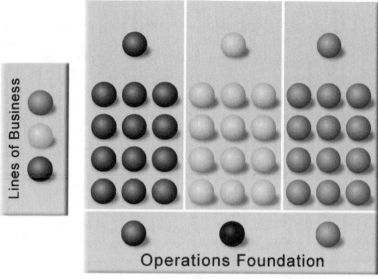

Lines of Business

Operations Foundation

(Manufacturing, Support, etc.)

Figure 7-5 One Solution to Billiard Ball Management.

this setting, then, a classic case of misalignment is a sales force goaled and measured on selling a certain dollar value of products or services into a channel, regardless of real end-user customer demand, resulting in products being temporarily sold or booked, only to be returned later.

This situation hit 3Com just after the US Robotics acquisition when a poor quarter was reported, due in part to channel stuffing (shipping products to distribution houses in the absence of real demand from end-user customers). The company got what it measured and rewarded. By crediting its sales people for goods booked or sold into the channel—even when those sales did not represent sales to an actual customer—the company motivated behaviors that did not achieve its true desired outcome. Companies get what they measure. To achieve alignment, it is critical to make sure to measure the right things.

As described in Chapter 5, Cisco faced channel conflict in 1996 when it decided to add a second tier to its highly successful direct sales force. The established sales team was unhappy about the decision because they believed that their own sales (and therefore their commissions) were at risk of a decline as a result. To appease the disgruntled sales force, Cisco reduced the attractiveness of the product sold to its new channel partners, which at first diminished the ability of these partners to be successful. Then, Cisco figured out how to parse the product by life cycle. It aligned its new, more technically complex, high-end product line with the existing direct sales force, whose knowledge and relationships could make the more complicated aspect of the sale work, it gave the older, less complex end of the product line to the second-tier channel, and it aligned its incentive programs to support this division of labor. In the new scheme, the desired *outcomes*, the *measures*, and the *anticipated rewards* were aligned, which drove the desired results.

Product Portfolio and Sales Channel Capacity Mismatch

As a company grows, the balance between its product portfolio and its sales channel capacity becomes harder to maintain. Aligning a configuration of sales channels to multiple technologies and hundreds, even thousands, of products is the extraordinary challenge of Stage 4 companies. The knowledge required and the complexity of the sales strategies are too great for one channel to handle well.

A significant example of product and channel misalignment occurred in AT&T's Computer Systems in the 1980s and early 1990s. After divestiture, AT&T Computer Systems had numerous products and a hunger for entering the network and computer world, unfortunately resulting in a "ready, fire, aim" development mentality. At the same time, a legacy of process inertia remained from the monopoly days of AT&T. In addition, the company lacked an effective distribution channel because the Regional Bell Operating Companies (RBOCs), which had "owned" the customer relationships, had been divested from AT&T. The R&D labs, then, were overinvested in development and thus were out of balance or misaligned with the sales channel's capacity to absorb new technology knowledge. In the late 1980s, AT&T bought NCR, in part for its distribution channel and what was thought to be a complementary product portfolio. The acquisition was not successful in expanding distribution capacity, however. By the 1990s, the acquisition was deemed a failure, and NCR was sold off to stop the financial hemorrhage.

For a positive example, we can look again at Cisco's channel organization. As the company's product portfolio expanded, it exceeded the capacity of the two channels it had successfully developed. Eventually the company expanded into a two-tier distribution, augmenting the existing Tier 1 partners and its direct sales force. The direct sales team focused on newer products and markets; Tier 1 integrators drove mature and mainstream products; and the Tier 2 channel sold more mature products, where timely fulfillment was paramount. This three-level structure allowed each level to keep up with the complexities of its portion of the company's product portfolio. By aligning its products and sales channel capacity, Cisco was able to outpace all of its peers.

Conflict Between Schedule and Quality

It is not unusual to find project teams focused more on schedule than on quality, as meeting deadlines is more urgent, more measurable, and more likely to be rewarded. However, when the scale tips too far in the direction of schedule, bugs and other quality shortfalls become prevalent. At the very early stages of an emerging market, time-to-market tends to outweigh quality in importance only because *customers'* success depends on beating *their* competition to market. When a customer is competing with other early adopters on the turf of time-to-market, a vendor can afford to work out bugs later. In this scenario, schedule takes precedence over quality. However, once the market becomes more established, the focus turns to quality. Then products have to be "clean" at the point of shipping them. It is all a matter of aligning with customer needs and expectations.

Aligning priorities with customer expectations not only results in satisfied customers, it helps resolve competing internal priorities. Unaligned or unresolved competing priorities of schedule and quality create thrash, just as in our earlier example of the software engineer who is trying to meet the goals of different organizations within a company. A lot of energy can get spent trying to address two opposing and unresolvable issues, without results. Understanding and aligning to customer priorities facilitates alignment of potentially competing priorities, like schedule and quality. The caveat is that customer intimacy is required to do this.

Conflicting Business Models

Alignment of diverse business models within the same company is most likely to be an issue in the wake of a merger or movement into a new market. To understand the fundamental nature of how a company's business model is essential to determining the nature of that company, consider the possibility of a merger in each of the following two examples:

- Two software companies have very different business models, each based on their separate markets, products, and position in those markets. One company has predictable growth, high-quality revenues (as judged by gross margin in excess of 80 percent), and high revenues per employee (in excess of $500,000 per year). The other company has lower growth, a 55 percent gross margin, and revenues per employee of $300,000. The former company might trade at a figure of between $5 and $10 per share in even a difficult market, whereas the latter might trade between $1 and $2.

- A hardware company creates a high-volume, simple consumer commodity, selling tens of millions of items per year, which returns a relatively low gross margin. This company's business model is in dramatic contrast to a company that sells a low number of units—thousands or tens of thousands—of an expensive and complex product that requires specialists to install it.

Different business models, as suggested in these examples, create different structural and operational requirements. The merger of two dissimilar business models into one organization is fraught with peril because the structural and operational elements in place for one model will be in conflict with those of the other.

In the real-life example of the 3Com/US Robotics merger, prior to the merger, 3Com had 55 percent to 60 percent gross margins, predictable growth, and sales of complex systems to businesses, as well as sales of high-end Ethernet adapter cards to high-end consumers and businesses. US Robotics, on the other hand, had a strong position in consumer modems, with a margin structure in the range of 10 percent to 30 percent. It shipped millions of low-complexity products through different channels, requiring specialized marketing strategies like advertising.

The merger of these two companies combined not only two different cultures but two distinctly different operating models. Mixing 3Com's higher margin systems business with US Robotics' lower margin modem business created a clash of structures and operating systems that required reconciliation rather than provided leverage. Ultimately, the merger was a failure, at considerable loss to the combined entity.

Misalignment can also occur between a company's business model and a changing market if the company does not change its model to fit the new world. As we discuss in various examples in this book, when the litigation against AT&T resulted in AT&T's divestiture, a new market was created—one in which anyone could build a phone and connect it to the AT&T network. Pacific Rim competitors quickly emerged, driving a decline in margins, creating competition in the actual design of telephone units and accelerating the time-to-market. The result was that AT&T's business model, which was based on a captive market, was now misaligned with the new, highly competitive market. This misalignment required AT&T to make fundamental changes in its operations—embracing completely new values—when it had once had tremendous success using a different model.

Monitoring and Measuring Alignment

Finally, we offer some observations with regard to monitoring and measuring misalignment.

Few Metrics Span Functions and Make Misalignment Visible

Attempting to measure misalignment by function will not work because the value chain in any company is cross-functional. A company will get what it measures, and separate measurement by functions will only result in silo-ing the organization.

Furthermore, measures have to change with the market, as the ultimate point of alignment is with the customer. Remaining static in what a company measures results in inertia—the systematic reinforcement of the organization's past. To stay aligned with a changing environment, it is important to do the following:

- recognize that change is a constant

- renew metrics for functional organizations

- develop metrics for cross-functional alignment

- be prepared to create new structures to bias results in favor of changing requirements

For example, in a relatively mature market, a manufacturing organization might choose to optimize its results according to inventory turns and customer lead times. In a new or exploding market, however, that same organization will need to focus on scaling and growth. At any one time, the question is, do these functional metrics serve the *larger* purposes of the company? It is always important to measure what the company is trying to achieve. Leaders must think carefully about the outcomes they are driving toward and align what is measured to those outcomes. Furthermore, to obtain useful measures, business systems must be aligned to deliver the measures the company is after. If the company is after cross-functional outcomes, then individual functionally based measures alone will not provide what is needed.

Accountability for Monitoring Alignment

Alignment, for all its potency, is not often examined or even talked about. Moreover, symptoms of misalignment are often ignored or "solved" by creating a new position—a person who typically tries to fix things through persuasion rather than through a more sustainable structural fix. This is equivalent to treating a systemic problem topically. An energetic individual can temporarily solve a local irritation, but if the problem is systemic, then it warrants systemic (structural) treatment for ongoing health. The wrong treatment only contributes to ultimate failure. If monitoring and measuring organizational alignment in the right way is not someone's job, then it is no one's job.

Examples of Where Misalignment Can Be Sensed

As we mention at the beginning of this chapter, alignment can be sensed as something not quite right. Paying attention to the right symtoms can develop that sense. Symptoms include the following:

- **glare conditions**—symptomized by not enough decision making due to leaders lacking the ability to see the problems

- **tourists**—too many observers who are not participants—people who come to a meeting, don't speak, eat the food, litter, then go away to tell others imprecisely what they heard and saw

- **unnecessary strain**—a sense that getting things done is *hard*—too many meetings, too many people, and too much difficulty getting decisions made

- **extras**—too many people in nonspecialized, go-between functions, trying to facilitate links between one organization and another (liaison to liaisons)

- **missing information**—lack of open feedback loops to and from employees, customers, and partners

- **use of pocket vetos**—no closure and no discussion

- **actions inconsistent with words**—what you hear is not what you get

When these kinds of symptoms exist, unwanted results can become the norm. This lack of predictability is the overarching *vital sign* indicating that there are problems in alignment across the company's value chain. Figure 7–6 summarizes the key points and lists the external indicators and internal vital signs associated with alignment.

Considerations and Antidotes

Remediation of misalignment can be expensive and difficult if the problem has been allowed to grow to significant proportions. One way to think about the complexity of remediation is to consider the balls-on-the-floor experiment—a mental framework for assessing the extent of remediation that is required.

Imagine three balls scattered on the floor. If you want them aligned, you need only move one to achieve it. In this simple case, remediation is but one step away. However, if the number of balls scattered on the floor is ten, the number of steps to align them all can be as many as eight. Clearly, structures that can be remediated in one or two moves tend to be more resilient and less resistant to change because remediation is one or two changes away. Structures that require many moves for remediation—steps affecting people, products, and processes—are much more complex and subject to failure.

Yet one of the most insidious paradoxes of human behavior is that procrastination seems to grow with complexity. Instead of preventing higher risk by measuring diligently and acting sooner, we tend to ignore potential bad news and hope for the best. We imagine we are avoiding risk while in fact we are letting it build. Assessing alignment is a *daily*, not an annual, activity. Here are some ways to keep the issues of alignment front and center:

The Challenge	Maintaining Alignment Across the Value Chain
Key Points	• alignment and misalignment can be sensed • alignment is crucial across the value chain, along its various axes • structure biases results • be ready to realign to keep pace with the market
External Indicators or Existing Problems	• forecasts that exceed actuals • loss of customers/market share • getting products to market late • declining revenues
Vital Signs Indicating Potential Perils	• thrash in the organization—flip-flopping from one perspective to another without coming to a conclusion • glare conditions—the inability to see problems and get them solved • lack of open feedback loops • lack of cross-functional metrics • mismatched channel capacity and technology potency • restrictive manufacturing processes compared to product portfolio potential

Figure 7-6   Alignment External Indicators and Vital Signs.

- Solve your biggest problems with structure.

- Look for opportunities to make structural change that will drive alignment across the value chain; don't wait for the weight of problems to force you to do it.

- Restructure at customer transition points when the business model changes or markets shift, causing change in the value chain.

- Make sure that efforts to achieve functional excellence occur with an eye to the business as a whole and that they are *customer driven*.

- Determine and apply a dominant or compelling logic to optimizing the structure when the business model requires change.

- Avoid recipes that never work; for example, move projects to people rather than people to projects—the former creating a win–win, the latter a lose–lose for people.

- Build a culture that thrives on change, and communicate change as a key leadership ingredient.

- Create a strategy grounded in metrics that will get you where you want to go, and use metrics to drive an organization to constant learning.

As customers' needs change, alignment must be reassessed; goals, structure, and process changed; and new alignment achieved.

Something to Think About

Consider the rules of thumb listed above and analyze your organization according to these suggestions:

- Where do you find your strengths?

- Vulnerabilities?

- What actions should you take to assess alignment and consider adjustments?

8
A Culture of Learning

Overview

- Culture is the most powerful governing tool for ensuring organizational health. It can neutralize unnecessary complexity and drive execution excellence.

- A healthy culture is, by necessity, a learning culture, and a learning culture is essential to competitive advantage.

- Lack of strong underpinnings for a learning culture in the earliest stages of an organization's development can lead to serious problems, especially as complexity grows.

- A learning culture has the following characteristics:
  - an appetite for fact-based feedback
  - open and active dialogue
  - planned experimentation
  - leaders who accept their responsibility as coaches and teachers

- Feedback, dialogue, experimentation, and coaching result in informed decisions—decisions made at the right time and with the right level of risk.

Born out of Bell Labs, Lucent Technologies was spun off from AT&T in 1996. Lucent's mission was to compete with the Internet equipment providers selling to telecommunications and enterprise customers. At that time, the focus of competition was on both a technology called packet switching (a method of managing data transmission over the Internet) and voice-over-IP (voice transmission over the Internet). It was the potential of future voice communication services provided over AT&T hardware that drove AT&T to establish Lucent as a stand-alone company—a separate business to address new markets and customers.

With its AT&T ancestry, Lucent knew the voice customers far better than any data-oriented Internet company. Consequently, its entry into the market was an enormous threat to the existing competitors, who were eager to expand their own stake in voice-over-IP. Not only did Lucent threaten this opportunity, but if the company were successful, it would be in a position to steal share in the faster growing data transmission market. Lucent's entry posed a particular threat to Cisco Systems, then the biggest competitor in the Internet market. Unlike Cisco, Lucent understood how to deliver the large, reliable systems required by voice customers. Lucent had the people and the infrastructure to support the highest quality system reliability.

Although Cisco saw competition with a company as large as Lucent as an indication of its own success, Lucent was nonetheless an enormous threat to Cisco's continued growth. Cisco was good at playing in the fast-paced early stages of the Internet market, when reliability was less important than time-to-market. However, Cisco's service model was still evolving and was considerably underdeveloped in comparison to Lucent's.

Nevertheless, Lucent's hardware development process was slow. Products were delivered through a centralized organizational structure. Cisco's advantage (and that of other companies like it, born to the Internet world) was in its ability to drive innovation through a decentralized organization, its skill in meeting aggressive time-to-market demands, and its highly reliable distribution systems.

Also damaging to Lucent's ability to compete were the company's roots in the Bell Labs culture, which had been founded on assumptions profoundly different from those of high-tech markets of the late 1990s. In the original monopoly world of telecommunications, for instance, customers could be told what they needed to do. Operating under the assumption that it knew best, given its history of success in the traditional voice market, Lucent missed the essential fact that customers of Internet transmission technology expected to tell their vendors what to do. In addition, Lucent had a tendency to be wedded to specific technologies, rather than remaining "technology agnostic" and therefore flexible in a developing market.

Finally, and as damaging, Lucent's culture promoted political safety as opposed to openness and learning. Leaders learned to evaluate their issues in private, to find out what would pass muster, and to bring to the table only surefire positions. Missing were the essential elements of a learning culture—listening, open dialogue, constructive confrontation—that is, a constant willingness to consider new ideas.

While Cisco and other competitors in the market were learning to deliver products that could perform at the highest reliability level that Lucent knew so well, Lucent failed to adapt to the cultural requirements of the new marketplace. AT&T had known that its culture was not suited to the high speed of the Internet marketplace and had spun off Lucent in the hope that as a stand-alone company, it could develop a new culture and compete in the new world. But the cultural makeover did not develop. Too much of the old world was inbred in Lucent processes and players.

Culture as a Governing Tool

Culture is both a popular and a slippery term. Everyone talks about it, books are written about it, and it has even become a legitimate subject in executive conversation. Few leaders, however, seem to have a practical understanding of how it works, much less how to develop and manage it.

Consider the following set of cascading tenets about culture as a governing tool:

- Culture governs by implicitly providing a compass for navigating complex situations, thus neutralizing complexity.

- A healthy culture is by necessity a learning culture, and a learning culture is essential to competitive advantage.

- A learning culture depends on four key elements:
  - an appetite for feedback
  - active, open exchange of views and information
  - planned experimentation
  - leaders who coach and teach

- Feedback, dialogue, experimentation, and coaching result in informed decisions—decisions made at the right time and with the right level of risk.

These tenets describe a learning culture. We explore each of these in the following sections.

How Culture Governs

A culture governs through "norms" of behavior—that is, through the implicit messages that communicate how people are expected to act in a given organization. A mature culture is visible in the *typical* behavior of individuals in the organization. That behavior is most important, of course, with regard to key aspects of performance— for example, responsiveness to customers, commitment to quality, and openness to change.

In mature cultures, it is as though invisible forces affect people's behavior, resulting in a collective understanding of "how we do it around here." Culture, then, can be defined as the *set of biases that impact what people do when no one is around* . . . what they do when they don't have anyone to ask. Thus, culture is the compass— both a powerful and an informal governing mechanism. It is reinforced and supplemented over time by more mechanistic means of governance, which we discuss in Chapter 10. But nothing substitutes for a strong set of built-in biases and informal expectations as a means of governance.

Let's look at an example. Imagine that employee John Jones picks up the phone and hears about a customer problem at six o'clock in the evening. The customer is very angry, believing that John's company has done something wrong. Solving this particular problem requires an employee more senior than John, but the senior managers whom John knows are traveling or have gone home and are not reachable.

Recommended Reading

L. Senn and J. Childress, *The Secret of a Winning Culture* (New York: TaylorWilson, 1999).

If at John's company customer focus is a genuine cultural norm, John will understand a few things without question—the customer needs to be heard and needs to receive a straight answer as soon as possible. John is not in a position to know whether the customer is mistaken or is communicating information crucial to the company. Both overreacting and underreacting on John's part can cause more problems than they solve. John's response could affect not only the issue at hand but also the company's relationship with this customer.

In this scenario, John can neither hand off the phone to someone who has more answers nor, if he acts according to the company's culture, put the customer off until tomorrow. Under the influence of strong cultural norms, John will ask enough questions to demonstrate to the customer that he is working on the problem and will follow up to make sure that it gets addressed. Even without the requisite knowledge to solve the problem or more senior guidance at hand, John will know how to handle the customer if the culture is truly customer focused.

Learning from Cultural Norms

How do employees come to know what a culture expects of them? When they enter a new workplace, they bring their personal biases about the right way to behave, including how they learned to do things at previous employers. But previous "norms" may be out of sync with those of a new employer, so an employee must have some way to learn what is expected at the new company. Yet norms are not the kinds of things that get written down.

As soon as employees enter the new company, their environment begins to affect them. Successful employees in a given culture instinctively observe and learn the behaviors reinforced by that system, both positively and negatively. The most important source of communication of cultural biases in an organization is the individual behavior of others, especially those with power to affect rewards and to make critical decisions. It is *executive behavior*, then, that counts the most in shaping culture because executives have the most influence over key decisions.

The Influence of Leaders' Behavior

One error that leaders make is to assume that culture is a function of what they *say*, not what they *do*. In fact, the more influential the leader, the more impact that person's behavior has on culture. For example, if the CEO—typically the most influential person in a company—treats customers as more important than anything else about the job, other employees are likely to realize that this kind of behavior is valued and are therefore likely to mimic it. On the other hand, if the CEO delegates concerns about customers to others in the organization and pays more attention to Wall Street, say, or to stockholders, others in the organization will tend to interpret this as a message about who and what is most important. This will be true no matter what the CEO says about the importance of customers.

To use another example, if the CEO—or any executive—avoids conflict, always tending to smooth things over at the first sign of contention, employees soon learn to avoid provoking or engaging in such activity. On the other hand, if executives are more interested in *learning* than about steering clear of contention, they will be willing to engage in constructive confrontation when it is needed because it is a source of learning. Their *behavior*—not their words—communicates what is important. For leaders to recognize this is crucial because the right leadership behavior must overcome natural tendencies toward protection of turf and reputation.

Culture Neutralizes Complexity

As organizational complexity grows, the value of a learning culture grows. As a growing number of employees enter the organization and affect outcomes, a culture that clearly communicates expectations of how to treat customers, how to make good trade-off decisions, how to operate cross-functionally, and so on, is of enormous value. A culture with strong biases toward healthy behaviors will unify employees as their numbers and diversity grow. With complexity come increasing and often competing demands that can be neutralized by a strong culture that helps employees know what to do "when no one is around to ask."

Let's look more closely at customer focus as a cultural feature to further illustrate this point. Companies often say that they are customer focused—that the customer comes first. On examination, however, the behaviors behind this claim don't seem to back it up. Customers might "come first" but only as long as they buy the right product. Or they "come first" except when it is apparently more important to please the boss. The real test of customer focus is in the moments of competing priorities. If customers come first, then they take priority over other things, period. If they come first, then executives—those in a unique position to exert their influence both internally and externally—will all be actively involved with customers on a regular basis and will guide employees to prioritize customer needs under even the most complex of circumstances. Again, *words* do not make culture; *behavior* does. So *real* customer focus will be characterized by consistent customer-oriented *action*.

Learning Culture: A Competitive Advantage

Successful cultures are not about what feels good but about what provides long-term health and competitive advantage. Healthy organizations are learning organizations because learning is what ensures that the company continues to adapt and stay ahead of the competition. Our fundamental proposition is shown in Figure 8–1.

As we discussed earlier, culture starts with the behavior of leaders. So, to develop and reinforce a learning culture, leaders must have a bias for learning—an appetite for feedback, listening, and adapting. The more leaders *demonstrate and expect* listening and learning, the more the company culture will be biased in the same way, where cultural norms implicitly expect employees to seek feedback, listen to it, and learn from it. For the top leaders to drive learning, they must be *learning leaders*. It is the consistency of leadership behavior that shapes culture, so the more learning leaders there are, the more chance there is of building a learning culture.

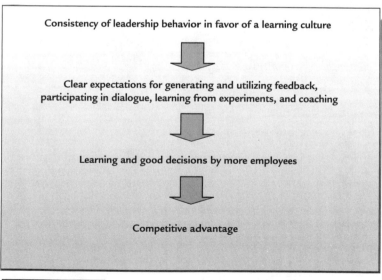

| Figure 8–1 | Culture and Competitive Advantage.

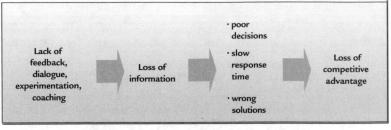

| Figure 8-2 | Lack of Learning Elements and Loss of Competitive Advantage. |

Figure 8–2 suggests the negative repercussions of a *nonlearning* culture. The lack of the elements listed on the left of the diagram means the organization has no way to ensure good information as a basis for good decisions. The quality of decisions is diluted, and competitive advantage is threatened:

The Elements of a Learning Culture

As we indicated earlier, a learning culture depends on four elements. Here we list them again, each modified by the kinds of behaviors that promote those elements:

- appetite for feedback
  - open listening—encouraging and respecting input from all levels
  - seeking underlying reasons behind trends
  - relentless questioning
  - regular review of progress
- vigorous dialogue
  - healthy exchange of ideas
  - constructive confrontation—open challenge while avoiding polarities
  - constructive humor
  - informality
- planned experimentation
  - constructive paranoia
  - constant anticipation

- willingness to change
- constant scrutiny
- coaching
  - using teachable moments
  - being direct and supportive
  - rotating of leaders for growth and to disseminate best practices

It is these behaviors, if consistent, that build a culture of learning and thereby establish a competitive advantage.

On the other hand, certain behaviors establish a culture that restricts learning—a dangerous thread of failure:

- politics (hierarchical safety before learning and contribution)
- ignoring or punishing carriers of bad news
- haphazard data gathering
- ignoring unpleasant information
- spending more time focusing inward than outward
- risk aversion—too much fear of making mistakes, lack of willingness to experiment
- more top-down than bottom-up communication

If our argument is sound—that feedback, dialogue, experimentation, and coaching are the critical factors that drive learning, and therefore good decisions and good governance—what does it take to ensure that they are present and utilized? How do leaders ensure learning behaviors in their company's culture?

Appetite for Feedback

If culture is primarily a function of how leaders behave, the most important question to ask if you are one of those leaders is, what is *your own* appetite for feedback? Building culture starts with self-examination and personal behavior. Consider the following questions:

- How much time do you spend with customers and employees?
- How well do you (personally) listen to them? If you think you do it well, do others agree? How well do customers think you listen? How do you know?

- How has customer input recently influenced you? What about employee input?

- What proportion of the time that you are meeting with others are you talking and what proportion are you listening?

- How readily do you allow constructive conflict to occur in meetings?

- How well can you distinguish between constructive conflict and wasted energy?

- How openly and frequently do those who work for you disagree with you and others they work for?

Examining and working on personal conduct can make a big difference. The next step, though, is to promote and support learning behaviors *in others*, especially other leaders, who will influence even more people. A learning culture depends on a set of leaders who consistently listen and learn. Again, some questions:

- Can you rate how vigorously the key leaders in your organization seek and use feedback? They might each do it differently . . . what do you know about their methods?

- What learning have you seen each of them demonstrate recently?

- How well do they promote obtaining and using feedback within their organizations?

The question of listening and learning on a personal level inevitably leads to the issue of *resistance*. Why don't leaders readily have an appetite for feedback? Why is listening such a challenge for leaders? One reason is a constant flow of feedback in a learning culture brings the bad news with the good. No one finds it easy to face bad news, especially if it is surprising. No one wants to hear that projected actuals are not likely to meet the forecast, or that the product schedule will slip, or that the competition is making design wins. Tying one's ego, however, to the proportion of good to bad news is a mistake. Bad news is critically important, as it informs leaders when change is required and what that change needs to be. Facing facts—good and bad—is both important and often painful.

Consider the scenario in which a company is developing a new product based on an aggressive market disruption strategy. During development, there are many discussions about the technical challenges and uncertainties. In the course of these discussions, the key leader involved has communicated clearly that no slip in schedule will be tolerated but has *not listened* to feedback in order to understand the challenges and uncertainties, despite the efforts of technology leaders to communicate them. Finally, imagine that the challenges cannot be overcome in the time allotted and the product's planned release date cannot be met. As a result of the leader's reluctance to listen to warnings and understand the facts of the situation, there is no contingency plan in place, and no one is in a position to establish a new and reliable release date.

Why did this leader not heed the team's warnings? Typically, in a scenario like this, discussions about the unwelcome challenges in the development of a product makes leaders uncomfortable. Leaders often do not know how to effectively balance the technologists' input with market information. It is a very inexact science. Regardless of the difficulties, however, ignoring useful information is of no help, whereas gathering *more* information is likely to be. *Listening carefully to the carriers of bad news gives the listener the very information needed* to diagnose and solve the problem.

Consider the results had the leader in this scenario found the answers to the following questions:

- Are things as bad as the engineers think? Do other informed experts agree? Should more experienced experts become informed and weigh in with their opinions?

- Could some creative brainstorming about the situation lead to a solution? If not, what steps should be taken to control the potential damage?

- What useful information can be learned about the product, the development process, customer commitment, and the employees involved?

The good news is that leaders can count on the fact that the human beings in competing companies will struggle with the same tendency to resist bad news. Good leaders, however, will make it a competitive advantage to be the *first* to gather and the *best* at facing *all* the news, good *and* bad.

Open and Active Dialogue

Of the four factors of a learning culture that we pose here—an appetite for feedback, open and active dialogue, planned experimentation, and leaders as coaches—open and active dialogue might appear to be the one most likely to be already in place. However, ask anyone what *dialogue* means, and you are likely to hear something like "people talking to each other." Rarely would the concept of *listening* enter the definition. Dialogue, however, is a matter of give and take, not just give. Even in the *strongest* organizations—dynamic environments full of highly intelligent, opinionated people—*listening* is often in undersupply compared to the volume of strongly voiced opinions.

The tendency to advocate more than listen is a common failing in leadership. Studies have shown that most people who hold leadership positions tend to do the following:

- communicate their convictions more than their questions
- be quick to reach conclusions
- be ready to get on with it, sometimes prematurely

Therefore, it is crucial not to *assume* that learning dialogue is occurring in an organization but rather to realize that dialogue needs to be *nurtured*. The results of nurturing it can make a critical difference in ensuring good decisions. Truly constructive dialogue that results in learning includes a number of important characteristics. None of these is a time-consuming activity, but rather a *frame of mind*:

- listening for new perspectives
- acknowledging other speakers
- speaking without judgment
- respecting differences
- suspending role/status
- balancing inquiry and advocacy
- focusing on discovering the next level of understanding
- letting go of the need for predetermined outcomes

Assuring dialogue in multiple forums—formal and informal—is *everyone's* responsibility, but it can be facilitated by leaders who

Going the Distance: Why Some Companies Dominate and Others Fail

Recommended Reading

Bert Frydman, Joanne Wyer, Iva M. Wilson, and Peter Senge, *The Power of Collaborative Leadership: Lessons for the Learning Organization* (Woburn, MA: Butterworth-Heinemann, 2000).

recognize its value and promote it for the purpose of learning and reaching better decisions.

Planned Experimentation

The third element of a learning culture is *planned experimentation*. This means taking specific actions designed to both achieve outcomes *and* produce learning. For example, in Chapter 5 we discuss an approach to inserting new products, designed to minimize adverse impact on current revenues. Any new forays into a market are, by definition, planned experiments; even if predictions are intelligent, no one *knows* what will happen.

However, if a product transition is considered simply as the best decision that can be made, take or leave the outcomes, a major opportunity is missed. To benefit from the opportunity, the strategy can also be seen as an experiment from which the organization can learn, whether it succeeds or fails. This attitude is the first in a series of steps to maximize both the company's position in the market and its learning about the market, the product, and its execution capability.

The difference between taking what comes and learning from what comes is both in the mindset and in the follow-up. With the mindset of planned experimentation, the decision is made, the action taken, and the results are mined for lessons. How close to the predicted outcome did they come? How big was the difference? What did the difference indicate about the market or the competition that was not already known? What adjustments can be made to improve the effort next time? And so on.

Another example of planned experimentation is in reorganizing in support of a new corporate strategy. Although it is important to make reasonably firm decisions about organizational structure, and certainly to provide sufficient clarity for employees about the changes, precisely how a new organization will work can only be discovered after that structure takes effect. The real results of reorganizations derive from the way they are implemented, not necessarily from how they are designed. Does the new structure end up driving the team in the direction of the new strategy? How will hand-offs work? Are there sufficient integrating mechanisms to drive lateral coordination? Again, first decisions can be seen as final decisions or as the beginning of an experiment, from which learning and improvements can be derived.

Planned experimentation does not mean either endless movement or indecision. Planned experimentation implies *careful* decision making and provides the option of taking more risks, planning those risks, and learning from them. Someone once described Cisco's bias for action and learning with the phrase "Doing 8 out of 10 things well is better than 5 out of 5 right." This is not just a matter of getting more done and accepting the downside of the risk. By going for 8 out of 10 with thoughtful effort, progress can be made on the 8 initiatives and good information gained from all 10, instead of limiting the potential to making progress on only 5.

Leaders as Coaches

To establish and nurture a culture that supports feedback, dialogue, and planned experimentation, executives and their teams have to use the influence of their personal and collective behaviors. They have to become coaches and teachers.

One of a teaching leader's most important tools is the timing of teaching behaviors with "teachable" moments in organizational life. Not only does well-timed teaching behavior develop people, it is key in shaping culture. Figure 8–3 suggests some examples of teachable moments that leaders can look for and exploit. It is *how* the executive responds to these moments that matters. Effective coaching means that leaders coach when others are in the best position to learn from it.

Unfortunately, teachable moments are also moments in which leadership behavior can reinforce the *opposite* of a learning culture. Punishing first-time mistakes and "killing the messenger" who brings bad news are two all-too-familiar examples of how *not* to coach constructively.

Our experience is that leaders give two reasons for not being active coaches—they don't have time or they don't know how. The first argument is an excuse. Not having time is a euphemism for the mistaken opinion that coaching is not important enough to replace other activities. The problem is *prioritization*, not availability of time. However, inexperienced leaders often think that coaching is very time consuming. It doesn't have to be, as we discuss shortly.

Teachable Moments	Teaching Behaviors
• mistakes • customer-based successes • evaluation of results • critical decision points • organizational changes • crises • conflicts • hiring decisions	• discussing mistakes objectively and thinking through alternatives for next time • asking questions that require answers based on recent feedback • holding people accountable to learn from experience • helping others learn to diagnose poor results • explaining the rationale behind changes and key decisions • facilitating constructive exchange of ideas at all levels • giving developmental feedback • relentlessly pursuing facts

Figure 8-3 Opportunities to Shape Culture.

The second argument—that they don't know how to coach—often implies a misunderstanding of what coaching is. Many leaders worry about how the input will be received, whether they can deliver it constructively, and so on. These are reasonable concerns, but to ignore the task because of the possibility of making a mistake is no solution.

Here are some ideas that can help for those who are not yet comfortable in a coaching role. The Recommended Reading will provide more ideas.

• Coaching does not have to take a lot of time. Often it can be done in a few minutes, and very informally. Do it on the way to or from a meeting at the end of a one-on-one or—with care—even in email (although truly tough messages should not be sent by email).

• Be objectively frank. Don't pull punches and don't make judgmental comments. *It is possible to be supportive and direct at the same time.*

• Think of coaching as providing *useful information*, not as evaluating. Describe what you see the person doing and what some alternatives might be, rather than trying to specify how right or wrong the person might have been.

- Use personal examples of how and what *you've* learned in similar experiences.

A key feature of organizations that develop their leaders as coaches is setting clear expectations for *coaching as a leadership responsibility* and subsequently *measuring leaders* by it. Jack Welch, former CEO of GE, is well known for remarking that GE's core competency is not delivering certain products or services but rather is the ability to find and delvelop strong leaders and motivate them to learn and grow.

Establishing Cultural Underpinnings

Because cultures are defined by everyday behaviors, they develop from the moment a company is born. Executives or executive teams cannot casually decide to form the company's culture later—say, after they establish a business presence in the market. Culture begins to develop from the moment there are individuals in the organization who *act with influence*. The first steps early members take with regard to customers and to each other begin to shape culture.

If the key players are more concerned about building the product they have in mind than in finding out what customers want, their company culture will be more technology driven than market driven. If they choose to suppress conflict and mitigate disagreements, their company culture will move toward narrow-mindedness rather than broad-mindedness—more closed than open. The consistency and quality of culture is where the choice lies, not the timing.

The stronger the roots of a culture of learning, the more chance there is for ongoing cultural health. Turning around an established culture—one that is not used to listening, learning, and adapting—is a long, difficult task best avoided by establishing strong underpinnings for learning from the start. A learning organization reinforces

---

Recommended Reading

James W. Robinson, "The Leader as Teacher," in *Jack Welch and Leadership: Executive Lessons from the Master CEO* (Roseville, CA: Prima Publishing, 2001).

---

itself both with the value of the learning itself and by attracting leaders with compatible values, who continue the learning process. A culture in which learning *is pervasive and active* is essential in avoiding all the other threads of failure that great companies face.

Early Learning

Not only does it behoove a company to develop early roots of a learning culture to ensure its existence later, but listening and learning are also essential to secure success in Stage 1. This is the stage at which leaders can become fixated on their original technology, whether it fits with current real customer needs or not. The original idea for the company's mission, which may fit perfectly in today's market, may not fit for tomorrow. Listening to feedback from customers and innovators (both internal and external) is essential; without this feedback, the company can miss the first turn in the technology racetrack.

Not listening to employees can also spell disaster right from the very beginning. Employees are often the first to realize how customers really feel and may well have the best ideas for responding to competitive threats. Certainly they are most likely to know the most about what is working and not working in the organization.

Later Learning

Making it successfully through the early stages of company development might suggest that a company has achieved a healthy culture, or at least that the culture has healthy elements. However, as complexity grows, the amount and kind of feedback needed increases. The number and variety of customers grows. Partners are important new additions. And the number of competitors to be aware of and learn about grows. A company's means of getting and absorbing information to ensure learning has to adapt as complexity increases.

In the increasingly complex environment of a later-stage company, culture often becomes *diluted*. The organization is no longer a tightly knit team of entrepreneurial individuals, initially drawn together by the early opportunity. New employees, many coming in through acquisitions rather than by personal choice, bring new cultural assumptions. The organization spreads out geographically, while local considerations are varied and influential. Again, early-stage underpinnings of culture make a significant difference in communicating expectations to new employees and in tying together a decentralized organization.

Too often, leaders make the mistake of believing that culture is a "soft issue," one that HR is responsible for. But culture is the job of line leaders, from the board and the CEO down to the first-line managers. Culture is one of the most potent tools any leader has to secure competitive advantage. Ignoring culture—or expecting someone else to be responsible for it—is like guiding a large group of opinionated people through unknown and dangerous territory without the authority of a compass.

Maintaining Culture During High Growth

In the 1990s, Cisco became well known for its unique culture. Its aspects included the following:

- relentless attention to customers
- extreme results orientation and commitment to "stretch goals" that were constantly measured
- planned experimentation in both organizational structure and process
- using a Socratic approach to provoke people's thinking
- using the art of the "and" rather than eliminating options with "or"
- belief in doing 8 out of 10 things well rather than 5 out of 5
- a commitment to people and empowerment—that with goals, tools, and autonomy, people will take ownership and make it happen
- a belief in the value of a decentralized "horizontal" organization, where the primary information flow is lateral rather than vertical

During its phenomenal growth in the 1990s, Cisco was able to spread this culture across a sprawling organization. How did Cisco maintain its culture during high growth?

First, the company believed strongly that the value it acquired when it acquired a company was in the *people*, not just in the technology or product. Success, then, was defined by retaining the new employees, so that, in turn, the new leaders could help Cisco continue to evolve. Second, Cisco saw what it acquired as part of an end-to-end business solution rather than an independent device or function. True integration was pursued, rather than leaving the acquired company alone, to be tolerated by the larger system.

Exhibit 8-1: A Leader's Musings

I believe strongly in the importance of culture. It is my job and the job of the leaders I work with to breed a strong culture through living it out, through selecting new leaders compatible with its expectations, and through coaching and teaching.

I feel passionately about all aspects of culture, but perhaps the one that means the most to me is learning through coaching. I've had the privilege of coaching the best and hope to continue this experience going forward. Coaching is an essential element of building and reinforcing culture. Coaches acquire talent, choose the rhythm, and ensure accountability, training, preparation, and alignment.

Effective teams work in the ambiguity of transition; that is, they keep working the ball around the court and cover for one another until one gets a shot. Coaches watch the court and decide when to play "man-to-man," switch to zone defense, and so on. Coaches set the tone as they nurture a team, helping people be all they can be through a mix of basic skills (defense, offense, and so on) and selfless teamwork.

Coaching can be both visible and invisible. In the end, coaches serve others. Players are where they are to make history. They will move on in time, but with good coaching, they also will have learned as if their work experience were a university.

Third, Cisco's selection process for acquisitions was both strategic and highly refined (see Chapter 6), based on size, cultural chemistry, and alignment. This way, the outcomes were heavily biased for success, including the potential for cultural integration. Cisco learned from the enormous number of acquisitions it has completed. As a result, it has developed a methodology and willingness to focus intensely on the integration process as a means of preventing cultural dilution.

As is true for all companies that have survived the downturn in the early years of this century, new pressures are providing new influences on culture. Cisco, like other companies, will have to work hard to maintain the strengths of its culture, weed out the emerging cultural elements that can limit learning, and develop new elements

Here are a number of characteristics of day-to-day company life—customers, delivery/meeting commitments, meetings, level of energy, involvement with employees—that are examples of places to look for the *vital signs of a learning culture*. Pick one or more of the numbered categories and use it to evaluate culture in your company.

1. Customers

   - How rigorously does the company collect customer data?

   - How many company leaders visit customers every month?

   - Are executives from all corporate functions involved in customer contact, or just Marketing and Sales—or just Sales?

   - How many customers do individual executives have strong relationships with?

   - What measures are in place to find out how customers experience contact from company leaders?

2. Delivery/meeting commitments

   - How routinely do you gather feedback on how product planning and delivery are coming along (e.g., through ops reviews)?

   - Are the forums for evaluating delivery effective?

     - Is only good news presented?

     - If there is bad news, is it "taken offline" or discussed openly?

3. Meetings

   - Is open and active dialogue a common feature of meetings or are people just exchanging individual points of view without learning from each other?

   - How effective is dialogue, as measured by advancing the process of creative problem solving?

4. Level of energy

   - If you were an outsider, how would you describe the level of energy in the company?

- Are people excited, moving quickly and in a focused way?

- Do decisions get made efficiently?

- How does the energy level at your company compare to your sense of it elsewhere?

5. Employees

- How often do you walk around the company and talk to people?

- What forums are established to get input? What do you learn from them?

- Do employees speak up in these forums? What do you learn from them?

- How do employees describe their experience at the company? Is it fun? Are they learning?

needed in a new environment. Like any successful company, Cisco's self-evaluation, learning, and change must be constant.

Lucent, again, provides a contrast. It has been much less successful at acquisitions. Acquisition selection and integration has been neither a core competence nor a part of an end-to-end system of growth. Rather, it has been a reactive response to internal nonperformance. Consequently, acquisitions have focused on products rather than on people. Furthermore, there was a fundamental cultural clash between Lucent and the companies it acquired. Lucent carried the Bell Labs culture, one result being that it failed to deliver its products in a competitive and timely manner. Consequently, it was forced to acquire companies that *could* do so.

Imagine the cultural integration challenges when Lucent acquired informal, speed- and delivery-oriented startup cultures. Lucent's cultural roots lay in a monopoly world, and many of its leaders (at least from 1995 to 2000) had participated in that monopoly environment—big in size, hierarchical in organization, and oriented to perks like corporate jets and golf memberships. The clash of Lucent with Silicon Valley, with its pride in egalitarian informality, has clearly been problematic.

The Challenge	Building a Culture That Ensures Good Decision Making
Key Points	<ul><li>appetite for feedback</li><li>open and active dialogue</li><li>planned experimentation</li><li>leaders who coach and teach</li></ul>
External Indicators or Existing Problems	<ul><li>stalled revenue</li><li>negative customer feedback</li><li>falling behind the competition technologically</li><li>loss of key leaders</li><li>missing strategic opportunities that require bold steps</li></ul>
Vital Signs Indicating Potential Perils	<ul><li>overly cautious decision making</li><li>inactive cross-functional exchange</li><li>little constructive challenge on critical issues and decisions</li><li>haphazard information flow regarding customers, sales, product delivery, and employees</li><li>lack of common language and principles about learning culture</li><li>employee cynicism</li></ul>

Figure 8–4   Culture of Learning.

Vital Signs

In Figure 8–4 we summarize the elements of a learning culture and list its associated *external indicators* and *internal vital signs*. To be able to see these vital signs when they appear means paying attention to behaviors in the organization that reveal them. See the Something to Think About box for more ideas.

9
Leadership DNA

Overview

- Leadership DNA is a company's ability to create its own leaders for the future.

- A company's leadership DNA engenders leaders with values and behavior patterns that can either help or hinder long-term success.

- A company whose leadership DNA produces leaders who are *authentic*, *oriented to service*, and *biased toward learning* has the essential ingredients for ensuring long-lived leadership strength.

- Leadership DNA of a great company also engenders leaders with additional characteristics specifically suited to that particular company's market drivers.

- Leadership DNA helps to shape a company's culture, which in turn affects the selection of new leaders.

- The responsibility of establishing the right leadership DNA in a company rests with its early leaders; maintaining it through hiring and developing of new leaders is essential.

A company becomes a great company for many reasons—well-timed, innovative products; a differentiating strategy; sustained customer focus; execution excellence; a culture of learning; and certainly its ability to ensure future leadership. Long-lived success requires that a company not only *hire* good leaders but also *develop* leaders for the future.

A company's ability to ensure strong leadership now, as well as in the future, is part of its DNA. A company's leadership DNA attracts certain types of leaders, repels others, and ensures the development of future leaders from its high-performing ranks. Without the right kind of leadership DNA, a company's ability to ensure strong future leadership is constricted, making it difficult for the company to weather major transitions and changing demands.

Healthy leadership DNA attracts and develops leaders with a common belief system about leadership. Once well established, leadership DNA then acts as an important governor in selecting new leaders, in setting expectations and sanctions that guide leaders' behavior, and in helping current leaders to grow and develop *other* leaders. A company's leadership DNA is most visible in the kind of leaders it grows, attracts, and retains.

Establishing the right kind of DNA in a company depends on the beliefs and traits of the most influential leaders. Are the leaders focused on themselves and their own successes or on the successes of others and the long-lived success of the company? Do they establish and reinforce a leadership DNA that is short-term oriented—high image, high talent, high turnover—or long-term oriented—strong capability, strong beliefs, strong commitment to others? Are strong leaders for the future emerging under their guidance?

Rock Star Leaders

There are two kinds of company leadership DNA that can develop into a thread of failure. One is a kind of weak DNA that produces leaders with little or no consistent belief systems and that results in uncertainty about the quality of leadership in the long term. The other kind is DNA that creates leaders with a focus on personal glory rather than long-term company success. At their most exaggerated, these are "rock star leaders." They illustrate how problematic leadership DNA in a company can lead to company failure in the long term.

Rock star leaders are typically very talented individuals. The success of their companies is built on their personal talent and charisma. However, unlike real rock stars, who *must* self-promote and can only be successful based on their personal impact, rock star *leaders* have the larger job of building a company, which can be of value for many people over the long term. When these leaders leave a company, success built on their personal talent leaves with them.

Rock star leaders are typically unsuited to industry downturns. They shine in the good times, but they often have difficulty leading to greatness in situations that do not feed their need for bright lights. This is because rock star leaders are concerned about impression first, substance second, and impressions hold much more currency in good times than in bad. The momentum of success can camouflage company deficits, including lack of substance in its leadership.

The industry that we know best—high-tech—has its own version of rock stars. Typically, they are competent leaders, having risen to center stage. They might even have proven their abilities over long periods of time and in different settings. However, they are by definition lacking in humility, the belief in the importance of being of service to other people, and a bias for learning—qualities oriented to contribution, not to self-aggrandizement. As we discuss shortly, *authenticity, orientation to service*, and *a bias for learning* are core to building a great company that is not dependent on any one leader for long-lived success.

The Rock Star Focus

Rock stars fuel their own identities, typically through the story of their own individual success. Their eyes are on the mirror, not out the window. Jim Collins suggests that an excess of ego leads to promises that cannot be met. He explores the history of several rock star CEOs, including Doug Ivester, who lost out at Coke when he didn't listen to either his team or the board; Rich McGinn at Lucent, who seemed unaware of the realities of the situation until the board made it clear it was time for him to leave; and Jill Barad at Mattel, who, as the company was failing, insisted on creating a CEO Barbie whose accessories matched her own.[1]

Early rock star success can be seductive. Leaders who find great satisfaction in their own charismatic talents as speakers and vision-

[1] Jim Collins, "Beware the Self-Promoting CEO," *Wall Street Journal*, 26 November 2001.

aries can be especially subject to this seduction. They find it hard to give up the glory once they first experience it. Telltale signs of a leader being a star rather than a leader of a team are statements like, "This is *my* company," or "Since *I've* been running this company . . ." Statements like these indicate a sense of personal contribution way out of balance with collective contribution. They imply an eye on the mirror and a focus on nurturing one's own identity rather than developing the talent of others, where the real value of a company lies. Feeding the public relations needs of a rock star leader drains energy from the organization rather than fueling it.

Carly Fiorina, the CEO of HP, has been perceived as nurturing a rock star persona. *Forbes* magazine in late 1999 showed her on its cover, with the headline "The Cult of Carly." Inside, the title of the article was "All Carly! All the Time," referring to her approach to leadership at HP as "The Carly Show." The article focused on the energy Fiorina spent appearing on television shows and starring in HP commercials—all before she had established a successful track record as a CEO. This is typical of the public impression she made early in her tenure.

However, as this book is being written, Carly Fiorina has proven herself a persevering leader. She is driving an onerous reshaping of a very famous company and has needed to communicate that broadly. If she continues on the road to success, she will have created a customer-focused company, not a CEO-focused company. She has gotten the world's attention and can use it for the benefit of many. It all depends on her fundamental focus.

A Different Kind of Focus

In contrast to Fiorina's early leadership style as described in *Forbes*, Collins gives the following examples of Charles Walgreen, of the Walgreen empire, and Katherine Graham, formerly CEO of the *Washington Post*:

> Mr. Walgreen not only had the guts, but he made his decisions without fanfare—quietly taking action based on understanding, not bravado. Yet despite these results, not once did Mr. Walgreen stand in front of the mirror and point to himself as a key factor, preferring instead to point out the window to credit the people he had on his team. When we confronted him with the undeniable fact of stupendous results created under his leadership and pushed him to discuss his own role in getting great people to make those results happen, he deflected again, and pinned much of the credit for his success on being "lucky."

When Graham became president of the Washington Post, she did not position herself as the great leader or savior. In her own words, she was "terrified." Shy, awkward and socially fearful, Graham did not launch "The Katherine Tour" or create "The Cult of Katherine." Reflecting on her early years atop the Post in her book "Personal History," she hardly gives herself any credit whatsoever, writing that she was surprised even to land on her feet.[2]

Fame, however, does not define a rock star. Consider Jack Welch of GE, an unusually well-known business leader, whose departure from GE generated tremendous publicity. Despite the hype and publicity—some of it negative—that accompanied his departure from GE, he cannot accurately be described as a rock star leader, by our use of the term. He developed many leaders, who went on to become famous in their own right. Although he was the chief anarchist, overcoming inertia at GE over the course of 20 years of change under his leadership, he would be the first to point out that others helped make GE great. His bureaucracy-busting dogma served others by setting them free to exercise their own leadership and be part of real change. His focus on creating great leaders served those leaders. As he transitioned control of GE to Jeff Immelt, he made it clear that his past success was now irrelevant. Immelt's courage and competency were what mattered now.

David Packard and Bill Hewlett are two other examples of leaders who earned individual fame while building a company with leadership DNA that bred leaders for the long term. HP was a great company long after their departures, not in small part due to the quality of leaders who followed them. Under Hewlett's and Packard's leadership, HP became distinguished by being a great place to work, with great products and great people, rather than by its founders' personalities and press. Their self-effacing qualities established a self-effacing element to the company's leadership DNA, which for a long time attracted leaders with the crucial willingness to focus on building the leaders of the future.

Leadership DNA Ingredients

Healthy leadership DNA has two kinds of ingredients:

- ingredients that are essential to long-lived success in any company, which we call *core ingredients*

[2] Jim Collins, "Beware the Self-Promoting CEO," *Wall Street Journal*, 26 November 2001.

Recommended Reading

Jim Collins, *Good to Great: Why Some Companies Make the Leap
. . . and Others Don't* (New York: HarperCollins, 2001).

- ingredients that are uniquely important to a company because of its particular mission and market and that define organizational "fit," which we call *specialized ingredients*

To introduce our definition of core DNA ingredients, we refer once more to the results of Jim Collins' research on great companies. In it he identified two consistent factors in the leaders who led companies of moderate success to become long-lived, great companies. These two distinguishing features are *humility* and *strong will*. In addition, these leaders believed in the importance of people and showed it by building the success of their companies first on the choice of people and then on vision and strategy. What distinguished leaders of Collins' "great companies" from all the others can best be summarized by a quote from one of them, Darwin Smith, longtime CEO of Kimberly Clark: "I never stopped trying to become qualified for the job."

Collins summarized his research conclusions as follows:

> We learned in our research that the most effective leaders never make themselves the center of attention. They are understated yet determined, quiet yet forceful. Most lack the *liability of charisma*. Indeed, the very best ones overwhelmed us not with their ego, but with their humility. They're ambitious, to be sure, but ambitious first and foremost *for their institutions*, not for themselves [italics ours].[3]

Our personal experience with hundreds of successful and unsuccessful leaders of high-tech companies bears out Collins' results. In watching the leaders we know help their companies reach greatness from whatever level of the organization they serve, we see them create emotional connections with people, build a following, achieve results in various settings, and grow themselves and others. We believe that these leaders bear very consistent traits. These are the core ingredients of healthy leadership DNA for any company— authenticity, an orientation to service, and a bias for learning in the company's leaders. Let's examine each, in turn.

[3] Jim Collins, "Beware the Self-Promoting CEO," *Wall Street Journal*, 26 November 2001.

Authenticity

Authenticity is a level of humility, openness, and maturity that results in the leader relating to others in a congruent way. What you see is what you get—consistently. An authentic leader walks the talk without having to try.

Authenticity is about accepting one's own human gifts, limits, and potential—and appreciating those of others. It is a matter of being true to one's own uniqueness. That's why authentic leaders do not look or act alike. Their primary commitment is to an internal integrity. They look to their own passion for motivation, although these passions are different from one leader to the next. Authentic leaders rely on an internal integrity—an internal source of self-governance. Guidance by this internal governance results in a consistent humility, trustworthiness, and courage.

Collins saw this in the leaders of great companies as unpretentiousness and a compelling modesty:

> They'd go on and on about the company and the contributions of other executives, but they would instinctively deflect discussion about their own role. When pressed to talk about themselves, they'd say things like, "I hope I'm not sounding like a big shot," or "I don't think I can take much credit for what happened. We were blessed with marvelous people." One Level 5 leader even asserted, "There are a lot of people in this company who could do my job better than I do."[4]

Collins contrasted this to "the presence of a gargantuan ego that contributed to the demise or continued mediocrity" of other companies he studied. He found "gargantuan egos," especially in those companies that did not show sustained or long-lived success—"the companies that would show a shift in performance under a talented yet egocentric . . . leader, only to decline in later years."[5]

For all their humility, however, the intelligence and self-confidence of successful, authentic leaders are very high. They have a mature appreciation and respect for the complexities of people, organizations, and industry dynamics, as well as a sincere realization of any one individual's very limited ability, highly intelligent or not, to know all the right answers in a complex setting. Instead, they believe in the possibility of discovering the right answers by working with others.

[4] Jim Collins, *Why Some Companies Make the Leap . . . and Others Don't* (New York: HarperCollins, 2001), p. 27.

[5] Ibid.

A good leader's innate respect for others also ensures nonhierarchical relationships, making room for others' creativity and influence. The resulting growth enriches the entire environment and advances the potential for better decisions, to the competitive advantage of the company. It also makes moot the concern as to whether the leader has "good interpersonal skills." Authentic, trustworthy, respectful interaction, even if it is rough around the edges, goes a lot further toward building a following than elegant interactive skills.

On the other hand, authentic leaders know when they need to make a decision whether they have the right answer or not. Because they are oriented to serving others, they know when the time has come to take the bull by the horns, make an executive decision, and get on with it. They calibrate risk taking to the needs of the business and of the people they are leading and not to their own personal comfort level.

Orientation to Service

This brings us to the second essential leadership trait that is bred by, and reinforces, the right kind of company leadership DNA—serving others. Leaders for the long term realize that by serving others they are also developing other leaders, those who will enable the company to thrive long after they have departed.

Some leaders who serve others might not even think of it as service. Providing an environment in which others can grow might be an intellectual principle as much as a deeply held value. The importance is not in how leaders conceptualize but in how they *act*. Do they act based on a concern for whether they are getting what *they* deserve or whether *others* are?

Service is a focus on others, not self, on give, not take, on obligation, not prerogative. Long-lived great companies need leaders who build for the sake of others, not for their own sake; who want to ensure that the company is great after they leave; and who spend their time and energy ensuring that over everything else.

A Bias for Learning

If leaders already have a strong bias toward authenticity and toward serving others, a bias for growth and learning naturally follows. When authentic leaders do not know the answer, they admit it without discomfort. It simply would not occur to them that they *could* know everything. And their egos are not tied to whether they know more than others. They believe that they have plenty to learn and are eager to do so, from whatever source that learning might come. At the same time, they are capable of projecting confidence.

Returning to our example of Jack Welch, former CEO of GE, Welch has publicly used the example of his decision to buy Kidder Peabody against the advice of his board to illustrate the problem of a leader who lets hubris get in the way of genuine curiosity to learn and, thus, good decision making. GE ended up selling Kidder in 1994, demostrating that those leaders with enough authenticity and service orientation to have a bias for learning aren't immune to mistakes—they just *learn* from them.

Specialized Leadership DNA Ingredients

Let's turn now to the idea of specialized ingredients in company leadership DNA—those that define the company's nature and to which leaders' natural and learned behaviors must find a reasonable "fit."

Levels of "Fit"ness

As a great company grows, its leadership DNA causes it to seek the kinds of leaders it needs and believes in, placing bets on people who have what it takes to build successfully in *that particular* company. Although these newly hired leaders might need some development, they are hired because they seem to be people whom others will follow within that unique company and because they have characteristics that are admired by the successful leaders already in residence.

Figure 9–1 contains some examples of opposite types of specialized leadership DNA ingredients. Each ingredient can be important in engendering the right leaders for the future, depending on a particular company's unique requirements.

```
Aggressive— — — — — — — — — — Cautious
Bias for action  — — — — — — — — — Bias for planning
Aggressiveness  — — — — — — — — — Accommodation
Comfort with ambiguity — — — — — — Need for predictability
Preference for change — — — — — — Preference for stability
```

Figure 9-1 Characteristics of Company Leadership DNA.

Different companies will need leaders with leadership characteristics closer to one end of these scales than the other. Exactly where on a given scale a company's leaders need to be depends primarily on the company's *mission* and *market*. A company with a single, very long-term mission and a reasonably predictable path to that mission will require leaders with characteristics more on the right end rather than the left end of these scales. A company in a fast moving market with multiple missions and unpredictable barriers along the way will, in general, need leaders closer to the left end. Let's look at some examples.

Slower Environments

First, consider a large company in an industry with little or no competition. Here the leadership challenge is managing size, nurturing slow and predictable growth, and maintaining stability. There is less need for innovation and more for service and cost efficiency. Here, hierarchies tend to work better than what these days is called "boundaryless" or "network" organizations. The ideal leaders are enlightened, compassionate, and very disciplined. They experiment less and use policy and dogma to teach how they have achieved success in the past.

In some sense this describes the leadership DNA in telecommunications companies before the advent of the Internet. For example, before its divestiture, AT&T was the largest nongovernmental organization in the world. It needed to be hierarchical, slow moving, and maternal; otherwise, chaos would have reigned.

Now consider the government as an employer. Here, leadership is defined by influence and political networking. Things get done, but very slowly and in very low volume. Considering ideas and building coalitions are more often the focus than achieving outcomes that change things. Government leaders create poles of identity with which to sway opinion and establish their own signature. They keep things from diverging too far in one direction or the other. This is leadership less of action and more of maintaining constituency through rhetoric and identity.

Faster Environments

High-tech environments, on the other hand, are very different. The driving force for this industry is intense competition through invention and the potential for wealth. Competition drives fast outcomes that are judged along the dimensions of time, quality, and features. High-tech leaders, then, must have a bias for action, a reasonably high risk-taking tendency, relative aggressiveness, and quick intelligence.

Survival and certainly long-term success in high-tech cannot be had without a requisite level of intellectual horsepower. Creative, highly intelligent engineers drive the world of high-tech. Their leaders must have intelligence sufficient to keep pace with these engineers' ideas and have the ability to read the complicated technical, competitive, and economic landscape.

Establishing and reinforcing specialized leadership DNA, then, is a matter of identifying and hiring those leaders who will nurture new leaders for the future—leaders who are well suited to a company's unique environment and its challenges.

Changes in Leadership DNA Over Time

The founders, board of directors, and early leaders of a startup shape the company's original leadership DNA through their own leadership behaviors and their early hiring choices. The quality and type of this DNA, then, influences the development of the company's unique culture, consciously or otherwise. Once that culture is established, it in turn begins to attract or repel certain types of new leaders. This interdependency of leadership DNA and culture can stabilize DNA for a long time, but it can also eventually mutate. This is most likely when a new CEO arrives with a set of beliefs and behaviors that are distinctly different from those that formed the original leadership DNA and culture. This only reinforces the fact of the potent influence of leadership DNA on culture: in its formation, resilience, and transformation.

Consider those cases in which company founders have led their companies for a long time. In these cases, there are fewer influences to counter the company's original leadership DNA. The stamp of these leaders' unique qualities, which have bred other leaders through the company, remains evident in the company's culture for a very long time. Obvious examples in our world of high-tech include HP, Intel, IBM, Oracle, and Apple.

Bill Hewlett's and Dave Packard's ongoing leadership influence at their company became famous industry-wide as "the HP Way." Both men were egalitarian, inventive, people-oriented, and famous for their personal philanthropy. The HP Way, in turn, was for many years very open, innovative, and socially responsible. However, after many years without the two founders at the helm, the culture at HP is changing. Its original leadership DNA has increasingly less influence as it is countered by the influence of new leaders with slightly—or significantly—different values.

In another example of leadership DNA affecting culture, consider Wind River Systems. Jerry Fiddler and David Wilner, two Berkeley graduates, began Wind River as a two-man consulting firm. Both were free thinkers, highly creative, and exceptionally egalitarian and personal. In response to market potential, they transformed their firm into the dominant real-time software competitor, but at the same time established and retained a unique, Berkeley-esque environment, hot tub and all. Despite their growth, they continued to consult with all employees by mass email when considering key decisions. This kind of open, consultative approach marked the company's creative culture for a long time. However, just as at HP, Wind River company culture is changing. Fiddler and Wilner relinquished their key line-executive roles, and the current culture at the company reflects a mix of original and new.

When founders leave a company relatively early, it is the first long-term leaders who establish the company's leadership DNA. John Morgridge was CEO at Cisco from 1988 to 1996 and is seen as the architect of the company's leadership DNA and the culture that took Cisco to its heights in 2000. Morgridge was a self-effacing, competitive, unassuming leader with strong beliefs and light rhetoric. Cisco's first 15 years, as a result of his leadership style, were marked by an egalitarian culture, strong results and metrics orientation, and technical agnosticism—and new generations of leaders who reinforced this. When John Chambers succeeded Morgridge, he focused on decentralized empowerment, which became a signature element of Cisco's culture during the 1990s.

Later leaders who rise to significant levels of influence can either strengthen or mutate the company's existing leadership DNA and culture through their own hiring choices and the extent to which they coach and develop leaders in a specific direction. Mutation is likely with a new CEO whose behavior demonstrates beliefs and traits different from those engendered by the existing leadership DNA. CEOs, by their ability to affect major long-term decisions, including the hiring of other key executives, are so influential that they can, in and of themselves, affect the quality of a company's leadership DNA. This can work both ways—improving or degrading a company's existing leadership DNA.

New York's Museum of Modern Art (MOMA) provides a non–high-tech example of new leaders affecting leadership DNA and culture. In the case of a museum, because curators have great influence over fundraising and are generally treated almost as if they have academic tenure, their leadership is nearly as influential as the director's:

> Like the art it shows, the museum itself has been going through changes in recent years. Glenn Lowry, the current Director, is a much more activist chief executive than Richard Oldenburg, his predecessor, who ran the place from 1972 to 1995. Oldenburg kept a fairly low profile in his dealings with the curatorial end of things, allowing the department chiefs to perpetuate what had long been described as a system of feudal fiefdoms within the museum. Lowry, an Islamic-art scholar who, in his previous directorial role, had steered the Art Gallery of Ontario through a serious financial crisis, brought considerable skill and energy to bear on breaking down the barriers between MOMA's departments and getting the curators to be more collegial. He also worked to break down the old-boy network, placing more women in top jobs and encouraging the many female members of the staff to believe that their voices were as audible as those of their male colleagues.[6]

Leadership DNA and Other Governance Challenges

In Chapter 1, we introduced the idea that there are four predictable governance challenges great companies face—a culture of learning, leadership DNA, governance systems, and boards of directors oversight—each of which can lead to failure or to competitive advantage. Figure 9–2 shows how leadership DNA relates to each of the other three governance challenges.

Leadership DNA and Governance Systems

Both leadership DNA and culture affect the quality of governance systems. Leaders with core DNA ingredients, for example, because they have an awareness of how the organization succeeds through others, are eager to establish the governance tools that empower others to make decisions well. They do not hoard information or decision-making power. On the other hand, leaders with a tendency toward high control and autocratic decision making are likely to

---

[6] Calvin Thomas, "The Modernist," *New Yorker*, 5 November 2001.

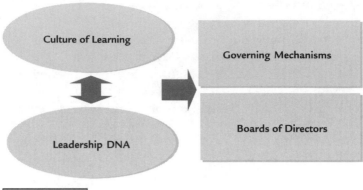

Figure 9–2 Governance Factors and Their Relationships.

develop governance systems that reflect that bias. We discuss governance systems further in Chapter 10.

Leadership DNA and Board of Directors Oversight

A company's leadership DNA is related to its board of directors in two ways. As we said earlier, a startup's board influences the establishment of leadership DNA through the hiring of the company's first CEO. Later in a company's life, its leadership DNA influences the quality of the board, primarily through the ways the CEO interacts with it. (In turn, later stage boards influence leadership DNA by their selection of and influence over the CEO. We explore this further in Chapter 11.)

Too often, by the time a person has made it to the CEO position, learning with humility is something of a distant memory. On the other hand, as we saw in the case of Darwin Smith of Kimberly Clark, some CEOs never lose their propensity to learn and grow. Such hunger for learning will show up in the formation of a board of directors. If CEOs want to learn, they will establish an open culture in which the boards as well as their executive teams are forthright in providing feedback, and they will make sure that they have a board that will be active and critical in support of their learning.

Meeting the Challenge

Once leadership DNA is established in a company, there are two avenues for meeting the challenge of reinforcing the right company leadership DNA—*hiring practices* and *leadership development*.

Hiring Practices

Selecting leaders who will build for the future and reinforce the strengths of a company's leadership DNA is an art—one that we think can be learned. But finding desirable qualities in others, which help perpetuate a company's leadership DNA and culture, depends on the hiring leaders having those qualities themselves. Consider the following description of one Cisco interviewee:

> When I interviewed with Cisco, I interviewed with John Morgridge [the former CEO]. He spent 90 minutes with me. He went down my two-page resume and asked me a question about every line item. Why were you born in Neptune, New Jersey? Why did you go to Wall High School after going to St. Catherine's Grammar School? Why did you become an engineer? Why would you or anyone get a PhD? What is the biggest mistake you ever made? Some answers were no more sophisticated than saying I was born in Neptune, New Jersey, because that's where my mother was and the hospital was. John was listening for the honesty and sincerity of the answer, not a wrong or right answer; he was looking for a key piece of leadership DNA at Cisco—being forthright when challenged.[7]

In asking these questions, John Morgridge was looking for a candidate with the type of authenticity and forthrightness that he himself had and valued. Candidates who have not learned to accept themselves will tend to give the answers that they think the interviewer wants. Their responses will be coated with misplaced irony, too much credit-taking, or false humility. Their focus is often more on what they accomplished than on what they were *part* of accomplishing.

The best measure of authenticity is not analytical evaluation; it is in the *feel* of the experience. It is not in the content of the person's words; it is in their actions, the *way* they handle the conversation. Those who lead with authenticity, service orientation, and a bias for learning recognize those same ingredients in others when they are there.

Leadership Development

In addition to hiring the right leadership DNA from the outside, the core and specialized ingredients can also be *developed*. Leaders engendered by the right kind of leadership DNA help their followers become better than themselves. If existing leaders believe in nurturing leaders for the future, they assemble and promote the essential traits in all who surround them. It is a philosophy that places a priority on leadership *potential*—not on just the latest accomplishment.

---

[7] Obtained from the author.

It is a philosophy of investment in existing employees with that potential rather than one of counting on just-in-time hiring.

Although leadership development should be proactive and deliberate, leaders who develop others also take responsibility for their own learning. In a culture of learning, authentic leaders proactively leverage learning opportunities. They either create them or take full advantage of those offered. This is true of leaders with tenure as well as newly hired leaders. The latter, however, have a unique challenge—learning to be successful in a new environment.

When Cisco decided to pursue the service provider business in 1995, it faced the difficult challenge of integrating a large new set of leaders from two sources. In the extraordinary market growth of the late 1990s and the competition for voice, video, and data transmission, Cisco acquired many small companies with technology leaders. At the same time, Cisco knew it needed the experience and customer knowledge of leaders from the large telecommunications carriers to help build infrastructure and teach Cisco how to operate in the telecommunications customer world. Integrating these two types of leaders into Cisco's particular culture was an enormous challenge.

Sometimes the acquired leaders had the right leadership attributes for Cisco's culture, and sometimes not. Many of the new management hires from the telecommunications world initially failed to adapt successfully to Cisco's culture. Exhibit 9–1 tells the story of how many of those leaders were helped to become successful at Cisco.

Exhibit 9–1: Developing Cultural Fit

A Cisco business unit (BU) leader—let's call him Ben—was concerned about why his team of leaders was not responding to urgent manufacturing problems called "line stops." A line stop is a temporary hold on the production of a product, thus impacting BU revenues. To Ben, whose leadership style was fully in sync with Cisco culture, the only proper response to a line stop was obvious—*all* attention should be given to solving the line stop problem, day or night, until the product was moving again.

Many of his leaders, however, were new hires, recently out of the telecommunications world. To them, this assumption made no sense. Manufacturing had the responsibility for line stops. The involvement of Ben's team members, who were Engineering and Marketing leaders, would not only be of questionable value but would also be interfering in someone else's business. They hadn't

---

grown up in Cisco's horizontal, decentralized organization. Cisco's culture was one in which if something was wrong and affecting your product, you were responsible, no matter where the problem existed.

One way to understand this feature of Cisco's culture is through a vignette told by Dave, a long-time colleague of Ben's. During a staff meeting in his location in southern California, one of Dave's team members complained that he couldn't accomplish a goal because someone in Manufacturing in San Jose (northern California) had not done his part. Dave's response provided a clear sense of Cisco's values in this situation. He asked, "If this problem isn't solved, then what are you doing in this meeting? Why aren't you on a plane on your way to San Jose to get that problem solved?" If a person needed hierarchy and formal authority within which to operate, Cisco was not for them.

Ben had asked for outside help in evaluating the alignment between his new leaders and Cisco's leadership DNA. Could the new leaders become successful in the Cisco culture? With some help, he eventually solved the problem through a series of leadership assessment and development tactics. The thrust of the solution, driven largely by Ben's own avid desire to learn and serve, was the evolution of a leadership model by which he taught and coached his new leaders and held them accountable to do the same. Some made it through the change process; some did not.

He arrived at the solution in the following way. He set out to clarify the leadership characteristics of those leaders who were not only already successful at Cisco but who were also adapting to the changing world required by the emergence of the service provider industry. This was done in the following three steps:

- by a simple clarification of Cisco's cultural drivers—what were the success factors for Cisco leaders?

- by an efficient method of obtaining an evaluation of all the key leaders through a 360-degree quantitative assessment of their capabilities according to these success factors

- by comparing the results of those leaders who were clearly top performers with the results of those who were struggling

From this comparison, Ben could see that there were three categories of performance: basic skills that were baseline for being hired, skills that were uniquely required in the Cisco culture, and skills that Cisco required leaders

Basic Competencies	Cisco Success Competencies	Senior Executive Competencies
• applies relevant technical knowledge for the good of the business • demonstrates an ability to meet difficult schedules while staying within budget • identifies and hires staff to ensure the right competencies exist for organization success and growth • shows a strong problem-solving capability • demonstrates the courage to act with integrity • displays a strong customer orientation	• uses influence rather than position to make things happen—in and out of BU • demonstrates 100 percent ownership of the whole business—gives and receives help readily • drives accountability through the organization fairly and effectively • is forthcoming with important facts, good or bad • is unafraid of authority and respectful of people at all levels • works effectively in uncertain conditions—takes initiative and adapts to changing needs of the business	• provides vision and communicates it effectively • brings order to an environment with chaotic challenges • demonstrates mature behavior as role model • ensures problems are fixed systemically • makes long-term development (people and organization) a priority, despite short-term pressures • provides an environment for others' personal success

Figure E9–1 Cisco Success Model—Leadership Competencies.

to gain as they grew in complexity and sophistication (see Figure E9–1). Each of these categories was given a different weighting, depending on the role of the person being evaluated. The more senior and strategic the role, the more the third category, for instance, was weighted.

Ben and his team used this tool for two purposes: first, as a sort of decoding ring for new leaders to use to learn what behaviors led to success at Cisco; and second, to promote discussion and self-assessment for new and existing leaders—separate from formal performance evaluations. It allowed leaders to determine their own suitability to the culture and to identify specific ways they could serve the business and their people more effectively.

Vital Signs

The evidence of a company's leadership DNA is in how its key leaders act, especially with regard to developing other leaders. Internal vital signs for a company's leadership DNA are not in what leaders say but in what they do and how that affects others. Figure 9–3 lists the key points of core leadership DNA as well as the external indicators and internal vital signs that indicate the lack of leadership DNA.

A Call to Action

The primary way a company can successfully scale and adapt is to focus on the quality of leadership. Are enough leaders with the appropriate value system developing at any one time to scale the company?

Ultimately, the characteristics of leaders that build for the long term—authenticity, service to others, and a bias for learning—result in the kinds of leaders who do the following:

- build emotional connections with people
- build a following and are often seen as natural leaders
- grow themselves as well as others
- achieve and overachieve results

When a company's internal vital signs suggest that these are not the kinds of results accruing from the current leaders, it is time to take action. If the signs apply to a very small percentage of a company's leaders, the problem is one of individual performance, which can be handled on an individual level. However, if the vital signs listed in Figure 9–3 are *typical* in the company, there is a problem in the company's leadership DNA, an emerging thread of failure. The problem, then, is likely to be especially difficult, as it rests in the quality of leaders currently in place. This is why establishing the right kind of leadership DNA from a company's inception is so critical. If a leadership DNA problem does exist, the solution will have to come from the top, possibly even from the board of directors. Assignment of responsibility to diagnose and solve an endemic leadership problem is essential before it becomes a long-term drain on success.

The Challenge	Creating a Healthy Leadership DNA
Key Points	• authenticity • orientation to service • bias for learning • success built on people first, then vision and strategy • leaders who coach and teach
External Indicators or Existing Problems	• difficulty in attracting seasoned, successful leaders • leadership churn (turnover)
Vital Signs Indicating Potential Perils	• focus on personal ambition over common goals • inability of leaders to build a following • leadership behavior that blocks learning in the organization • inability of leaders to scale with company growth • lack of interest in and response to developmental efforts ("no time" for development) • unproductive competition between leaders

Figure 9-3 Leadership DNA.

1. What are the most typical behaviors you see in your company's leaders?

   • listening? advocating? a balance?

   • coaching and teaching?

   • inspiring and helping? or mainly doing?

   • timely weeding out of misfits or avoiding the tough calls?

   • humility or hubris?

   • strong lateral relationships or active infighting?

2. How fast are the leaders scaling?

   • How fast are the current leaders expanding their capabilities to meet new and larger challenges?

   • How quickly are leaders ready for broader and higher positions?

3. How confidently and soundly do they make decisions?

   • What is their track record in making tough decisions?

   • How good is their timing in making decisions?

4. How consistently do their words fit their actions? Is their self-image consistent with others' views of them?

5. How readily do they admit errors?

   • How willingly do they bring forth bad news when it is there?

   • How do they handle their own mistakes and others'?

6. What are they learning? What are the indicators of their learning?

10
Governance Systems

Overview

- The increasingly complex environment of a successful company requires more formal or systematic means of governance than culture and leadership DNA alone can provide.

- Governance systems, however, often develop into a thread of failure when they are not well executed.

- The purpose of effective governing systems is to ensure good governance decision making based on good information.

- Good information is provided by built-in, active feedback loops. Good decisions are reached through disciplined use of that information.

- The right kinds of governance systems can ensure empowerment—information, decision making, and accountability in the right hands.

Jim Frank is a CEO faced with a tough decision about his company's strategy. A recent announcement by a competitor brings the situation to a head. Jim thinks he knows the right way to go but needs the executive team's buy-in. The wrong decision could lead to some very uncomfortable conversations with the board of directors . . . or worse, a public fiasco. Whichever way he goes, one or more key projects will likely be terminated, threatening both careers and livelihoods. Some of the executives he is about to consult have tied their reputations to the projects they are sponsoring.

Jim explains the situation to the team and suggests they do some homework and bring their arguments to a meeting a few days later. During the intervening week, the team members spend time collecting data for their arguments and lobbying each other as well as Jim. In these various one-on-one encounters, the executives figure out the political landscape. If their efforts to influence people to support their own projects fall short, they shift to making sure they understand Jim's views and to figuring out how to align with those. A few deals are cut, and by the time the team comes together the following week, the outcome is essentially a fait accompli. Each executive has a "safe" argument to support the predictable outcome.

Although the ultimate decision—a key moment in the company's governance—is one everyone agrees to, it is also one with significant potential for failure. The executives' primary goal has been their own safety—first in trying to preserve the projects they are already sponsoring and then in aligning with the winds of power— not in getting to the best answer to beat the competition.

Many questions can be asked to explore the inherent problems in this scenario:

- Why was the CEO the one calling the question about the product? Why did another executive closer to the problem not raise the issue?

- Why was the decision on the table only *after* a competitor's announcement?

- Who had the most information to make the right decision?

- What were the grounds of the arguments that differed from the CEO's?

- What were the important facts, and how were they used?

- What could have been learned by a freewheeling, open discussion of the pros and cons of the situation?

A Second Scenario

Imagine a different CEO grappling with a consistent disparity between the sales forecast and actual revenues. For several quarters in a row the company's revenues have come up short, and the disparity has raised questions at the board level about the capability of the Sales VP. Rumors of "heads rolling" are heard in the hallways. Employees are scared because their stock price is dropping, and they are not sure the organization is being run well enough to fix the problem. The CEO knows that if the problem does not get fixed, she will be next on the board's list.

The CEO has tried pushing the Sales VP, to the point of threatening him, but things have not improved. The Sales VP has yelled at Marketing about the forecasting process and at Engineering about the product, which was not shipped on time. Still, the revenues come in significantly under forecast. The best answer that the Sales VP can come up with is to "sandbag" his forecast even more than before, thus lowering the company's sights for growth.

Again, such a scenario raises critical questions:

- Who should be accountable for an accurate forecast?
- Who is responsible to ensure that the forecast is met?
- What measures are being taken to understand the cause of the missed numbers?
- What is the right process to ensure useful and accurate forecasting?

A Third Scenario

Finally, imagine a scenario in which a formal mechanism for reviewing engineering schedules is in place. On a routine basis, Engineering representatives report their progress against the schedule to senior management. Sales and Marketing are concerned about customer expectations; Manufacturing is concerned about parts inventory and production scheduling; and Customer Support needs to develop its resource plans.

Meetings are held regularly, and the data reported are accurate. But the meetings do not seem to *make a difference*. Information that shows that schedules will be missed is explained away. No one raises questions beyond the explanations given. Although the meetings are informative, and each function can go back and adjust its plans to the information provided, schedules continue to slip. No real *governance* comes out of the meeting. No brainstorming is done about how to get on track in the future, no improvements are made to the analysis of the problem, no lessons are learned, and no change occurs. The process is *informational* but not *educational*. The outcome is adjustment, not governance.

Governance System Problems

These three scenarios depict the kinds of corporate problems that governance systems are put in place to address. In each scenario—in both formal and informal settings—we can see a number of problems that result in ineffective governance systems. Examples follow:

- motives of political safety
- decision making driven to the center, away from the customer and local leaders
- clouded sense of accountability
- "silo mentality"
- weakened performance standards
- unconstructive internal competition

However, just because governance systems can become dysfunctional is no reason to avoid them. They are critical to a company's success as complexity increases.

Complexity Drives the Need for Formal Governance Systems

With company growth, the informal governance of culture and the behavior of strong leaders remain critical, but they are insufficient to ensure adequate governance. By Stage 3—when a company is public and has a breadth of products and markets—informal means of ensuring that decision makers have the information they need and that this information is well utilized are simply inadequate. There are too many people, spread across too many geographies, with too many complex tasks to accomplish, to count on informal governance alone. Even if, as happens in great companies, strong leaders decentralize decision making and breed other strong leaders throughout the organization, increasing complexity drives the need for formal methods of data collection, review, and problem solving.

To illustrate this, consider a company that sells products that are mission critical for the customer—a networking company or an e-commerce software house, for instance, that sells products to Schwab, the discount stock trading company. Because Schwab has developed a significant dependency on service to customers over the Internet, the equipment and software that ensures the reliability of that online service has become mission critical for Schwab.

If the vendor for the e-commerce software, for instance, runs into delivery or support problems, it will need to demonstrate exceptionally fast response time in solving the problem or risk loss of a very large customer . . . and some reputation with it. Sometimes in emergency situations, solutions require decisions that run counter to the way the company usually does business. If this kind of exception decision making has to run up the chain of command and then down again, the possibility of fast response is doomed. Speed and customer focus drive the need for local decision making in companies operating in fast-paced markets and offering mission-critical products.

At the same time, *uncoordinated* local decision making can create a kind of centrifugal force in the organization, resulting in problems like internal competition for the same customers and duplicate investment of time and money. A company with many business units can find itself spinning out of control if the well-intentioned entrepreneurial efforts of those units are not coordinated to a larger purpose. Different product groups end up competing for the same customers, products lose interoperability when it's needed, or the company loses the opportunity for a longer term, stronger, and more lucrative solutions approach.

How Effective Governance Systems Work

How can governance systems make the difference and be effective? Silicon Valley is full of engineers who have sought startup environments to get away from bureaucratic governing systems that restrict innovation and are typically associated with size. We believe, however, that although size can create a bias toward bureaucracy, healthy companies can scale to tens of thousands of employees and billions of dollars of revenue efficiently and nonbureaucratically, if they are managed and grown with the right culture and the right kind of governance systems.

Traditional thought suggests that there are two kinds of governing environments that appear at first to be mutually exclusive:[1]

- autonomous, independent, creative, and chaotic environments, like those in small companies or startups
- safe, orderly, dependent, and bureaucratic environments, like those in many large companies

Great companies are, by definition, large and complex. But to succeed in an Internet economy, they cannot afford the viscous creep of bureaucracy. In slower, low-tech economies, large companies can depend primarily on vertical communications—communications up and down the hierarchy of the organization—to provide information. Leaders often know more than their teams, and governance can be achieved by a leader asking "How do I get others to do what I know is right?"

In too many companies, however, that approach does not work. For large companies in faster markets, focus has to be on *lateral* communications—communications across the organization. It is impossible for one leader to know all that is needed to make good decisions. Leaders must ask, "How do I support the *team* in making good decisions?" Teams that can operate efficiently become critically important.

Effective governance systems facilitate lateral communication. For these systems to be effective, however, several key tenets apply, each of which we discuss in detail in following paragraphs.

- Effective governance systems promote *both* local autonomy and enterprise-wide coordination.

- The creative tension that emerges as each organizational function develops operational excellence and gains confidence is natural and can be managed to the advantage of the company.

- Customers are the uniting force in focusing creative tension.

- Feedback loops, which provide critical information from the customer and other external sources, as well as from employees, are the foundation of effective governance systems.

[1] These ideas were first developed by David Bradford and Allen Cohen and published in *Power Up: Transforming Organizations Through Shared Leadership* (Hoboken, NJ: John Wiley & Sons, 1998).

- Rigorous use of the information from useful feedback loops makes governance systems work.

Autonomy *and* Control

To manage complexity, organizations need to promote both local autonomy and enterprise-wide control.

- **autonomy**—to ensure that decisions are made closer to the customer, to promote creativity and innovation, and to provide a motivating environment
- **control**—to ensure coordination and consistent customer satisfaction, quality control, and cost containment

Good governance systems need to promote local autonomy while facilitating the success of the whole enterprise. Business units, regions, and functions are all examples of local organizations that need a sufficient level of autonomy with which to make good decisions. In each case, there is specialized, local knowledge about the business, the customer, and the discipline that requires the unique expertise of the local decision makers. On the other hand, if in each case the local organization goes about its business without an understanding of its impact on the larger enterprise, governance for the good of the whole is lost.

Creative Tension

The inherent conflict in governing for both local and larger ends is less problematic than it might seem. Creative tension is bound to occur between talented and aggressive local builders and any efforts to restrict local actions for the good of company-wide goals. But it is precisely this creative tension that can enhance the quality of decision making. Governance systems that promote both autonomy and coordination take advantage of the creative potential in the inherent conflict. Let's look at an example.

Imagine a business unit management team. As any good team would be, it is passionate about its own products. Information obtained through good feedback loops suggests that the company should accelerate efforts to sell one of the unit's products in a specific market segment. At the same time, it is obvious at an enterprise or line-of-business level that the company needs to balance sales of that same product with a more solutions-oriented approach to the business, involving a multiple product sale.

A complicating factor is that the business unit's leaders are given strong incentives to ensure products sales. Arguments to slow down, coordinate, or share responsibility outside of their unit are likely to be less compelling than the motivation to succeed in the area over which they have direct control. Without the help of good governance systems, these local leaders are not likely to keep in mind the goals of the larger system and remember their part in those goals. However, when a governance system exposes these leaders' dual accountability not only to win locally but also to use their products to help the larger system win *collectively*, they can find their place in making the larger system a greater success—and succeed better themselves in the bargain.

In large, complex companies, local leaders can operationalize this dual accountability by participating on cross-functional teams, sharing responsibility for achieving larger goals and aligning reward systems. But the critical point is that the inherent creative tension between local goals and collective accountability for larger goals can find resolution in customer solutions—achieving outcomes most advantageous to the customer.

Customers as the Unifying Force

Keeping the primary focus on customers helps channel the creative tension between local autonomy and enterprise-wide control. For instance, in establishing new markets, there are what is sometimes called "beachhead customers," who represent the future. These customers can be the unifying force. Rallying around them, focusing a coordinated effort to win them, and measuring success by those collective wins are the kinds of dynamics that distinguish a great company.

Customers are the common denominator in those situations in which local and enterprise-wide goals might otherwise be at apparent odds. Rather than *systems* engineering, this is *customer-insertion engineering*—that is, focusing on how customers embrace a new technology and insert it into a network or market rather than focusing on how to interest customers in a specific product. The approach is to identify the beachhead customers, decompose their issues into local concerns, then rejoin the solutions to those issues to meet the whole customer need.

Feedback Loops

If effective governance systems simultaneously support local autonomy and enterprise-wide interests, and they manage the inherent creative tension, on a practical level, how does this work? Let's examine the two critical elements of effective governance systems in some detail.

- *good information*, obtained through built-in feedback loops that ensure ongoing, useful information

- *rigor and discipline* in bringing the information to the table and using it

Useful information is the lifeblood of constructive governance systems. It has to be collected and distributed regularly and accurately to all relevant organizations to allow them to respond quickly while keeping an eye on larger system goals. Information is provided through a set of well-designed feedback loops. Let's look at this a little more closely.

A feedback loop in great companies is the artery along which crucial data flow. The flow of information comes *into* the company from critical external sources and flows *through* the organization, enhanced by critical internal information. The distribution of information through the organization helps tie together the local and disparate elements of the company with common information. A list of the kinds of information effective governance depends on, as well as the sources of that information, is shown in Figure 10–1.

The most essential feature that makes feedback valuable in any company is that it be provided in a way that depicts *trends over time* and *actual versus planned result*. Information that offers only a current snapshot, no matter how factual, is inadequate.

In great companies, information does not flow through these feedback loops haphazardly. There are disciplined processes and accountabilities to ensure the effective information gathering and evaluation. If a company's culture is a learning culture, its leaders and employees will already be involved in informally gathering and reviewing critical information. Governance mechanisms simply formalize this—that is, they provide *organization* and *predictability* to this informal process across the increasingly complex organization. Individuals are identified as responsible to collect, organize, and report specific kinds of information; time is spent developing critical

Good Information	Key Sources
accurate	**External**
timely	customer accounts
trend-oriented	beachhead customers
unfiltered	emerging as well as existing
evaluative of the past	competition
converted into lessons learned	new technology and standards
helpful to the future	
	Internal
	alignment of local and larger
	system goals
	forecasts vs. actuals
	operations review
	employee satisfaction

Figure 10-1 Elements of Effective Governance Systems.

external and internal relationships to ensure access to and exchange of valuable information; and individuals who need the information have ready access to it.

In an organization with a genuine commitment to customer satisfaction, for instance, employees from the CEO on down will be actively involved in getting customer feedback, and their performance will be measured by it. In such a culture, key leaders and sales people meet frequently with customers to maintain an understanding of their needs at different levels. Others gather survey data and analyze it. And as the company grows, mechanisms are developed to ensure that the approach to gathering feedback is coordinated and put to productive use.

Using the Information with Rigor and Discipline

Although data coming through feedback loops provide valuable information to individuals or units, the information from an interdependent set of individuals or units needs to be coordinated and used for larger purposes. This again requires accountability and predictable, efficient processes.

Even when they are small, great companies establish effective, routine forums to ensure good use of the information. When fed by useful feedback loops and run with discipline and rigor, these forums result in effective governance. The kinds of forums we are talking about include the following:

- customer critical account evaluations
- weekly sales forecast meetings
- operations reviews
- project reviews
- design reviews
- strategic planning offsites

In great companies, these kinds of forums are rigorous in their regularity, in the organization of information for reporting, and in the objective evaluation of the information presented. Through the expectations established by this rigor, leaders learn and accountability is enhanced. Accountability is not about blame. It is a function of good information. What is the goal? Who is accountable? What happened? What can be learned? What is the corrective action to be taken? How should responsibility for what happened be addressed? Who is responsible for next steps? This kind of objective approach to accountability is essential for an environment to be motivating to high performers and a source of learning to everyone.

Given the right agenda, real governance is achieved through effective *leadership behavior* in the meeting, which drives the right processes—processes that promote learning and open problem solving. This is where discipline comes in. In the third scenario at the beginning of this chapter, we described a situation in which the company had regular forums but not much came out of them. In our experience, this is all too typical. To make forums useful, an atmosphere of *openness* and *frank exchange* must be promoted and reinforced. If this doesn't come naturally in the culture, it takes careful attention to the process. Effective governance ensures this kind of frank exchange to make the most of the information that is available. All too often in business forums, the participants offer their points of view, but it is more like a series of monologues than an exchange. When true exchange of information happens, mutual influence occurs. People learn and change their perspectives in a positive direction if the exchange is healthy. Better solutions are found. Better decisions are made.

1. Consider the following list of desirable outcomes of high-quality governance systems:

   • problems defined

   • weak points discovered

   • accountability exposed

   • potential solutions developed

   • lessons learned to be applied to future situations

   • good decisions made

   Think of a governance forum in your company. Are these outcomes achieved?

2. If the answer is "no" or "not enough," it is time to revamp the forums. If you are the leader, make the changes and get others involved in executing those changes. If you are a participant, find an effective way to point out the problems and recommend changes. Take the risk to make improvements.

Teams or groups of people in meetings often avoid this kind of real exchange for various reasons. Sometimes the implicit "norms" in the culture are not supportive of open disagreement. People are sometimes afraid they will get mired in conflict rather than reach constructive conclusions. Often, participants want to avoid subjecting their points of view to debate and influence. Constructive dialogue does improve with practice, but it is primarily a matter of understanding what it takes and being willing to try it. Figure 10–2 suggests the elements of what it takes—the kind of data and behaviors that make interpersonal exchange productive. Productive results will, in turn, reinforce the behavior.

Recommended Reading

Peter Senge, "Team Learning," in *The Fifth Discipline* (New York: Doubleday, 1990), pp. 233–272.

Data to Feed Dialogue	Behaviors That Make Dialogue Productive
• facts (e.g., real numbers) • realistic estimates • clear logic chains • competitive analyses • descriptions of applicable personal experience • perceptions, defined as such • opinions/attitudes, so defined • personal reactions	• suspension of role/status—acting with a sense of joint accountability, no matter what your role • speaking objectively and frankly based on concerns for the right outcomes, not for political safety • listening for new perspectives • building on others' ideas • respecting differences • balancing inquiry and advocacy • focusing on learning—discovering the next level of understanding

Figure 10–2   Data and Dialogue.

A final point about rigor and discipline—although effective governance mechanisms solve problems and ensure goal achievement, they can go one step further. In addition to solving today's problems, they can contribute to solving tomorrow's by being *teaching forums*. To be more specific, consider a group of people involved in a meeting designed to assess results and solve problems. They can operate based on today's realities, use factual data, rigorously review it, share in the problem-solving process, and walk away with useful outcomes. However, this same group can also use the same forum to move to a second level of advantage. In addition to solving problems, they can jointly mine the learnings available from the information and how it was reviewed, *including the way they tackled the problem*. This is how a learning culture is formalized in effective governance systems.

An Example of Successful Informational Forums

Cisco developed a strong culture of learning through its focus on measurement and rigorous operations reviews with decentralized and cross-functional accountability. As the company grew, the expectation of regular, fact-based reviews of progress by individual organizations became built in.

New leaders encountered this expectation immediately. Their calendars automatically included the key operations review dates, and templates identifying the information required in ops reviews were supplied from a leader's employment start date. If a new director or vice president were assigned an assistant who had worked for any period of time at Cisco, the assistant knew the ropes about ops reviews and helped the newcomer understand the expectations.

The network of ops reviews ran both horizontally and vertically. The horizontal thread was that a business unit ops review would cover not only marketing and R&D information but also relevant information on sales, manufacturing, and support issues impacting the unit's revenues. The vertical thread was that ops reviews were required at every level in the organization. If a BU was large enough that the leader could not stay on top of all the information daily, that leader held ops reviews to scrutinize the local information, which was then summarized at the BU level to be reported up to the line-of-business level. Line-of-business leaders held ops reviews to hear reports from the business unit leaders and to consider and discuss cross-BU issues. Meanwhile, leads for Manufacturing, Customer Advocacy (Services and Support), and administrative functions held reviews to ensure fact-based scrutiny and governance in their areas. Finally, John Morgridge and John Chambers, during each of their tenures as CEO, held operational reviews to study and discuss the information that migrated up through all the company's organizations.

Perhaps the most notable aspect of the company ops reviews was the teaching orientation. The audiences for the data-driven reviews were cross-functional, so that learnings extended beyond one's own area. At the close of each CEO review, John Chambers summarized results he deemed excellent and identified areas for improvement. Experiments were recognized, failures admitted, and lessons learned noted. A culture emerged that had a bias toward action, a bias toward risk taking, and a bias toward learning.

Governance Systems and Culture

As can be seen in Figure 10–3 (similar to Figure 9–2), a culture of learning and leadership DNA guide the quality of governance systems. In this version of the figure, we show a two-way arrow, not

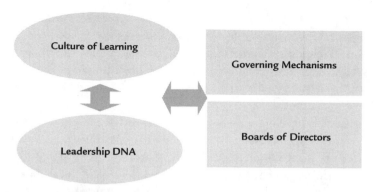

Culture of Learning

Governing Mechanisms

Leadership DNA

Boards of Directors

Figure 10-3 Governing Challenges and Their Relationships.

only between leadership DNA and culture but also between these first two governing solutions and governing *systems*. We want to enrich the point made in Chapter 9—not only can leadership DNA and a culture of learning lead to the development of high-quality governance systems, but governance systems can also strengthen (or weaken) culture and attract (or repel) certain kinds of leaders.

Look again at the list shown earlier of the results that can accrue from dysfunctional governance systems:

- motives of political safety

- decision making driven to the center, away from the customer and local leaders

- clouded sense of accountability

- "silo mentality"

- weakened performance standards

- unconstructive internal competition

Each of these examples implies cultural problems. Although effective governance systems are important to ensure good decisions, they are also critical in promoting the kind of culture that attracts creative decision makers. As we discussed earlier, people leave larger organizations to retrieve a sense of autonomy in their work and feel more independence from hierarchy. Many leave growing companies feeling a loss of the autonomy they experienced in earlier stages of company growth. The assumption is that because growth and complexity necessitate controls to drive consistency through the organization, local autonomy will necessarily be diminished. If, however, controls consist of good information in the hands of local decision makers, where accountability is motivating and a team process ensures coordination for larger purposes, creative employees can find it satisfying to stay with great companies as those companies grow.

In addition, new leaders learn implicitly from the structure and process of governance. They learn how important accountability is in the organization, whether open exchange and argument are valued or suppressed, and the importance of the quality of data and analysis. They learn about the company's attitude toward self-critique and learning. In return, effective governance systems demand the right company leadership DNA. In a great company, leaders have to show unit integrity, be prepared for any other leader to be the hero of a specific battle and pass the ball when needed, to achieve wins for the larger organization.

To make governance systems effective, a culture in which conflict is addressed openly is essential. Strategic leaders who can articulate internal conflict are necessary to ensure rapid resolution. Skill on the part of the leader to whom escalations come if issues cannot be worked out laterally is critical. Conflict management that breeds "favorites" or winners and losers will only feed the motives of political safety (and dysfunctional governance) rather than customer success.

In addition, rewards—both formal and informal—which are key aspects of a culture and an element of governance themselves, must be aligned with the dual goals of local and company-wide concerns. Governance in a learning culture—one that is constantly open to employee feedback, that experiments thoughtfully, and that is rigorous about analyzing how things are really going—will find the right reward system and keep it current with company needs.

Vital Signs

The outcomes of high-quality governance systems can be monitored. Effective outcomes include the following:

- problems defined
- weak points discovered
- accountability exposed
- potential solutions developed
- lessons learned and applied to future situations
- good decisions made

The Challenge	Formalizing the Governing Tools to Manage Complexity
Key Points	• autonomy *and* coordination • customers as the unifying force • rigorous and disciplined use of good information • exposing accountability
External Indicators or Existing Problems	• falling behind the competition with technology • too many critical customer accounts • missed schedules • forecasts greater than actuals
Vital Signs Indicating Potential Perils	• organization "thrash"— decisions made inefficiently or made and remade • glare conditions—the inability to see problems and get them solved • decision making based on "how we've done it before" • no predictable flow of data from customers and the field • lack of routine events for assessment and self-critique • lack of active give-and-take argument and learning in those events

Figure 10–4 Governance Systems.

A summary of the key points, external indicators, and vital signs, which are early indicators of failure due to dysfunctional governance systmes, are listed in Figure 10–4.

Summary

Good governance systems are not about autocratic control; they are about constantly renewed information in the hands of the right decision makers. They ensure distribution of information through the organization to those who are in the best position to coordinate and

1. Consider the idea of organization thrash, exemplified by the following:

   - the same decisions made over and over

   - decisions not getting made

   - slow decision making

   a. When and where have you seen organization thrash?

   b. What is at the heart of it?

   - lack of good information?

   - lack of clear understanding of the critical nature of getting the decision made?

   - lack of clear accountability?

   - some other root cause?

   c. How can you determine the root cause?

   d. How will you know you've solved the problem?

2. Look at the other vital signs of dysfunctional governance systems.

   a. Which of these vital signs concern you the most?

   b. How are your current governing systems helping or hurting?

   c. Does the company have the right ones in place? Too many? Too few?

   d. In what way could they be more effective?

deliver. Through feedback loops at all levels, good governance systems inform decision makers and expose accountability. Multiple minds assess data. As a result, experiments based on accurate information can be planned and implemented. Feedback on how experiments are working is built in. Expectations of learning and change can be made explicit. Ownership and accountability are exposed, motivating strong performers. Collective intelligence is developed and commonality of purpose assured. Good governance systems neutralize complexity.

11
Board of Directors Oversight

Overview

- In Stage 1 of a company's growth, the oversight provided by a board of directors is typically an active part of a company's governance.

- In later stages, board oversight is a "lagging" governance tool, a backstop to the leading tools of a learning culture, leadership DNA, and internal governance mechanisms.

- At all stages, board members' attention to the business of a company is often diluted. Thus, board oversight can be reactive when it most needs to be proactive.

- In addition, CEOs too often select board members who see the world in the same way that they do, rather than in ways that complement and challenge their own views.

- The changes in business climate caused by the business failures of 2002 demonstrate that boards must embrace a stronger model.

- We suggest solutions to strengthen board oversight, especially in later stages of a company's life, when complexity drives exceptionally high risk.

We live in a time when it is imperative that corporate boards learn to embrace discipline or else government intervention will choke what can be an excellent system for economic growth. It is not just the independence of board operations that is at risk. More important, the management and board failures we have witnessed in the early years of the twenty-first century threaten the system that has been the foundation of the Information Age. This system allows large, established companies that manage operating capital well to focus on long-term growth while venture-backed companies and privately financed small businesses develop new ideas and bring them to the marketplace rapidly.

Neither of these elements of the system can do both well, and without both elements, the marketplace that makes jobs and creates the foundation of economic stability will be weakened. It is not the *system* that has been in error. Rather, it is the failure of a few human beings in positions to impact many others, without the *right kind of oversight* in place, that has been in error.

An example of proposed legislation that could hurt this system is the expensing of stock options. The innovation of stock options as a part of employee compensation originated with Robert Noyce (a founder of Intel and a Silicon Valley pioneer), who brought it to the technology community to promote employee ownership, risk taking, and a focus on the future. This was in contrast to the structure of compensation in larger, established companies that paid pensions and dividends, based on the past.

We believe that the system, which takes advantage of the strengths of both of these kinds of companies, is fundamentally strong and necessary to ensure technological competitiveness in the United States. However, any system can be abused, and the right measures need to be taken to monitor and prevent such abuse. It is with this backdrop that we discuss the dynamics of boards of directors oversight and offer specific ideas about how boards can bring greater discipline to their companies. Great companies discipline themselves rather than waiting for government legislation.

A Board's Evolution, from Startup through Stage 4

Boards have various roles and certain proclivities, based both on the nature of the companies that they serve and the stages those companies are in. Boards are typically proactive with venture-based startups and reactive or lagging in more mature firms.

In startups, boards are often made up of venture capitalists, who are representatives of the initial investors. These boards evaluate the founding CEO, ensure the hiring of a strong leadership team, audit financial results, make sure the strategic direction of the company is clear, and actively select the first CEO's successor, as needed. Through these actions they engender culture and help establish the company's leadership DNA.

Early boards also often help establish the company's business model, as well as define strategies for liquidation, whether through sale or going public (IPO). Sometimes early-stage boards engage in business development with customers to help fast track their investments and encourage stronger valuations. It is because of the level of risk of their investment and (often) the inexperience of startup management teams that these early-stage boards tend to be more proactive than boards of more mature companies.

Once a board has ensured that a professional management team is in place, however, it has to bow out of involvement in the company's day-to-day operations. From this point through Stage 4, the full bloom of a company's success, board oversight rarely involves day-to-day issues but rather focuses on key strategic concerns. Later-stage board oversight tends to be reactive to the recommendations of company leadership, thereby becoming a lagging—and too often weak—governance system.

The Role of a Board of Directors

Boards of directors in all stages can and should play an important role, not only in ensuring governance oversight for a company but also in nurturing the direction and force of a company's momentum. To the public eye, their participation is normally invisible, as a gossamer thread. Yet the role is important—engendering culture and perpetuating leadership DNA while fulfilling their more traditional fiduciary responsibilities of oversight and capital investment.

Board members have a unique perspective on a company, different from that of any of the internal leaders involved. The CEO has a similar vantage point—seeing across all the aspects of the organization and being more or less equally involved in each—but even the CEO cannot see with the eyes of board members. The CEO makes daily decisions impacting the company, and by this greater involvement, necessarily loses some objectivity.

Board oversight plays a crucial role in many areas of corporate health:

- partnering with the CEO and the executive team in evaluating the strategic landscape and envisioning the future
- ensuring the viability of the company's strategy and approving significant shifts in direction or business model
- ensuring operational integrity through audits
- evaluating major capital investments, such as acquisitions
- evaluating CEO performance and ensuring proper succession
- providing a backstop to the CEO's frailties and missteps
- mentoring the CEO and other company leaders

Obviously, the caricature of a board as a rubber stamp, approving any motion that comes before it, reflects the too-often-true case of board members not taking full responsibility for their role. A strong and well-functioning board of directors is needed to *complement* and *challenge* management's views, based on depth and breadth of experience and knowledge.

Weak Board Oversight

All too many examples of weak board oversight exist. Several stories illustrate different ways board oversight can fail. One of the consistent elements in these stories is that although the evidence of impending failure is often apparent, it is often ignored by those closest to it. The importance of the board's role in independent assessment is apparent.

Nonaction in the Face of CEO Failure

In the late 1990s, Lucent had set itself a target of achieving a double-digit, billion-dollar shift in revenue source, moving from voice communications products to data communications products. However, because Lucent's culture had developed in a noncompetitive environment, the speed and nature of the technology shift required was countercultural. Given the company's technology inertia, the new growth target was highly unrealistic. Unfortunately, Lucent's CEO was not able to see past his company's existing mindset, and the board proved itself slow to see the risk.

Despite the fact that Lucent's chosen strategies began to fail publicly, the CEO persisted as executive after executive left the company. After 18 months of executive turnover, shareholder lawsuits, and public embarrassment, the Lucent board finally replaced the CEO. Its action demonstrated one of the axioms of any governing body—Better Late Than Never. But where was the board oversight when a significant portion of the loss could have been prevented?

Evaluating Mergers

Consider again the merger of 3Com and US Robotics, as discussed in Chapter 6. Although some analysts held high hope that this union would bring about unrivaled competition for the likes of Cisco and others, there were board-level considerations that should have called the merger into question. First, the track record of large mergers is inherently poor and bears special scrutiny. In addition, a merger between companies of significantly different cultures and different business models raises serious questions. Last, geographic barriers (northern California versus Illinois) added considerable risk.

Active board members, who see their role as a complement and not just as a support or rubber stamp to the CEO, might have added up these material factors and concluded that this merger had a low probability of success. As history shows, 3Com was never again the same; it has a market cap today that is a fraction of its previous value and that of its former competitors. How well did 3Com's board scrutinize, debate, and challenge management at the point it was presented with the proposed merger?

Lack of Guidance through Difficult Passages

Another example of weak board oversight can be found in Stage 1, in the earliest days of a company's life. As is not uncommon, start-ups can reach a strategic cul de sac and find themselves targets for acquisition. As we discussed in Chapter 6, startup leaders and boards will sometimes pass on early acquisition offers because they believe the value of the company is higher than the offer. If, however, the company has reached a point of no return and its value can only be retrieved through acquisition, waiting for a better offer is a losing game. Strong board oversight can prevent this kind of loss by applying an objective assessment—that is, an independent, informed, and tough evaluation of the situation.

This same point can be seen from another direction. One startup familiar to us was the object of acquisition interest by a large company. However, a number of serious problems were discovered in the due-diligence process—the startup's CEO had been fired, key talent was leaving the company, a recent acquisition had diluted the culture, and there was a lack of consistent leadership DNA. In addition, product development was split across four markets, with declining-to-zero revenues in each. To top it off, additional acquisitions had been approved. Suffice it to say, the acquiring company passed on the opportunity. Earlier offers, which had been rejected, now looked attractive.

Although this startup's board of directors had exercised one of its duties by firing the former CEO and hiring a new one, it clearly had failed to fulfill its guardianship role. It lacked the ability to help the small company focus, stabilize a strong culture, and exercise some hard-nosed financial planning. The fledgling startup's momentum had been squandered. Now this board faced an even greater decision—find a buyer at a price it did not like (in which case some lead investors would lose money) or keep the experiment going and hope for a better day. With valuations near an all-time low as this book is being written, the startup is continuing to struggle with acquisition offers at distress values.

Protecting Shareholder Assets

The year 2002 brought to public light a series of spectacular corporate failures. Most of these were heavily influenced by the recent economic decline and the impact of September 11, 2001. However, Enron represented a company that had simply run amok. Its failure was not just the result of market hubris or bad luck. Could Enron's board of directors have prevented the failure? What was its liability in what was momentarily America's largest bankruptcy and governance scandal? What were individual board members responsible for? How could the head of the board's audit committee, considered one of the top five academic accountants in the United States, have missed the mark so widely? As the size of the impact on small investors was revealed, the public's thirst both to understand what happened and to take revenge grew. How culpable was the board? What punishment should board members incur?

Protection of shareholder value is a board's primary duty. When those assets are put at risk by "creative" management action—*even if those actions temporarily earn the company a great deal of money*—additional levels of scrutiny are in order. Not all new ideas are bad, but the good ones will withstand additional scrutiny. In Enron's case, the board's perspective was clouded by the apparent collusion of the company's auditors. On the other hand, experienced board members who are paying close attention and who ask for enough information to reassure themselves that management practices are sound are likely to find the fly in the ointment if it is there.

Strong board oversight, at any stage of a company's life, is one with *engaged* members, who see their role as *complementary* rather than subordinate to the CEO and who have the *courage to act* when needed. This is particularly poignant when the risks—and losses—are high. One expert board watcher described the pressures on Enron's board members by pointing out the following:

> When a company is booming in the capital market, it takes a tremendous amount of courage, a tremendous amount of bravado, a person with thick skin to say, "Hey, wait a minute, stop this train, this thing is an illusion, it is not right."[1]

Why Is Board Oversight Often Weak?

Too often, boards do not engage fully in their oversight role. As a result, they add to its company's potential for failure instead of preventing it. Weak board oversight, however, may exist at successful companies for many years. This can work as long as that company faces no sharp turns in the road that the CEO and executive team cannot handle. However, as history shows, that condition will not always hold.

There are a number of reasons why board oversight tends to be weak, including the fact that board members

- do not see their board roles as their primary job (except possibly for venture capitalists, although they tend to be on so many boards, no one board is central to their sense of purpose)

- have a level of ownership in the company that is not a big enough factor in their financial portfolio for the sense of risk to drive more serious involvement

---

[1] Kathleen Pender, "Ex-dean of Stanford Business School Led Enron Audit Panel," *San Francisco Chronicle*, 7 February 2002, Business Section.

- have been chosen because they are friends of the CEO and mis-understand that to mean "don't disagree with the CEO" . . . at least not in the "public" forum of board meetings

- have been selected for cosmetic (celebrity) rather than substantive reasons

- can act as if they are part of a board "fraternity" (i.e., "I'll be on your board, you be on mine"), whose rules are more about not making waves than about making a difference (e.g., venture capitalists working as board members for several companies, which they hope will become partners or customers of one another in the future)

However, the new world of board exposure in the wake of the failures in 2002 will—and should—create pressure to change these typical dynamics.

Antidotes

We believe there are a number of actions boards can take to strengthen their oversight.

Board Subcommittees

Board subcommittees are standard elements of a board structure. In fact, it is at the subcommittee level that much of the real work of board oversight really occurs. When committees do real work, they are likely to bring forward issues or positions that cause tension at the board level. Boards must respect and *take advantage* of the potential in this tension to provide real help to the company.

To accomplish the real work, every board needs at least the following activity areas or committees, each with the focus described:

- compensation subcommittee—compensation decisions and benchmarking for the CEO and key officers, and the compensation structure for employees

- audit subcommittee—the nature, reporting, and compliance of accounting practices

- corporate governance—roles, policies, and execution of corporate authority

- corporate development—the initiatives that drive corporate futures, including but not limited to mergers and acquisitions

Most critically, each of these subcommittees should serve the shareholders by ensuring that the right discussions, fact-based considerations, and decisions *are reviewed and made visible.*

New Policies

It goes without saying that in the post-1996 stock market surge and the ensuing economic decline, there are numerous practices that should be assessed, inventoried, and abated by corporate boards:

- **Both private company boards and regulators should insist on sound criteria before allowing a company to go public.** Prior to 1997, it was typical for startup companies to achieve at least three quarters of profitability and other positive business metrics before successfully executing an IPO. At this point, the management team had produced a minimum level of predictability, the market was well enough developed to have a reliable future, and the public could invest without undue risk. However, by 1999—this criterion for going public having been long abandoned—companies were going IPO before they had a product in the market, before profitability was achieved, and often with incestuous customer endorsements (explained next).

- **Financially motivated customer endorsements should be heavily discounted or even outlawed.** During the post-1996 economic boom, startup companies in the telecommunications industry increasingly offered larger telecom companies and influential individuals in those companies stock options, "friends and family" stock, and pre-IPO stock positions. This meant that if the larger company made an endorsement of the startup company's product, it (and any individual "beneficiaries") would receive accelerated stock and/or option appreciation if the startup were successful. This option appreciation could more than pay for a telecom company's equipment expenditure. For the individual in the company, this meant the potential for substantial personal gain. Although it is apparent that this practice leads to the wrong behaviors, the approach was not unusual.

This approach was exceptionally toxic because it not only led to risks taken without regard to what was best for shareholders, it also created a *culture* focused on the following:

- pursuit of personal gain over shareholder long-term value

- acceptance of false valuing of startup companies, based on the appearance of greater customer and market traction than is real

- distortion of the market's sense of value creation reached by a new company.

In addition to independent board action, we also recommend that the SEC requires boards to make visible stock and stock options approved for customers or individuals that work for customers. Investors could then appropriately discount the extent of the new company's traction in the market. In addition, companies could be asked to produce their own policy and disclosure requirements surrounding this kind of activity. A more extreme approach from the government would be to outlaw this conduct altogether.

- **Boards should ensure that revenue recognition is driven by real absorption and product use.** During the post-1996 Internet boom, some companies counted revenues that were not associated with customers' real use of products. One form of this is classically called "channel stuffing"—that is, the recognition by a company of sales of product to a channel partner who, in turn, *holds* that inventory without a final sale to an end-use customer. When this occurs, a company *appears* to have revenues and the market *appears* to be growing at a faster pace than is real. Another form of counting revenues before they are real is in the sale of software licenses to customers far in advance of the real use of that software by the end-user community. Accounting practices that allow acknowledgment of revenues on a "sell-through" basis, rather than on the basis of actual absorption or use of a product by real customers, should not be allowed.

- **Boards should ensure reported revenue is not based on revenue swapping.** Another practice that some companies have embraced involves one company buying something from the first company if the first company buys something from the other. These end-of-quarter strategies designed to create the *appearance* of reaching revenue goals only create a misleading indication of company and market growth and are inherently unsustainable. Open disclosure of any such transactions is a minimum requirement.

- **A company's statements about the future should be overtly reviewed and approved by boards.** Companies' announcements about the future typically address forecasts of market growth and a company's view of relevant market and economic trends. It is true that a company that consistently makes inaccurate forward-looking statements will eventually be discounted, but both institutional and individual investors can be hurt if at any point in time they invest on the basis of such inaccuracies. Boards have to look at each forward-looking announcement and ensure there is a sound basis for it. What do we know? What do we not know? What assumptions support our business? This practice will encourage more debate and minimize the number of self-promotional predictions.

Although we recognize that this is not a comprehensive list of antidotes, we believe if boards truly *embrace* these kinds of actions and not just comply with those that are mandated by regulatory agencies, the level of market volatility could be genuinely dampened. Companies that act on the basis of genuine concern for shareholders and employees will tend toward more earnest internal disclosure and more effective action. Responsible behavior begets more responsible behavior; whereas the reverse is likely to be true as well. A company that recognizes revenues based on swaps, individual customer incentives, or channel stuffing is more likely to camouflage its operating expense, quarter after quarter, thus distorting profitability, eventually leading to a wall of reckoning.

Too many employees, shareholders, vendors, and others affected by company failures have been disillusioned and hurt financially. This is the purview of boards—their protection. Boards must drive company discipline or else the government will help with blunt instruments that are not likely to benefit an otherwise successful system.

To embrace these kinds of ideas and not just take steps to *appear* stronger, a board may well have to change its culture. Here are some ideas that help in making that kind of change:

- Ensure board diversity, in knowledge as well as interest.

- Discuss and establish mechanisms to ensure the role of board oversight as a feedback loop and a forum for material, productive discussions on critical company business.

- Replace members who operate primarily as rubber stamps.

- Have the board develop and review a record of its decisions—for instance, conducting measurements on the success of acquisitions.

- Ensure that the board conducts a formal, independent assessment of the CEO's performance twice per year in a highly volatile market—once per year in a more predictable market.

- Routinely obtain confidential input from board members to assess their view of their role, of the company's current situation, and of how the board can improve its effectiveness.

- After they have served on the board for one year, assess board members' knowledge of the operation. If they have not demonstrated value after their first 12 months, they are not likely to do so over the next 12. (This can be accomplished by the board chairperson if that person is not the CEO. Here is an example of how the European bias toward appointing non-CEO chairpersons enables a stronger sense of accountability. We believe that U.S. companies would be well served to embrace this approach.)

Vital Signs

How can you tell if a board is strong or weak? As with the other seven challenges that we have discussed in this book, there are internal vital signs that you can be read long before board oversight, if it is becoming a thread of failure, grows to the point of exposure through external indicators. Figure 11–1 includes a list of relevant vital signs.

The Challenge	Building a Board That Takes an Active Role in the Success of the Company
Key Points	• complementing and challenging management • sound policy to drive sound practice • scrutiny where practices are not tried and true • self-scrutiny to improve board effectiveness
External Indicators or Existing Problems	• loss of market share • loss of key acquisition opportunities
Vital Signs Indicating Potential Perils	• little meaningful discussion at board meetings • avoidance of painful reality • little or no argument with management's views • little or no substantive consultation with board members by the CEO • slow board action in the face of tough facts

Figure 11–1   Board of Directors Oversight.

Something to Think About

Based on your answers to the following questions, what are the first two changes you would make to strengthen the board you are evaluating?

1. What improvements has the board made in its functioning, given the lessons learned in corporate failure in 2002?

2. Is there a well-understood set of principles used by the board for assessing the company's operating model, risk tolerance, and acquisition strategy?

3. How clear are the members of the board as to their role? How common are their expectations as to their obligations?

4. What mechanisms are in place to ensure that the board receives and discusses *critical* and *relevant* information?

5. Do the board members raise *important questions* and offer *productive ideas* to encourage building corporate longevity and venture return?

6. Is dialogue at board meetings *lively, open, and candid*? Do board members, including the CEO, ensure that key issues are openly explored and discussed?

7. What happens if a board member raises an uncomfortable issue? Is it skirted or taken "offline"?

8. What challenges has the board posed to the CEO and the leadership team? How often does this happen?

9. What is the track record of board members rubber stamping management's recommendations? (They might agree with management, but have they asked tough questions and insisted on *fact-based, well-researched* arguments before agreeing?)

10. Does the board look beyond strategy and financial data and show concern for internal vital signs that can indicate problems?

11. Is there a dominant logic for the makeup of the board (depth and diversity of expertise, objectivity with regard to the CEO, etc.)?

12. Does the board assess the CEO twice a year?

13. Do board members give the CEO anonymous/collective feedback? How often? What happens if that feedback is ignored?

14. Does the board obtain an assessment of its effectiveness every year?

15. How accountable do board members feel for corporate success? How do you know?

12
Putting It All Together

Overview

- Meeting the four *execution* challenges is essential in achieving dominance, which depends greatly on meeting the four *governance* challenges.

- Furthermore, the challenges are interdependent, and responses to one reinforce the outcome of others, for good or for bad.

- Understanding the predictable challenges as well as monitoring their vital signs are essential in a company's ability to turn them to advantage.

- A review of the thesis of the book summarizes the way complexity can be both exploited to advantage and can also cause failure.

- Constant assessment of vital signs for both individual threads of failure and as a comprehensive review of organizational health is essential.

- Measurement of vital signs should focus on *trends* in the information obtained.

Robert Litan of the Brookings Institute described the Enron debacle this way:

> a massive failure in the governance system. You can look at the system as a series of concentric circles: from management to Directors, and the Audit Committee to regulators and analysts and so forth. This was like a nuclear meltdown where the core melted through all layers.[1]

In this short quote are indications of Enron's complexity, the ingredients of its leadership DNA, and its culture. More implicit is the sense that the company's governance systems were inadequate, its strategies misguided, and its board either complicit in the bad decisions leading to the company's downfall or asleep at the wheel.

In terms of our model, the Enron debacle can be seen not just as a failure of the CEO, the CFO, or the board of directors, but of *all* the governance challenges a company faces—lack of an open, learning culture, poor leadership DNA, inadequate governance systems, and weak board of directors oversight. As we have discussed throughout this book, if one or more of these predictable governance challenges becomes an untreated thread of failure, a company faces serious risk of demise.

Furthermore, if a company isn't able to meet its governance challenges, it increases its risk of not meeting its predictable execution challenges—innovation, poor product transitions, misguided strategy, and misalignment. The ability to meet execution demands *depends on* strong governance capability. And strong execution is the foundation for taking full advantage of the dimensions of complexity.

What might have happened at Enron if there had been a culture, leadership DNA, and governance systems that supported open debate, constant learning, and service to others? In such an environment, it is far more likely that the oversight provided by its board of directors—especially its audit committee linked to independent auditors—could have played more effectively its role as final backstop in a system of checks and balances. Had these governance elements been in place, might they not have led to reliable differentiating strategies, alignment, and other execution successes that enable healthy results?

---

[1] Richard Stevenson and Jeff Gerth, "Multiple Safeguards Failed to Detect Problems at Enron," *New York Times*, 19 January 2002.

That wasn't Enron, however. When its internal checks and balances failed, it is not surprising that the board did not do any better. A company's potential threads of governance failure—weak culture, weak leadership DNA, dysfunctional governance systems, and weak board of directors oversight—are intricately related to each other. And they are linked directly to the execution threads—technology inertia, poor product transitions, misguided strategy, and misalignment. Without a solid governance foundation, execution will fail.

Although the various threads can appear with greater or lesser probability at different phases of a company's life, as we posed in Chapter 2, if one or more threads are left to develop, others follow and then *reinforce each other*. This is especially true in later stages of growth and complexity. Consequently, managing the various risks of complexity simultaneously requires constant discipline and vigilance. More specifically, execution challenges become much more difficult to remediate if governance isn't effectively addressed.

Through the previous eight chapters, we have treated each of the threads of failure individually, referring to only some of the interdependencies. In this chapter, we focus on the interconnections among the challenges and the process of assessing them simultaneously. As we review the basic thesis of this book in the next section, we begin to weave the threads together.

Review of Our Thesis

Complexity is the inevitable result of company growth and success. It is exacerbated by industry shifts and transitions. Complexity can overwhelm both leaders and companies and thus cause corporate health and dominance to be fleeting.

At the same time, complexity can *help* a company achieve competitive advantage and dominance. By understanding complexity and the threads of failure that emerge out of it and then acting on this understanding, a company can turn potential for demise into long-term advantage. Thus, complexity is a double-edged sword— an agent of failure as well as an agent for achieving dominance.

We have attempted in this book to help companies address this doubled-edged challenge more successfully. In Chapter 1 we briefly described a way of *taking advantage of complexity* to effectively beat the competition. For the greater part of this book—for each of the eight predictable challenges—we have discussed turning the inevitable threads of failure to advantage. Let's address these two approaches, again, in order.

Using Complexity to Beat the Competition

As introduced in Chapter 1, we can look at complexity as through a three-dimensional prism, shown here again in Figure 12–1. A company differentiates itself on one or more of these three dimensions:

- product/technology—products or technology positioned to fulfill an unfulfilled need

- sales/distribution reach—efficient access to customers that maximizes customer satisfaction

- economies of scale—achievement of cost structures that are measurably better than the competition's

Substantive differentiation occurs when a company is ahead of the competition on two of the three dimensions—that is, on one of the three possible planes, where a plane is the "surface" between two of the dimensions in Figure 12–1. Innovating on any *one* dimension can create a competitive gap of differentiation but tends to be insufficient for long-term success, at least in highly competitive, fast-changing markets like high-tech. When differentiation occurs

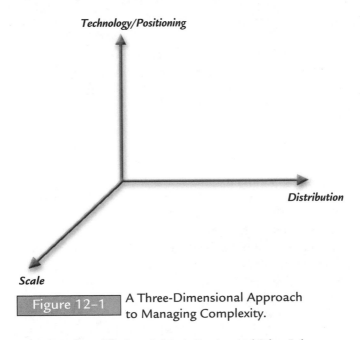

Figure 12–1   A Three-Dimensional Approach to Managing Complexity.

simultaneously on all *three* dimensions, a company enjoys the equivalent of monopoly benefits, as we have all seen in the case of Microsoft. However, this level of success carries its own risks, which is not the case with differentiation on two dimensions (a plane). Market dominance for a company for five years or more (our definition of a "great" company) generally requires ongoing differentiation on at least *two* dimensions—for instance, having greater reach of distribution and greater technical/product advantage.

This "planar" advantage will not be achieved unless a company meets its predictable execution challenges. Dominance through successful exploitation of planar differentiation requires execution excellence. If a company differentiates itself on two dimensions, it will have a differentiating strategy, an aggressive yet pragmatic attitude toward new product development (market disruption), effective product transitions, and sufficient corporate alignment. If the four execution challenges are well met, a company is in a position to take advantage of complexity on two dimensions. And, as we argued previously, meeting these execution challenges rests on strong governance elements throughout the years of success.

Turning the Threads of Failure to Advantage

We have proposed and illustrated eight predictable challenges that great companies face, and we showed how each can become a thread of failure or can be turned to advantage. The potential for failure through weak cultural underpinnings, for instance, is turned to competitive advantage by establishing a strong foundation for a culture of learning.

A company's long-term success starts with the foundation of its culture, which thrives on feedback loops—a constant flow of input, especially from customers and employees—and promotes constant learning. This foundation nurtures a leadership belief system that results in a diverse set of experienced leaders who all identify with that particular culture, who reinforce its strengths, and who grow other leaders to continue the process. This is the company's leadership DNA, which assures development of the right leaders through the company's lifetime—specifically, leaders who are humble; who are oriented to serving customers, employees, and shareholders; who have a bias for learning; and whose style is suited to the market-driven needs of their particular company. A learning culture and learning leaders ensure a constant readiness for change.

As the company grows, this learning environment and the leaders who thrive on and nurture it provide the basis for more formal governing systems, systems capable of ensuring the right flow of information in a more complex environment. The ultimate element of a set of governance systems is the oversight of a strong board of directors.

When these four governance challenges (culture, leadership DNA, governance systems, and board of directors oversight) are well met, a company can face its predictable execution challenges (innovation, product transitions, strategy, and alignment). Furthermore, given an *understanding* of these challenges and their dynamics, each can be turned to advantage.

As we have discussed, technology inertia, often the result of a company resting on the laurels of growth and success, can limit a company's ability to anticipate, lead, and adapt to market changes. However, if the right culture is in place, the leaders who reinforce that culture will be alert to the challenge of inertia. First, their focus on constantly *listening* to feedback helps overcome a tendency toward complacency. Second, their *understanding* of a successful company's tendency toward inertia can ensure that they are watchful for it. If the company is in a fast-paced market with aggressive competition, if its foundation of governing elements is strong, and if its leaders *understand* the dynamics of technology disruption, those leaders will embrace the disruption that is critical for their company to gain a competitive advantage.

Equally challenging and perhaps less well understood are the implications of poor product transitions, which can stall or even depress revenues. Again, the right kind of culture, leaders, and governing systems anticipate this challenge. An established accountability for understanding the dynamics of product transitions can lead to their artful execution so that the effect on current revenue streams is managed and market forces exploited. As logic would suggest, the *double jeopardy* of technology inertia and poor product transitions are not uncommon. Managing both well requires diligent understanding and assessment by leaders equipped with a bias for learning and expert execution knowledge.

Differentiating strategies and alignment, the other two predictable execution challenges, also require constant assessment, learning, and an understanding of their dynamics. We addressed in Chapters 6 and 7 the particular complexities of the dynamics of strategy and alignment, which, as with the other execution challenges, are far more likely to be addressed successfully if the company is meeting its governance challenges well and if the company's leaders understand the dynamics of these particular challenges.

None of this is easy, but it is all possible with the right foundation. Little is possible without the foundational elements of listening and learning and the reinforcing elements of learning leaders, effective governing systems, and strong board oversight. With these foundational elements, however, what companies accomplish in execution is the essence of becoming and remaining dominant.

Meeting the Challenge in Difficult Times

Although we believe that the eight challenges that we have cited in this book are predictable at any time, significant shifts in external circumstances can increase the level of risk. Thus, it is all the more important to understand them for managing through difficult times. To illustrate this, let's look at a specific example.

In 2001, revenues in the computing and telecommunications industries fell dramatically, even though those sectors had led the technology and stock market boom of the late 1990s. Both industries had been on steep growth curves in the 1990s because of the advent of the Internet. The transition from one technology generation to another drove a huge transition of products, services, and revenue streams. Although the greatest part of that boom era was based on solid new technology with long-lived market benefits, some was built on air and when the bust of that part of the market occurred, an enormous contraction occurred for companies in both the computing and telecom industries.

This market shift put additional pressure on these companies' execution challenges. The tendency toward technology inertia became harder to recognize, and product transitions were more difficult to accomplish successfully in declining markets; differentiating strategies were harder to devise when market movement was unfamiliar, and alignment became a greater challenge in shrinking organizations. Furthermore, declining business conditions stressed corporate cultures and leadership, especially when companies had to reduce their workforces—some for the first time and some, like Lucent and Nortel, to the level of less than half their employees.

In good conditions or bad, the predictable challenges are unavoidable. Under more difficult circumstances the pressures of those challenges are simply greater. The challenges result from the inevitable complexity that results from growth, and complexity itself can increase with large external shifts in technology and market economies.

Vital Signs Assessment

Figure 12–2 compiles the vital signs of all eight challenges that we discussed in this book.

An essential element of our thesis has been that vital signs— internal early warning signs—are the key to catching the emergence of threads of failure early. The list in Figure 12–2 can serve as a checklist for those interested in assessing how a company is doing relative to the eight challenges. However, reading these vital signs in isolation might not be sufficient. Focusing on the evidence and treatment of one thread at a time does not allow for their interdependence and the ways in which they reinforce each other, for good or ill.

As we said in earlier chapters, although any one thread of failure might not in and of itself result in disaster, a chronic case of not listening and learning will eventually allow multiple threads of failure to coexist and reinforce each other. Over time, this can result in real failure. Recognizing the links between the threads of failure through their common vital signs allows a more comprehensive approach to diagnosis and treatment.

For example, vital signs showing that a company's culture is developing resistances to learning can also suggest that the ability of the company's leadership DNA to grow learning leaders is declining. In this case, do you treat the culture, or do you treat the leadership DNA? Clearly, addressing both can help prevent the growth of multiple distress threads, and improvement in one area can reinforce the other. Addressing only one runs the risk of any gains being eroded by the continued existence of the other thread.

Consider another example in which there are signs of dysfunctional governance systems. Such evidence is also likely to suggest problems in execution, as governance systems are key to guiding execution. Treating governance systems can help, but it would be wise to assess the current state of execution challenges as well and address the likely emerging threads.

The Challenge	Associated Vital Signs
Innovation	• lack of planning for disruption • being surprised by competitors' moves • inflexible market strategy in response to market changes • lack of common understanding of disruption methodology • company culture loathe to partnership • cultural resistance to change
Product Transitions	• lack of explicit product transition planning • no regular postmortems on product transitions • mismatch between actual and planned product absorption rate • inconsistent understanding among leaders of how to make effective product transitions • tendency to introduce new products only into existing markets • little product insertion expertise in the company
Strategy	• glare conditions—the inability to see problems and get them solved • organization thrash—decisions made inefficiently or made and remade • lack of consistent, shared understanding of strategic direction by key leaders • strategic decisions made without critical assessment • lack of multistep strategic plans, including contingency plans • technology "religion"
Alignment	• thrash in the organization—decisions made inefficiently or made and remade • glare conditions—the inability to see problems and get them solved • lack of open feedback loops • lack of cross-functional metrics • mismatched channel capacity and technology potency • restrictive manufacturing processes given product portfolio potential

Figure 12–2 Summary Vital Signs for All Eight Threads of Failure.

The Challenge	Associated Vital Signs
Culture of Learning	• overly cautious decision making • inactive cross-functional exchange • little constructive challenge on critical issues and decisions • haphazard information flow regarding customers, sales, product delivery, and employees • lack of common language and principles about learning culture • employee cynicism
Leadership DNA	• focus on personal ambitions over common goals • inability of leaders to build a following • leadership behavior that blocks learning in the organization • inability of leaders to scale with company growth • lack of interest in and response to developmental efforts ("no time" for development) • unproductive competition between leaders
Governance Systems	• organization thrash—decisions made inefficiently or made and remade • glare conditions—the inability to see problems and get them solved • decision making based on "how we've done it before" • no predictable flow of data from customers and the field • lack of routine events for assessment and self-critique • lack of active give-and-take argument and learning in those events
Boards of Directors	• little meaningful discussion at board meetings • avoidance of painful reality • little or no argument with management's views • little or no substantive consultation with board members by the CEO • slow board action in the face of tough facts

Figure 12–2   continued

Measuring through Vital Signs

Measurement of anything can become a strictly analytical, ultimately meaningless exercise—simply seeking numbers. In our thesis, the importance of measurement comes in the sense of the *journey*—seeking an understanding of a company's ability to stay on course over time:

- Is the leadership team doing what it set out to do?
- Does it gather and use the information it needs regularly?
- How is it using that information?
- Is it responding flexibly and appropriately to outside pressures?

Questions should always probe *trends* or *longitudinal snapshots*:

- Are monthly business metrics improving or getting worse?
- Is the quality of leadership getting better or being eroded over time by the neglect to develop it and by the "cloning" effect, where like hires like?
- Is the culture changing and, if so, in what ways? For better or for worse?
- Are new efforts to install governing systems making a difference? In what ways?

Too often, leaders worry more about the absolute value of a metric and not enough about the *trends* in those metrics. Turning again to the personal health metaphor, if we monitor our weight at any one moment, it will only tell us whether we are in a range identified by experts as healthy. However, watching weight over time allows us to realize whether we are gaining, losing, or staying the same and how close we are to our targeted weight. When we are exposed to information that keeps our attention on the issue, it can be crucial to our long-term health. It is measurement over time—and connecting the dots between those moments in time—that counts.

In the measurement of corporate metrics, it is important to seek an understanding of several key features. By taking frequent readings it is possible to identify whether things are getting better or worse by the following:

- the *direction* in which things are going
- the *biases* that seem to be in place
- the *comparison* of information over time

Taking regular measurements provides the discipline that can allow a great company to continue on its path of greatness and to sustain dominance over time.

An Integrated Approach—A Tool for Diagnosis

Figure 12–3 is a measurement tool, in the form of a questionnaire, that can serve two purposes:

- It can be used informally by leaders, investors, board members, and so on as a checklist by which to regularly evaluate a company's health relative to all the predictable challenges.

- With the addition of quantitative measurement (e.g., a scale of 1 to 5), it could be used formally as a survey instrument to collect data on leaders' and/or employees' views on the existence and strength of vital signs in your company.

Although this questionnaire is based on the full set of vital signs listed in Figure 12–2, it is not organized by the predictable challenges; rather, it is intended to be used in assessing the state of affairs with regard to all eight of the challenges. Probing on individual challenges should be done with the lists of vital signs provided for each challenge in its relevant chapter. The tool in Figure 12–3 is designed for *comprehensive* diagnosis, to accomplish the following three purposes:

- gathering trend information (by establishing a baseline, then re-using it too periodically)

- ensuring accountability for expertise for the predictable challenges

- gathering information on interdependent threads

The order of the questions is purposely random to provoke thinking about the issues from different vantage points.

If the answer to any one of the questions is negative, especially on a trend basis, an investigation of the appropriate challenges is indicated. Where to start looking would depend both on the individual and the collective set of answers. Primary dependencies to be aware of include the following:

- Problems in execution suggest problems in governance.

- Problems with the more formal levels of governance (governance systems and board of directors oversight) suggest problems in culture and leadership DNA.

- Alignment is insufficient without the right strategy, whereas the right strategy cannot be executed efficiently without alignment.

- After an initial product success, further market disruption requires effective product transitions.

Does your company have a way of assessing its organizational health? If not, why? If so, can a tool like Figure 12–3 improve how your company is going about it? Whether this particular tool is the right one for the company with which you're involved isn't the critical issue. What's important is that your company has a way of *assessing its health over time*. Constant measurement of *emerging* problems and coaching the leadership team to focus on them is essential for a great company to maintain its dominance over the long term.

Let's compare a company to a basketball team. All successful coaches watch their teams' vital signs constantly. Aside from the external indicators—points scored, games won and lost, the number of offensive and defensive rebounds, the number of turnovers, shot percentages, time with possession, and so on—these leaders also watch internal vital signs: the attitude and health of each player, subtle shifts in the quality of team play, energy levels, whether the players are doing their homework, and so on. Good coaches go back to fundamentals to create *biases* that engender success and differentiation. Attending to vital signs allows those biases to be developed sooner and better.

Tenets for Managing Vital Signs

Here is a summary providing several tenets for tracking and following the vital signs that we discussed at various points in this book:

- **Don't wait for external indicators.** Measure vital signs regularly. Start early, and make this measurement part of the corporate culture—an expectation of all leaders.

Vital Signs Questionnaire

1. How seriously does the leadership team take the idea of recognizing predictable challenges and being ready for them?

2. How well do new leaders develop a following of team members?

3. How much glare exists in the organization—the inability to see problems and get them solved? Is it getting better or worse?

4. To what extent do leaders tend to rest on the laurels of past successes?

5. How often does the leadership team spend time mining the learnings from failures and successes? What signs are there of learning?

6. To what extent are decisions made on the basis of well-analyzed facts?

7. How open is the dialogue when leaders are making decisions involving significant risk?

8. To what extent do actual results match planned results?

9. How efficiently are decisions made? Are they made and remade? Does it take too long for decisions to get made?

10. How well did the last product transition meet predicted results?

11. How often does the leadership team review plans for the execution challenges?
    - innovation
    - product transitions
    - differentiating strategy
    - alignment

12. How active is the exchange of useful information cross-functionally?

13. How often are leaders surprised by competitors' moves? Is this getting better or worse?

14. How disciplined is information flow regarding customers, sales, product delivery, and employees?

15. Is there a common understanding about predictable challenges and how to meet them?

16. What systems are in place to integrate new leaders into the culture and teach them how to lead in this environment? How well are these systems used?

Figure 12–3   A Comprehensive Diagnostic Tool.

17. To what extent do leaders grow to meet changing company requirements?

18. How much Brownian motion is there—activity disproportionate to progress?

19. How disciplined is the team in holding routine forums for assessment and self-critique?

20. What expertise is in place with regard to each challenge?
    - innovation
    - product transitions
    - differentiating strategy
    - alignment
    - learning culture
    - leadership DNA
    - governance systems
    - board of directors oversight

21. How productive are the major governance forums? How many "tourists" are there in these sessions? Does learning occur?

22. Do metrics focus on functional results or cross-functional results?

23. How is alignment being measured?

24. How much meaningful discussion goes on at board meetings? To what extent are real issues discussed?

25. Are changes in plans driven by internal or external pressures?

26. How much open dialogue about management's views occurs at board meetings?

27. How open and freewheeling are debates about important issues? Do people learn in these exchanges?

Figure 12-3 continued

- **Understand the predictable challenges.** Don't wait to learn about problems after they arise. Consider the merits of the idea we pose in this book—that many of the most powerful challenges, which can become either dangers or opportunities, are predictable. Understand them before they emerge.

- **Develop an intuitive "feel" for each challenge.** Many of the vital signs we suggest in this book and repeat in this chapter can be "felt" as well as measured—the level of openness in debate, the amount of cross-functional "ventilation" or communication, and so on. Develop your intuition by both studying the nature of these challenges and paying attention to their vital signs, then follow this intuitive sense of things with more analytical measurement.

- **Focus on trends in measuring.** Measurement is essential but don't measure threads in isolation or at one moment in time. Measure *trends*.

- **Ensure accountability of expertise for predictable challenges.** As with personal health, frequent assessment is necessary (in a fast-paced environment, about quarterly is best), using the company's vital signs. To make this responsibility real for leaders, formal accountabilities should be established. Leaders must be actively coached for the task and held accountable if and when they lose their ability to learn, adapt, and propel the company forward.

- **Recognize the interdependency of threads of failure.** Don't think about and measure vital signs in isolation. Recognize the ways in which they affect and reinforce each other. Use the vital signs of one thread of failure to learn about other potential threads of failure.

The Last Word

We hope you've found reading this book to be informative, thought provoking, and useful. We have tried to challenge your thinking with fresh observations, theories, and questions that we believe are both complementary and contrary to some of the best writings of the day on this topic. As a result of publishing this material, we hope that more great companies continue to Go the Distance, meeting their demise only in natural old age and avoiding the all-to-frequent threat of fleeting dominance.

Appendix
Background to Chapter 5: Product Transition Case Study

The following material serves as background to the case study in Chapter 5, Product Transitions—"A Successful Product Transition and the Lessons Learned: A Case Study."

Background: Cisco's Product Transition History

Cisco began by selling high-end routers that served as part of the network "backbone" for large companies. These large routers, called the 7R family, commanded very high margins.

In the early 1990s, Cisco struggled with whether to make smaller routers that could be sold to small businesses and to the regional/remote offices of larger businesses. There was not an obvious answer to this question. The market opportunity was huge, but the smaller routers could also reduce Cisco's overall margins and hurt its market capitalization.

Cisco did decide to expand its router product lines, and by 1992 it had introduced the 4R series, a cost-effective router for regional and branch-office environments. Then, in 1994, Cisco introduced the 2R series, a low-end router for very small satellite offices and price-sensitive customers. As it turned out, Cisco was able to achieve strong margins on the sales of these less expensive routers, similarly to those it had achieved on its larger scale products. Eventually, the smaller 4R and 2R routers accounted for 33 percent of Cisco's revenues.

This successful product transition was an application of Cisco's strategy for transitions from one generation to another of its large router products. The company would introduce a new class of products at a particular price point and then raise the average sales price (ASP) of that class based on new software and hardware improvements. After a successful introduction, Cisco would then introduce another new class of products, at a relatively low price point, with more narrowly scoped functionality. Again, the ASP would be driven up over time on the basis of software and hardware improvements. The lower priced products allowed Cisco to continuously increase market penetration.

By applying this approach in introducing the smaller routers, the 2R and 4R families increased in price/performance over time, as depicted in Figure A–1.

Despite the success of the 2R and 4R router families, however, by 1996 some new challenges had developed that signaled the need for a new approach:

- The 4R family could no longer grow in performance or capacity due to technical limitations.

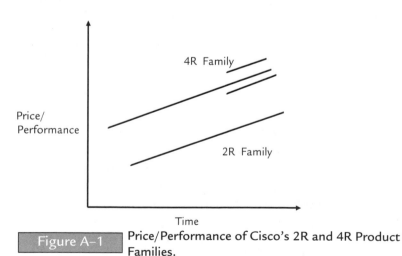

Figure A–1 Price/Performance of Cisco's 2R and 4R Product Families.

- The 2R family, which involved 25 modules, had become onerous for Cisco's distribution channels to manage. These dealers had to inventory all 25 versions of the 2R router to ensure that customers could get what they wanted quickly, an expensive process for a small distributor.

- Development of each of the application-specific 2R modules, done in parallel, had become more costly than it would be to develop a single, modular architecture.

At the same time, new markets and technologies had begun to emerge, providing new opportunities that Cisco did not want to miss. The company had only a minimal presence in these new arenas —the market of individual users who wished to reach a data network (the user access market) and the market for telephone service over data networks (the data telephony market). Previously, Cisco's products had focused only on connecting networks to each other. To gain market share in these new arenas, Cisco's products required greater architectural performance and flexibility. Cisco leaders decided that the solution to these problems was to develop a 3R product family that could be inserted between the 2R and 4R families.

The Development of the User-Access Market

The user-access market developed in a series of phases. The first phase occurred at the "department" level—individual employees, using a modem, could dial from home or satellite offices into their individual department's access server. The next phase in access market development was public dial-in. Individuals could use ISDN lines or modems to dial into a service provider such as AOL, PSINet, and UUNet to reach the Internet. The products that enabled this access were called access concentrators.

From 1995 to 1997, the majority of dial-up traffic was email. Typical users were "road warriors" (traveling employees) dialing into their company's network and sending and receiving email. But by the time Cisco faced the dilemma of adding a new product line to the 4R and 2R families, this usage pattern had begun to change. Increasingly, dial-in users wanted to send and receive various kinds of files—not just text messages—and this required 6 to 10 times the performance of email. In addition, users were beginning to explore conferencing and other video applications.

Access Server Market Share—Early to Mid 1997				
	Mid-range Routers	Low-end Routers	Access Concentrator	Access Servers
Cisco	78%	62%	18%	39%
Next Competitor 1	10%	8%	36%	18%
Next Competitor 2	3%	6%	33%	14%
Market Size in $B	1.197	2.294	1.912	0.451

SOURCE: Instas Routers/Access Server Unit Market Share Quarterly Reports

Figure A–2 Networking Products Market Share in 1997.

Meeting the Competition

By introducing a 3R family of products, Cisco would be offering a much stronger access product that could effectively compete against access specialists such as Ascend, Livingston and Shiva, Bay Networks, and 3Com. Ascend was one of the larger of these companies and was very aggressive in its marketing strategy. It was the first to sell to ISPs and had built their initial infrastructure. Figure A–2 shows market share for the access server market by mid 1997.

As customers began to use the Internet to transfer files and video and not just send email, the Ascend infrastructure installed at the ISPs became increasingly overburdened. This pressure in network usage offered an opening to a competitor who could replace the slower Ascend infrastructure with a product that could handle the higher performance required by the new applications. The Cisco 3R routers offered just such performance.

Sales and Distribution

The distribution channel by which a new product is sold to customers can determine the success of a product transition. Cisco was famous for its knowledgeable, talented sales force, which also provided consulting to its customers. This sales force had such a high degree of technical knowledge that it often knew more about networks than the customer did. Consequently, it could be counted on to influence customers' buying choices. By the time of the 3R product introduction, Cisco had thousands of sales staff in the direct sales force.

However, in addition to using this sales force, Cisco also sold products through Tier 1 integrators—Cisco partners like AT&T, EDS, and Cap Gemini—who both sold and serviced Cisco products, and Tier 2 integrators—the distributors that excelled at fulfillment, like Ingram, Micro, and Tech Data. By 1997, only 16 percent of 2R sales and 15 percent of 4R sales were made through the direct sales channel. The salient characteristics of each channel are compared in Figure A–3.

The sales of a product over its lifetime typically rise, peak, and then decline, making an upside-down U-shaped curve. In the past, with the strength of its influence in the market, Cisco could stretch out a product's sales curve. However, although Cisco had a lot of sway in the market, its use of the Tier 1 channel made it more difficult to influence the rate of absorption of new products. Tier 1 integrators tended to resist new products because of the expense of retraining their small sales forces. The Tier 2 integrators, on the other hand, were more flexible; they did not provide the same level of specialized support, so employee retraining required only a nominal investment.

Let's look at a quantitative way of understanding these dynamics. There are two important measures of influence that distribution channels have over product transitions.

- **Absorption coefficient:** This coefficient represents the fraction of a year that it takes a particular channel to train its sales force,

	Direct Sales	Tier 1 Integration	Tier 2 Integration
2R Sales	16%	72%	12%
4R Sales	15%	79%	6%
Purpose	To create new markets / To provide "high-touch" sales to large accounts	To scale the high-touch sales effort in mainstream (developed) markets	To provide product fulfillment in mature markets; provides brand information and local inventory
Who	Company sales personnel—thousands of account managers	More than 100 large companies who resell with technically knowledgeable sales teams	Houses of distribution with trained phone personnel and calibrated stocking for quick fulfillment

Figure A–3 Channel Characteristics and Share of Router Revenues.

educate the market, and absorb a new product. Based on a one-year outlook, a score of 0.5, for example, means it would take approximately six months (0.5 year) to begin to see real results—that is, quarter-over-quarter growth—in sales of the new products.

- **Disenfranchisement coefficient:** This is a measure of how quickly a channel is likely to stop selling a product. A score of 0.1, for instance, means that in five weeks (0.1 year) an existing product is likely to be stalled in a channel because the channel is now anticipating a new product.

Take, for instance, the situation in which Tier 1 integrators have the most influence over new-product sales. Let's assume that the *absorption* coefficient for Tier 1 integrators related to the new product is very high. This means that the integrators are not likely to be ready to sell the product very soon. In addition, assume the *disenfranchisement* coefficient for the same integrators regarding the same new product is low. This means that the integrators are likely to stop selling the existing product very quickly, most likely because they would be afraid to build up inventory on a product soon to be cannibalized. Clearly, a combination of a high absorption coefficient and a low disenfranchisement coefficient spells disaster for the product vendor.

Let's go back to the real situation Cisco faced with its Tier 1 integrators, the channel with the greatest influence over potential 3R sales. As can be seen in Figure A–4, compared with the direct sales force and Tier 2 integrators, Tier 1 integrators had the highest coefficients for both absorption and disenfranchisement. Although this was not a disaster scenario, it was clear that the risks were high in introducing the 3R products directly into the markets served by the 4R and 2R products.

	Direct Sales	Tier 1 Integration	Tier 2 Integration
Absorption Coefficient	.25-.5	.5-1	.33-1
Disenfranchisement Coefficient	.25-.33	.5-1	.1-.33

Figure A–4   Absorption and Disenfranchisement Coefficients by Channel.

Background to the Choice for the Right Option

In Chapter 5, in the discussion of the 3R router case study, several options were defined before a decision was made. The following material clarifies the reasoning behind the choice of Option C + D.

Historically, Cisco had introduced a new generation of products every 18 to 24 months. Its goal each time was to decrease price by a factor of 2 and to increase performance by a factor of 3, giving a combined price/performance increase of 6 every generation. The 3R product line was no exception to this rule. However, because of the significant price/performance improvement, the insertion of the 3R between the 4R and the 2R would have to be precise, or "surgical," to manage the impact on sales of the existing products.

Figure A–5 shows the intended price/performance positioning of the 3R family. Remember that the 3R product had been designed to provide a price/performance improvement factor of at least 6. As a result, based on this actual position in relation to the existing routers, introduction of the 3R could be managed such that it would strategically cannibalize the 2R family. However, to control the cannibalization impact that the new routers would have on the higher-powered 4R product line, it would be important to introduce the 3R products as having half their real capability. Otherwise, the market would be inclined to move too quickly from the 4R to the less-expensive 3R. If the market perceived that the 3R contained only half its real power, however, it could be

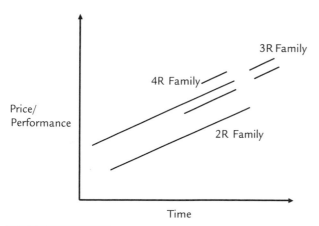

Figure A–5 Intended Positioning of the 3R Family.

managed such that it would gradually, and thus strategically, replace the 4R market.

See Chapter 5, Product Transitions—"A Successful Product Transition and the Lessons Learned: A Case Study"—for the complete case study.

Index

culture, 206–208, 207f
culture of learning, 13–14, 155–164
  vital signs, 13
effective systems, 197–199, 202f
  autonomy *and* control, 199
  creative tension, 199–200
  feedback loops, 201–202
  information utilization (rigor/discipline),
    202–205
  primary focus on customers, 200
governance systems, 15–16
informational forums case example, 205–206
leadership DNA, 14–15, 175–178, 183–184
as perils/opportunities, 4f, 196
  scenario one, 194
  scenario two, 195
  third scenario, 195–196
Graham, Katherine, 175
Growth (organizational), 40f
  and alignment, 131–133
  and challenges, 38–39
  and complexity, 1
  and formal governance systems, 196–197
  and culture maintenance, 166–169
  and momentum, 39
  and recycling, 39
  stage length, 38
  stages of, 21–22
    stage 1/single focus, 22–27
    stage 2/adding products, 27–29
    stage 3/multiple product lines, 29–32
    stage 4/multiple business lines, 33–38

H

Hewlett, William, 22, 175, 181
HP, 94, 174, 175
  AHP Way, 181–182

I

IBM, 61, 62, 181
  and Cisco, 25
  and governance systems, 16
  PC announcement, 72
  proprietary software mistake, 37
  and SNA (systems network architecture),
    52–53, 108
Immelt, Jeff, 175
Inertia, 23
  case example, 24
  learning inertia, 26
Information Age, and market instability, 6
Information gaps, as sign of misalignment, 145
Innovation, 9–10, 51–52
  change categories, 57
  considerations worksheets, 55, 59
  see also Disruptions dimension
Intel, 6, 108, 109, 181
  as disruptor company, 56
Intergraph, 53
Ivester, Doug, 173

J

Jobs, Steve, 10
Juniper Networks, 68, 73, 113

K

Kaufman Footwear (Ontario), 24
KayPro, 72
Kimberly Clark, 176, 184
Kroc, Ray, 23

L

Laws of Market Disruption, 59, 60f
  disruption as structural change driver, 61–62
  driving forces alignment and disruption,
    60–61
  entropy inevitability, 65
  kinetic structures prevail, 62–63, 68
  predictable patterns of opportunity, 63–65
Leadership, 189
  authenticity, 177–178
  case example of developing cultural fit,
    186–188
  considerations worksheet, 191
  development of, 184, 185–186
    hiring practices, 185
  DNA, 14_15, 171, 184f
    and boards of directors oversight, 184
    changes over time, 181–183
    and governance systems, 183–184
    ingredients, 175–176
    specialized ingredients, 179–180, 179f
    vital signs, 189, 190f
  faster environments, 180–181
  leaders as coaches, 162_164, 163f
  learning bias, 178–179
  rock star leaders, 172–173
    alternative focus, 174–175
    rock star focus, 173–174
  service orientation, 178
  slower environments, 180
Litan, Robert, 226
Longaberger, 6, 7, 8f
  as disruptor company, 56
Lowry, Glenn, 183
Lucent Technologies, 7–8, 68, 114, 115,
    150–151, 173
  board oversight/CEO failure, 214–215
  culture challenges, 169
  and TDM technology, 73–74

M

McDonald's, 23
  as disruptor company, 56
McGinn, Rich, 173
Marketing, guerilla marketing, 25
Markets
  dimensions of disruption, 9–10, 54–55, 54f
    technology inertia, 52–53
  physics of, 59
  and turning points, 9

defining direction, 11, 89, 106, 119–121
external indicators/vital signs, 120f, 121
inflexible or fluid vectors, 116–117, 117f
as misdirected vectors, 107, 108f
  make vs. buy, 110–111
  perils of misguided acquisition strategy,
    111–112
  positioning error, 107–108
  undersized/inadequate, 109, 110
  valuation hubris, 109
as self-defeating vectors, 113, 113f
  competing with customer, 115
  pricing errors, 113–115
  waking sleeping giants, 113
shallowly-rooted vectors, 115–116
timing of, 118
as vectors, 106–107, 107f
Structure biases, 29, 131–133
Success, 2
  and complexity relationship, 1
  and future success, 172
SynOptics, 68

T

Tandem, 65
Technology inertia, 9, 52–53, 53f, 230
  vital signs, 68, 69f
Thrash, 12–13
3Com, 139, 142, 215
Tourists, as sign of misalignment, 144
Tupperware, 6

U

UCLA basketball dynasty, 42
Unisys, 61, 65
US Robotics, 111, 139, 142, 215
UUNet, and Ascend, 7

V

Value chain
  mapping by alignment, 129–130, 130f
    in large companies, 130, 131f
    through change, 131
  start-up, 126, 127f
Vital signs, 13, 43–44, 225, 232, 233f–234f
  and alignment issues, 146f
  board of directors oversight, 222, 223f
  considerations worksheet, 49
  of culture of learning, 170, 170f
  developing differentiating strategy, 120f, 121
  formalizing approach toward, 48–49
  governance systems, 208–209, 209f
  in growth stage, 1, 26–27
  internal, 44–45
  leadership DNA, 189, 190f
  management tenets, 237, 239–240
  measurable vital signs and trends, 46,
    235–236
    diagnostic tool, 236–237, 239f
    outcome metrics, 48
  in product transitions, 87, 87f
  public/external indicators, 44
  see also Glare

W

Walgreen, Charles, 174
Welch, Jack, 164, 175
Wellfleet, 68
Wells Fargo, 22
Western Electric, 52
  PBX/VCS case example, 124
Wilner, David, 182
Wind River Systems, 182
Wooden, John, 42
WorldCom, 16
Woziak, Steve, 10

8 reasons why you should read the Financial Times for 4 weeks RISK-FREE!

To help you stay current with significant developments in the world economy ... and to assist you to make informed business decisions — the Financial Times brings you:

❶ Fast, meaningful overviews of international affairs ... plus daily briefings on major world news.

❷ Perceptive coverage of economic, business, financial and political developments with special focus on emerging markets.

❸ More international business news than any other publication.

❹ Sophisticated financial analysis and commentary on world market activity plus stock quotes from over 30 countries.

❺ Reports on international companies and a section on global investing.

❻ Specialized pages on management, marketing, advertising and technological innovations from all parts of the world.

❼ Highly valued single-topic special reports (over 200 annually) on countries, industries, investment opportunities, technology and more.

❽ The Saturday Weekend FT section — a globetrotter's guide to leisure-time activities around the world: the arts, fine dining, travel, sports and more.

FT FINANCIAL TIMES
World business newspaper